Sound Alliances

SOUND ALLIANCES

INDIGENOUS PEOPLES, CULTURAL POLITICS AND POPULAR MUSIC IN THE PACIFIC

Edited by Philip Hayward

CASSELL

London and New York

Cassell
Wellington House, 125 Strand, London WC2R 0BB
370 Lexington Avenue, New York, NY 10017–6550

First published 1998

British Library Cataloguing-in-Publication Data
A catalogue record for this book is available from the British Library.
ISBN 0-304-70055-X (Hardback)
      0-304-70050-9 (Paperback)

Library of Congress Cataloging-in-Publication Data
Sound alliances : indigenous peoples, cultural politics, and popular
   music in the Pacific / edited by Philip Hayward.
        p.   cm.
      Articles previously published in Perfect Beat, the Pacific journal
of research into contemporary music and popular culture.
      Includes bibliographical references and index.
      ISBN 0–304–70055–X (hardcover). — ISBN 0–304–70050–9 (paperback)
      1. Popular music—Pacific Area—History and criticism.
I. Hayward, Philip.   II. Perfect Beat.
ML3505.P16S68   1998
781.63'099—dc21   97-46111
                                                                      CIP
                                                                       MN

Typeset by BookEns Ltd, Royston, Herts.
Printed and bound in Great Britain by
Biddles Limited, Guildford and King's Lynn

Contents

About the Authors

Philip Hayward is Head of the Department of Media and Music Studies at Macquarie University in Sydney, Australia. He is editor of *Perfect Beat: The Pacific Journal of Research into Contemporary Music and Popular Culture*. He has written several books, including, most recently, *Music at the Borders: Not Drowning, Waving and their Engagement with Papua New Guinean Culture 1986–96* (1998).

John Castles lectures in Philosophy and Cultural Studies at Huron International University in Tokyo. He formerly taught Cultural Studies at the University of Technology, Sydney and Anthropology at University College, London.

David Goldsworthy is a senior lecturer in Music at the University of New England, Armidale, Australia. He has published widely on Pacific and Indonesian music, and performs in a Sundanese gamelan group.

Tony Mitchell is a senior lecturer in Cultural Studies at the University of Technology, Sydney, Australia. He has written several books, including, most recently, *Popular Music and Local Identity* (1996).

Karl Neuenfeldt lectures at Central Queensland University, Rockhampton, Australia. He has published widely in a number of journals and is editor of *The Didjeridu: From Arnhem Land to Internet* (1997).

Lisa Nicol is an Arts/Law graduate from Macquarie University in Sydney, Australia and was one of the co-ordinators of 'Loud' – 'Australia's First National Media Festival of Youth Culture and the Arts'.

Don Niles has been an ethnomusicologist at the Institute of Papua New Guinea Studies since 1979. He is the editor of the journal *Kulele* and has most recently edited *Mission and Music* by Heinrich Zahn, concerning the development of a Lutheran hymnody based on traditional Papua New Guinea melodies.

Malcolm Philpott lectures at the University of Southern Queensland, Australia and initiated the Music Archive for the Pacific, at Southern Cross University, Lismore, Australia in 1996.

Robin Ryan recently submitted a doctoral thesis on Australian gumleaf music at Monash University, Melbourne. She has contributed articles on Australian Aboriginal music and popular music to various journals and encyclopedias. She is currently a specialist advisor/consultant and assistant to the editors of the *Companion to Music and Dance in Australia* (forthcoming, Currency Press, Sydney).

Amy Ku'uleialoha Stillman is Associate Professor of Music at the University of Michigan. She is currently researching the history of modern hula.

Andrew N. Weintraub is an assistant professor in ethnomusicology at the University of Pittsburgh, where he also leads the gamelan ensemble. His geo-cultural areas of specialization are Indonesia, Hawai'i and the US.

Helen Wilson is a senior lecturer in Media and Communication Studies at Macquarie University, Sydney, Australia.

Acknowledgements

Many thanks to the members of the editorial boards, contributors and referees who have worked on *Perfect Beat* during the period 1992–97. Without their contributions neither this book, nor the journal itself, would have been possible.

Similarly, I would like to thank the Department of Media and Music Studies at Macquarie University, Sydney, for their unwavering support for the journal over the last five years. Without their financial assistance and facilitation the publication could not have been realized or continued.

Particular thanks to Tiffany Hutton and Mark Evans for their dedicated editorial and production assistance. Claire Butkus, Michael Flint, Jan Knapman and Andrew Murphie also deserve honourable mentions for their various assistances at various times. The much-missed Manic Exposeur distribution organization also played a significant part in distributing the journal in Australia during 1992–96 and keeping the cash flow ticking over; their efficiency and honesty was much appreciated.

In 1991, when I was developing the initial idea for *Perfect Beat*, Steven Muecke, Sonia Leiber and Mackenzie Wark all gave sober, sensible and valuable advice. Without their encouragement I might well have decided not to go ahead with the publication. In the following years, the support, advice and friendship of Steven Feld, Bruce Johnson, Tony Mitchell, Karl Neuenfeldt, Don Niles, Michael Webb and John Whiteoak has also been particularly appreciated. My daughter, Rosa, has grown up in a house filled with the sounds of various Pacific musics. By dancing and singing along with all manner of sounds she has continually reminded me that music is about joy and spontaneity (as well as more reflective appreciations).

Thanks also to Arthur Baker and Afrika Bambaata for providing the title (and implicit anthem) for the journal. Afrika Bambaata and the Soul Sonic Force's single 'Looking for the Perfect Beat' was originally released on the New York label, Tommy Boy, in 1983 and is also featured on the Polydor/21 Records album *The Perfect Beat (Compilation)* (1993) (and it still sounds brilliant).

Every effort has been made to contact all the copyright holders of material included in the book. If any material has been included without permission, we offer our apologies to all concerned and will happily include acknowledgement in any future edition.

Biggest thanks of all to my wife, Rebecca. Her support has been invaluable and her contribution to the management, production, distribution and administration of the journal has, hitherto, gone unrecognized. For all these reasons, and many more, this book is dedicated to her.

Introduction: Beyond the Axis

Philip Hayward

Over the last fifteen years Popular Music Studies has become an established field within (anglophone) Western academia. It now has an international umbrella body, IASPM (International Association for the Study of Popular Music), which holds major biennial conferences; has a series of national ASPMs which hold their own conferences and arrange events; and is affiliated to a series of institutions, principally in the form of university departments offering courses and/or research programmes in the subject. This groundswell of activity has also resulted in the publication of an increasing number of scholarly books and the production of several journals, such as the UK-based *Popular Music*, which began publishing in 1981; the US-based *OneTwoThreeFour: A Rock 'n' Roll Quarterly* (published in the first half of the 1980s); the sporadically published journal of IASPM USA, *Tracking* – relaunched in 1993 as *The Journal of Popular Music Studies*; and *Perfect Beat: The Pacific Journal of Research into Contemporary Music and Popular Culture*, which commenced in 1992.[1]

But while Popular Music Studies may have become established as a discipline, it shares a central characteristic with its parallel, and partially parental, disciplines, notably Media Studies and Cultural Studies, in that it primarily represents the aggregation of various approaches to the field of popular music (rather than a discrete and coherent discipline in its own right).[2] With notable exceptions, most obviously the work of Wallis and Malm,[3] Popular Music Studies has primarily applied itself to what might be termed a North Atlantic axis – seeing the music cultures of the USA and United Kingdom (and, to a lesser extent, those of Canada and western Europe) as constituting its essential culture and focus. In this regard, it has underexplored regions outside its original context, most notably those of Asia and the southern continents. These have remained, by and large, the province of Western ethnomusicologists. Yet here, too, there have been significant oversights. While the traditional and/or classical musical forms of non-Western cultures have been subject to various degrees of scrutiny over the last 30–40 years, the majority of new forms of popular musics which have resulted from cultural contacts, specifically, transactions between Western and non-Western cultures, have only recently begun to receive attention.

These forms are often referred to by ethnomusicologists as *syncretic*. The term itself derives from the medieval notion of syncretism, of 'the attempted union or reconciliation of diverse or opposite tendencies or practices',[4] and was a notion that, in its earliest usage, referred to the attempted reconciliation of distinct religious and/or philosophical concepts. The derivation of the term emphasizes ethnomusicologists' perceptions of the 'deep-rootedness' of forms of traditional music in their communities; and ethnomusicologists' perceptions of their complex natures and the difficulty in hybridizing them with imported forms.

Study of syncretic musics became more prominent in the 1980s, largely due to the rise of the 'world music' phenomenon (i.e. the Western marketing of musical products produced by musicians from non-Western locations) and, more specifically, a series of individual collaborations between Western and non-Western musicians. One of the most influential early studies of these collaborations was Steven Feld's article, 'Notes on World Beat', published in *Public Culture Bulletin* in 1988. In this piece Feld discussed the significance of the (then) novel phenomenon of Western recording artists producing albums which drew substantially on African and various non-Western musical traditions and resources.[5] Paul Simon's *Graceland* (1986) is the paradigmatic example of this. (NB. Feld identifies this specific kind of musical collaboration as 'world beat', to distinguish it from the variety of global musics yoked together under the generic marketing term 'world music'.)

Articles such as Feld's, and the continuing production and popularity of a series of albums subsequent to *Graceland*, resulted in discussions of world beat and world music coming to the fore in both Popular Music Studies and (in one wing of) Ethnomusicology. In the case of the former, this did not so much represent a globalization of address but rather the reinscription of the North Atlantic axis as a point of cultural mediation: the context for the creation of world beat and for the identification of diverse cultural commodities capable of being (re-)presented as world music. In this model, the North Atlantic axis became both a curator and a facilities house for world music/world beat production and the originator of an (essentially domestic) discourse about such production.[6]

In all this, certain parts of the globe seemed more part of the 'world' projected by these (musical) definitions than others. Much remained *terra incognita*, areas out-of-focus, more characterized by scholarly indifference than perceptions of cultural in-difference. One such area was that of the Australia–Western/Central Pacific region. This is an area easily characterized by the *inbetweenness* of its major anglophone settler nations, Australia and New Zealand (so remote from their notional 'mother' axis); the pre-mediated and touristified music culture of Hawai'i; the discrete obscurity of a scattering of small island cultures; and the complexities of Papua New Guinea (with its 800 languages). *World Music: The Rough Guide* (Broughton, S. *et al.*, 1995), for example, a 697-page book which contains detailed and largely accurate and uncontentious accounts of a range of global musics, relegates Papuan and Pacific musics to a final seven-page section (690–7). Aside from its brevity, the section is poorly researched – to the point of absurdity – and appears to be based solely on research undertaken by the British composer David Fanshawe during a couple of brief visits to the region. Given that writing tasks for other regions were assigned to local writers, it is baffling why the job of writing this section was not given to a (Papua) New Guinean, Hawaiian, New Zealander or Islander writer.

Perceptions about the marginality of Australia–Western/Central Pacific concerns to the project of Euro-American Popular Music Studies were graphically reinforced in 1993, with the relaunch of the IASPM US journal, *Tracking*, as *The Journal of Popular Music Studies*. Timed to coincide with the first international conference of IASPM to be held in the US, the first issue of the retitled journal featured a significant cover design. This attempted to represent IASPM's international address by depicting the world as two spheres, overlapping around the mid-Atlantic. The left sphere showed North and South America, the right Europe, Africa, the Middle East and Central Asia. Filleted out from this global representation was the slice of the planet comprising the islands of the North and South Pacific, Australia, New Zealand and East and South-East Asia.

Perfect Beat was founded in 1992 by a group of Australian-based academics, specifically to address this kind of marginalization and to develop regional music studies. As the publication's subtitle, 'The Journal of Research into Contemporary Music and Popular Culture', indicated, its focus was the broad multidisciplinary tradition of Popular Music Studies (described above). From its inception, the journal addressed itself to contemporary music and its broader cultural and media contexts. Early issues featured articles on a range of topics, from improvisatory musics in pre-jazz Australia (Whiteoak, 1993) and the use of the didjeridu in recorded music (Neuenfeldt, 1993), through to the promotional function of music videos (Battersby and Valtwies, 1992) and the music policy of Australian public radio (McManus, 1992). By the fourth issue it became increasingly evident to the editorial board that a series of common concerns linked the music cultures of Australia, New Zealand, Papua New Guinea, Hawai'i and the other islands of Melanesia, Micronesia and Polynesia. From volume two, issue one, the journal formally announced its expanded, pan-Pacific focus by describing itself as 'The *Pacific* Journal. . .' in its subtitle. Since then, *Perfect Beat* has published articles on aspects of the music cultures of Australia, Hawai'i, New Caledonia, New Guinea and New Zealand, Yap and the international diffusion of regional musics such as Hawaiian and Ambonese/Eurasian pop.[7] In recognition of the enhanced internationalization of music – as well as of the music industry, fandom and simple *communication* – it has also addressed itself to the growing diffusion of communities of (previously) localized taste within broader contexts (Neuenfeldt, 1997; Mitchell, 1997; Stahl, 1997). What is notable about these studies is their emphasis on how the local/ regional is not simply *dissolved* by the Internet, but *reconstituted*.

Over five years and ten issues (1(1)–3(2)), *Perfect Beat* has published an extensive and varied body of research and has encouraged authors who have subsequently published books on regional music issues.[8] Despite this resource, the majority of English-language popular music texts that continue to be written (outside the Australia–Western/Central Pacific) generalize about a variety of forms of popular music, music radio, music video, etc., with almost total recourse to North Atlantic examples. They thereby comprise a highly selective – and consequently flawed – scholarly tradition. Indeed, so pervasive is this tendency, so many are its examples, that almost any book on popular music by a North Atlantic-based Popular Music Studies author – with notable exceptions such as Garofalo (1992), Lipsitz (1994) and the work of Wallis and Malm[9] – will stand as an example.

This anthology brings together a selection of material from *Perfect Beat* addressing aspects of the relationship between indigenous peoples and popular music. Fifteen years ago, Margaret Kartomi published an article in the journal *Ethnomusicology* specifically addressed to Western scholars' perceptions of syncretic musics. In her article she emphasized that 'Western writers have tended to disapprove of [such] musics ... ignoring them or dismissing them as objects unworthy of attention' (1981: 227). As she also emphasized, this was based on a particular (educated and class-based) inflection of 'Eurocentric prejudices'. Surveying a range of ethnomusicological (and musicological) material written from the 1950s to the 1970s (as detailed in her bibliography (*ibid.*: 245–9)), she argued that although

> blatantly discriminatory statements about these [i.e. syncretic] musical genres are made less frequently today than a few decades ago ... With a few exceptions, musicologists have hardly given themselves the opportunity to begin to understand the forces at work in culture contact situations (*ibid.*: 228–9).

As part of a detailed examination and critique of the uses and connotations of the term 'acculturation' (and its suitability as a description of cross-cultural musical styles and processes), Kartomi made a strongly argued point about notions of musical 'purity', namely that

> there is a strong likelihood that all musics are syntheses of more than one cultural and (in some cases) class influence ... intercultural musical synthesis is not the exception but the rule. Conflict and change are part of the nature of reality, even in seemingly timeless, static societies (*ibid.*: 230).

Sound Alliances addresses issues of 'intercultural musical synthesis' and issues of 'conflict and change' not only in music cultures but also in the social groups and circumstances which originate them. As a result, the studies of indigenous people(s) and their engagements with popular music included here are orientated towards politics, the media and mediation, and music industry issues, in addition to the music itself.

The book is divided into three parts: I – Music, Identity and Cultural Politics; II – Music, Commerce and the Media Industries; and III – Access to the Mainstream: The Case of Yothu Yindi.

As with any anthology of its kind, the separation of chapters into discrete sections is somewhat problematic, since the themes of each interact and interrelate with each other. Part I comprises a series of broad historical analyses of the development of Australian Aboriginal Rock (Chapter 1), Maori and Pacific Islander music in Aotearoa/New Zealand (Chapter 2), and Kaneka music in New Caledonia (Chapter 3); along with more specific studies of the Koori (Aboriginal) music scene in Melbourne (Chapter 4) and contemporary Hawaiian musics (Chapters 5 and 6). Part II complements these by examining the way various industrial and media aspects interact with and/or facilitate contemporary syncretic musics. Individual chapters address the relationship between radio broadcasting and music culture (Chapter 9, on Maori radio), the development of locally-orientated music video production (Chapter 10, on the case of Papua New Guinea in the 1990s), the nature of particular music industry initiatives (Chapter 11, on New Zealand music in the mid-1990s), and the significance of (the absence of) copyright legislation for music cultures (Chapter 8, with reference to Papua New Guinea). Chapter 7 provides a broad overview of how a variety of industrial factors have affected the development of contemporary (Papua) New Guinean pop.

The final part comprises a case study of the Aboriginal rock group Yothu Yindi, who first rose to prominence in Australia in 1991 and then went on to attract international acclaim through tours of North and South America, Africa, Europe, Asia and Oceania in the mid-1990s. The section begins with a discussion of the significance of the band's roots in the Yolngu community of Yirrkala, Northern Territory and the high profile of that community in Aboriginal rights issues over the last two decades (Chapter 12). Chapters 13 and 14 then provide contrasting readings of the political significance of the band's best-known single and music video 'Treaty' (1991) and the broader issue of the political position, function and effect of Aboriginal music in a national and international context. The concluding chapter engages with these debates in a discussion of the band's career and its increasing multimedia orientation, including the presence of traditional Aboriginal culture on the Internet.

Neither this introduction, nor any of the individual chapters, attempts to draw on the research offered here to make overarching hypotheses about the complex interaction of Western, (post)colonial cultures and indigenous peoples across the Australia-Western/Central Pacific region. Rather, the anthology attempts to provide fragments of a holistic perception of the issues involved in late twentieth-century regional popular music culture – a series of studies from a research project currently still in an early phase, one of mapping diversity and documenting and/or reconstructing a largely unrecorded history. In this manner, *Sound Alliances* offers itself as a resource. By making a specific selection of material from the first ten issues of *Perfect Beat* available to North American and European readers, through bookshop distribution, the anthology attempts to identify and foreground a range of specific issues as both of intrinsic interest and as examples. It offers a series of case studies with which North Atlantic-orientated scholarship can engage, or, at the very least, *include* in its own generalizing hypotheses. This in turn should identify the last five years of the journal – and its continuing publications – as a further resource and a signpost to the rich musical cultures of a region which deserve to be both firmly on the map of Popular Music Studies and on the CD and record players and radios of global culture.

Notes

1. *Perfect Beat – The Pacific Journal of Research into Contemporary Music and Popular Culture* is a biannual publication, published in January and July, which commenced in July 1992. Further information about the journal can be obtained from: The Editor, c/o Department of Media and Music Studies, Macquarie University, NSW 2109, Australia (Tel: +61 (0) 2 9850 8786; fax +61 (0) 2 9850 8240; e-mail < phayward@ocs1.ocs.mq. edu.au >; or by visiting the journal's Web site < http://www.mcs.mq. edu.au/pbeat >). Subscription information can be obtained from John Libbey and Co., Level 10, 15–17 Young Street, Sydney NSW 2000, Australia (Telephone +61 (0) 2 9251 4099; fax +61 (0) 2 9251 4428; e-mail < jlsydney@mpx.com.au >).

    Perfect Beat has published two previous books: Hayward, P., Mitchell, T. and Shuker, R. (eds) (1994) *North Meets South: Popular Music in Aotearoa/ New Zealand* (contact < mevans@pip.engl.mq.edu.au > for purchase information), and Neuenfeldt, K. (ed.) *The Didjeridu: From Arnhem Land to Internet* (1997), co-published with John Libbey Pty (Sydney) (contact < jlsydney@mpx.com.au > for purchase information.

2. This is as much to do with the strategic and opportunistic nature of the establishment of the discipline in various 'cramped' or interstitial spaces as it is with any conscious decision to opt for pluralistic interdisiplinarity. Indeed, it might prove highly productive, if contentious, for Popular Music scholars to hypothesize an ideal and coherent Popular Music Studies discipline and then try and work towards this from their various locations and positions.

3. Two authors who have developed their work in Scandinavia, at the fringes of the (anglophone) North Atlantic axis.

4. *Shorter Oxford English Dictionary* (1975: 2223).
5. Though it should be noted that this tendency dates back to the late 1960s, at least, with Brian Jones and his attempts to record with various Moroccan performers and the more collaborative recordings undertaken by Ginger Baker and Mick Fleetwood in the 1970s and early 1980s.
6. As is well known, the term 'world music' itself was invented by a group of small record label owners in 1987, who were trying to find more effective ways of marketing and, particularly, retail shelving, the non-Western music they were releasing.
7. Along with broader studies of topics such as the nature of hip hop as a form of contemporary avant-garde (Wark, 1992); the significance of the theoretical work of Deleuze and Guattari for popular music analysis (Murphie, 1996); and a series of feature reviews of international books on contemporary music topics.
8. Such as Mitchell (1996), Shuker (1996), Hayward (1998), Neuenfeldt (1997) and Whiteoak (1997).
9. See Bibliography under both Wallis and Malm *and* Malm.

PART I

Music, Identity and Cultural Politics

1

Tjungaringanyi: Aboriginal Rock (1971–91)[1]

John Castles

The traditional–contemporary problem

Discourses about Australian Aboriginal music are often generated through ideas about authenticity, and they display all the paradoxes associated with the term. Proponents and promoters of Aboriginal music claim an original identity for it, but this original identity only emerges in relations with the outside. Aboriginal tribal groups have played music for many thousands of years, but 'it' wasn't 'Aboriginal music' then. 'Aboriginal music' began in 1899, when a white anthropologist first recorded it.

The habitual structuring of discourses about Aboriginal music through the terms 'traditional' and 'contemporary' expresses a wish to deny the irreversibility of this contact. These terms can still be made to signify at the level of content, they can be used to speak about a particular instrument, song structure or style as having originated amongst Aboriginal or non-Aboriginal people. But at the level where these parts of musical composition or performance articulate with meaning, for instance where they are played by a group which might have members who have partially integrated with other musics or languages, a fundamental dislocation has taken place. Today many Aboriginal people can play tribal music, but can any of them play it in such a way that they utterly banish an awareness that the act of performing it has taken on a layer of meaning that it did not have prior to the white invasion? To what extent do people play music with an awareness of the tradings and borrowings of styles current in traditional societies, and how can their audiences be aware that this sort of fusion was always already taking place?

Under these conditions, the meanings of 'traditional' and 'contemporary' have shifted. Under the gaze of those eager to hold them apart, each side starts to take on the meaning of the other. For Euro-Australians, maintenance of the category of tradition holds open the tantalizing possibility of making contact with the origin they are not. In a movement which accelerated after ethnomusicologists began their recording work in the 1960s and 1970s, tribal music is drawn towards the coastal cities and beyond. Liberal urbanites became interested in hearing tribal sounds, even if they have to resort to predominantly white bands like Gondwanaland or Neil Murray and the Rainmakers to hear them live.

So when Yothu Yindi went and sat with their elders, and then with Mushroom Records president Michael Gudinski, to thrash out a special deal which waived company copyright for the tribally-owned music, comprising half of their debut album, *Homeland Movement* (1989), they did so confident that it was these songs which would feed into the burgeoning world music movement and eventually sell the album in America and Europe.[2] International interest in Aboriginal music, like interest in Aboriginal art, gravitates towards the isolated locale; it seeks out artists from communities remote enough to lay claim to authentic lines of tradition. In this sense the 'margin' or the 'minor' is the creative space when opposed to the 'mainstream', the deterritorializing movement becomes creative.

The images of the most prominent Aboriginal bands are often about moving along these lines in the other direction. Yothu Yindi, the most prominent Aboriginal band of recent years, is based in Yirrkala in Eastern Arnhem Land, where tribal links remain largely undisturbed (see Part III of this anthology for further discussion). The band's lead singer, Mandawuy Yunupingu, is from a leading family in the Gumtaj clan. And it is because of this that the band's image is summed up by the phrase 'Into the Mainstream' – both in and away from the marginal. In an ABC (Australian Broadcasting Corporation) TV documentary of that name, which followed their 1988 tour of the US supporting Midnight Oil, shots of Howard Johnsons and freeways are overlaid with the sounds of didjeridu and *bilma* (clapsticks). The band, sometimes adorned with tribal body markings, are shown in buses, motels, fast food joints and backstage in anonymous auditoriums. The traditional and the local attain their specific significance on the way into a 'placeless' modern world.

If you think of contemporary culture as 'mass' culture, as music that leaves its own locale to become part of the background of an amorphous urban life, then the 'traditional' side of Aboriginal music is furthest on the way towards it. The loping convolutions of the didjeridu meet up with ambient music, TV commercials, computer screen-savers. But if you define 'tradition' as something sovereign to a bounded community, unaffected by a compulsion to have a meaning beyond it, then it is a 'contemporary' style, Country and Western, which most closely approximates this role for many Aboriginal people. Country and Western (C&W), Gospel and hymns, legacies of the 'pastoral' incursion (in both senses), the later side that the searchers for origin pass over, are, perhaps partly for this very reason, the musics that many Aboriginal communities come home to.

Country and Western, and CAAMA

In the cities and big country towns a tradition of family-orientated C&W outfits stretches back to Harry and Wilga Williams and the Country Outcasts, who began playing around Fitzroy in Melbourne in the 1960s. Sometimes the lyrics are about anguish and alienation, but precisely because the recordings these bands make are not expected to circulate far outside Aboriginal neighbourhoods, there is less concern with grounding everything in a predetermined Aboriginal domain, and a greater interest in simply exploring the styles and pleasures that attract, regardless of their origin. So, to take only a New South Wales example, when Roger Knox from Tamworth spoke to the Bicentennial Authority about funding a series of cassettes featuring Aboriginal artists he hoped to produce, he expressed a wish to 'sing songs that linked ... with something more spiritual, like in the Dreamtime stories' (Breen, 1989: 79). But the flavour of the *Koori Classic* series he went on to produce does not have much to do with the gravity and cultural purity of white nationalist constructions of the Dreamtime. Volume 1 features covers of Chuck Berry's 'Maybelline' and Dolly Parton's 'Jolene'. On the jacket, the 'Koori Classic' lettering mimics the Coca-Cola logo. On Volume 2, *Aboriginal Artists Present the All-Australian Fifties Party*, Roger and other band members are standing in front of a Cadillac with tail fins. The general atmosphere on the *Koori Classic* series is relaxed and warm. Light-hearted novelty songs about romance predominate, featuring everything from Hawaiian twang to rapid-fire, surf music-style instrumentals. In these genres, and in Gospel, women singers (e.g. Serina Andrew, Sharon Mann, Kathleen and Lucy Cox) are prominent, though all but inaudible in the music that reaches the cities.

Music from the Centre has a very different feel, but it is similarly dominated by C&W. Bands gravitate to the CAAMA (Central Australian Aboriginal Media Association) complex in Alice Springs. CAAMA was founded in 1980 and now comprises a television station, radio station (8KIN–FM) and recording studio. It is here, and at the annual (since 1989) 'Sing Loud, Play Strong' festivals at the Darwin Amphitheatre, that most of the new Aboriginal music reputations are being forged. Mudrooroo Narogin (now Nyoongar) has pointed out that not one of the cassettes released on the CAAMA label, Impartja, features traditional singers (Narogin, 1990: 67). *From the Bush*, a compilation of songs recorded at CAAMA and released on CD in 1990 (through PolyGram) contains a plethora of styles and emotions, from resignation (Bill Wellington's

'Dreamtime Blues') through self-affirmative rock (the Wedgetail Eagles' 'We're the Wedgetail Eagles') to celebrations (Blekbala Mujik's 'Don't Worry Just Be Happy'). But the prevailing sound, even in the songs sung in Aboriginal languages, is Gospel-tinged C&W. Often the 'lost lover' strand of C&W is adapted and made to speak of a stretch of country instead of a person (you can hear this surfacing in the Warumpi Band's 'My Island Home' (1987)). Aboriginality comes across not in the song structure itself but in the lyric themes and in the 'grain' of the voices. As Narogin observes, by the 1960s, to 'many Aboriginal people, Country and Western was traditional Aboriginal music' (1990: 63).

Receiving rock

My aim here is not to survey in detail the range of traditional and contemporary musics performed by Aboriginal people. This has already been done comprehensively in the work of Catherine Ellis and in the *Our Place, Our Music* project, edited by Marcus Breen (1989). Instead I offer an interpretation of the Aboriginal musical category variously called 'Aboriginal music' or 'Aboriginal rock', which emerged in the 1980s and gathered momentum in the 1990s, as a crucial moment in the ongoing process of negotiating this tangled relation of traditional and contemporary. This new music recognizes itself as 'contemporary' in the sense that at some level it aims to address a general, as well as Aboriginal, audience. With this in mind I (as a mainstream Euro-Australian) have not set out on a quest for authentic origins. Instead, I attempt to enter the dialogue this new music opens up by offering an interpretation of the cultural and political images of its most prominent exponents as they reached me in Sydney during this period.

The field of meaning through which this music was produced and received was constituted by two basic interpretive strategies. In the first, which tended to characterize the early 1980s, the contemporary music played by Aborigines is explicitly recognized as a *de facto* traditional music. In the second, now more prominent, move, Aboriginal music comes to represent an ideal fusion of traditional and contemporary and all the qualities they signify.

CASM, No Fixed Address and the silent majority

The formation in 1971 of what was to become (in 1975) the Centre for Aboriginal Studies in Music (CASM) at the University of Adelaide was the first important catalyst in Aboriginal music's renaissance. CASM was instrumental in the formation of many of the leading bands to emerge in the 1980s. Members of No Fixed Address, Coloured Stone, Kuckles and

Scrap Metal have trained there at various times in their careers. One of CASM's primary aims was to put urban Aboriginal musicians back in touch with the tribal musicians from whom they had been separated by genocide and assimilation. In her 1985 book on the CASM project, Cath Ellis stresses the resistance she initially encountered amongst urban Aboriginal people to the idea of learning from tribal musicians. Many of them had been brought up to despise tribal music or anything it implied, to distance themselves from the past and to move into the assimilated future. They considered Ellis's suggestion that they 'hadn't left', that they had some sort of connection with tribal Aborigines, to be insulting (Ellis, 1985: 148). The fact that now, increasingly, the suggestion that any Aboriginal person, urban or not, does *not* maintain some sort of link with a prior Aboriginality would be considered insulting, reveals the general shift in orientation through which the very possibility of a new Aboriginal music emerged.

The CASM idea, as Narogin says, was that the two musics 'might fertilize each other, develop side by side, or merge into one music of Aboriginality' (1990: 65). So the CASM bulletin was named *Tjungaringanyi* ('coming together as one') by the tribal musicians (Ellis, 1985: 167). Although a number of bands began incorporating traditional instruments as a result of this contact, its significance lay not so much in any comprehensive merger but in the opening up of a way of thinking about the role of non-tribal musics through the prism of tribal ones.

Through CASM, urban music students began to see their own musics as a 'new tradition'. For generations before, the idea that Aboriginality could express itself in contemporary styles was not canvassed. The terms were habitually constructed in stark opposition. So, for example, a 1958 report on traditional music in Wilcannia had the children distancing themselves from tribal music as much as possible: ... 'the younger generation don't like to hear these songs. They giggle and say it makes them feel "shamed". "We're like white folks now," they say' (Breen, 1989: 14). In 1981, Clive Yunkaporta of Aurukun complained that 'most of [the young] only want to learn the American country and western music from cassette tapes. I won't let them learn our traditional songs that way' (*ibid*).

The generation gap came to be regarded as a microcosm of the tragedy of assimilation. White meanings have wedged themselves between old and young as they represent the traditional and contemporary. While this division persisted, it can be compared with the following appreciation of the band, Coloured Stone, by CASM teacher Doug Petherick in 1989. Petherick refers to Coloured Stone's musical Aboriginality, contending that 'they play rock and country rock, but often break accepted white rules, such as square phrasing and constant rhythms, even when doing cover versions of popular standards' (Breen, 1989: 65). Or *On The Street* reviewer Stuart Ewings on *Koori Beat*: 'Reggae doesn't sound like rock, it's not usually laced with country and western sentiment, nor does it sound like rockabilly – CS (Coloured Stone) do' (1989: 12). Here we see the effects of a historically specific and wide-ranging interpretive turn. The emphasis has shifted from the second to the first term, from Aboriginal *music* to *Aboriginal* music. Unlike blues or rap in America or reggae in Jamaica, Aboriginal music has not coalesced into a single identifiable style. So Aboriginality is detected as a non-specific force which flows through and shapes eclectic contemporary blends.

No Fixed Address was the first band to gain widespread attention within the new listening formation opened up by CASM. Since its inception CASM had actively encouraged student interest in foreign indigenous musics as a way of raising interest in the preservation of their own. In the early 1970s there was an arrangement between CASM, then located at Port Adelaide, and the Seamens' Union, whereby visiting sailors (from Malaysia, the Philippines, Korea, Sweden, Indonesia) performed regularly for Aboriginal groups (Ellis, 1985: 169). It was in this context that Bob Marley's 1979 Adelaide appearance became the inspiration for No Fixed Address and a generation of CASM bands.

For No Fixed Address (NFA), reggae became Aboriginal music. The band is best known for the AFI (Australian Film Institute) jury prize-winning 1981 film and LP soundtrack *Wrong Side of the Road*. Lead singer and drummer Bart Willoughby's boast, 'You can't change the rhythm of my soul', from the anthemic 'We Have Survived', captures the new mood. The band's reggae rhythm already expresses the flow of an Aboriginality which racist whites are trying to block. The film has two interlocking stories. In one, a band member's search for his mother is hindered by a government department. In the other, the attempts of NFA and Us Mob to connect with their audience are repeatedly interrupted and intercepted by police.

By embracing reggae as an expression of solidarity with black people everywhere, NFA presented its Aboriginal audience with the possibility of a way out from under this oppression. They were, in effect, turning the logic of Australian individualist nationalism against itself. In this logic, each person becomes an equivalent, interchangeable unit of a given race or nationality. The numbers are then tallied up to produce terrifying entities variously called the 'yellow peril', the 'white majority', etc. By way of an arithmetical abstraction the majority realizes its power and the minority its oppression (see Kapferer, 1988). NFA's articulation with black music simply ups the ante within this logic. Instead of shrinking from the gaze of each and every white, or futilely attempting to cross into this national majority, they stay with the Aboriginal minority but present the threat of its linking up with an international majority. In 1981 (the same year as *Wrong Side of the Road* was released) Canberra hosted the World Council of Indigenous Peoples congress.

This challenge to entrenched white racism is a founding moment for Aboriginal rock. But its fruitfulness as a cohesive political platform seemed to diminish as the 1980s progressed. NFA continued to play internationally, but produced only one more mini-LP, *From My Eyes* (1982). The road to the black majority remains open, and it is still travelled in both directions. When Yothu Yindi were in New York in 1988, they went to Marcus Garvey Park in Harlem for an interview with a black radio station. And when Redhead Kingpin, who featured on the soundtrack for Spike Lee's *Do the Right Thing* (1989), came to Sydney in 1990, he visited the Aboriginal community in Redfern. But one limit of this more militant black discourse is that it is ultimately one of exile and diaspora; it cut across the recent articulation of indigenous cultures with the environmental movement with which many Aboriginal people were more comfortable. For Yothu Yindi, Harlem was just a stop-over on their tour 'From Diesel and Dust to Big Mountain' (a native American reservation in Arizona), a journey joining one indigenous community to another as witnesses to white destruction of the land.

In addition to this, the tendency in *Wrong Side of the Road* (and NFA's more polemical lyrics) to lump together all the levels of the Australian state – country publicans, the police, the government – under the rubric of a single censoring racism, no longer seems to be a productive base from which to negotiate the subtleties of current struggles over Aboriginal identity. Whilst the level of local day-to-day racism amongst whites shows little sign of abating, the Australian state, far from trying to repress Aboriginal cultural expression, is increasingly seizing opportunities to draw it (or a particular version of it) out. Aboriginal rock after all, like most other aspects of Australian art and culture, was generated with the active support of the state. The repressive hypothesis is inappropriate to a landscape dominated first by CASM (largely funded by the Aboriginal Arts Board of the Australia Council), then CAAMA (funded by Aboriginal Affairs and DEET (Department of Employment, Education and Training)), and by bodies such as ARIA (Australian Recording Industry Association) and the AFI (Australian Film Institute), who seldom miss opportunities to present Aboriginal artists with awards. The increasingly important part played by indigenous peoples in constructions of national identities, observable in international films such as *Crocodile Dundee* (1986) and *Dances with Wolves* (1991), and the political stakes this drawing-out produces, cannot be addressed through NFA's songs alone.

While the Australian state offers special funding for Aboriginal cultural projects, funding for Aboriginal music can also be understood within the context of a general move from 'assimilation' (through 'integration' in the 1970s) to 'multiculturalism' in the 1980s. This move is not as radical as is generally suggested. Multiculturalism is not so much a break with the logic of assimilation but its diffusion or postmodernization. Both share the idea that an identity is ideally constituted in an environment inhabited by like others. But where there was once supposed to be only one such environment, now they are permitted to multiply. Urban Aboriginal people were initially forced to become 'like' whites and, when this did not succeed, institutions like CASM encouraged them to become 'like' Aborigines again. Without suggesting that the move does not represent an improvement, that 'self-determination' is not real, it should not be forgotten that, to some extent, anti-assimilation is a form of re-assimilation. It is the modification or fine-tuning of a logic which originated in, and continues to shape, white visions of Aboriginality, rather than the radical abrogation of a defining role which it is sometimes touted as (see Kapferer, 1988: 205–7, and also Morris, 1989).

Coloured Stone

If you keep this in mind, then white encouragement of the category of 'Aboriginal music' as a reconnection with, and expression of, a prior Aboriginal community continues to hold a dangerously essentializing potential. Aboriginal musicians must steer a course between the cliffs of essentialization on one side and assimilation on the other. The career of Coloured Stone, the longest-lived and most prolific Aboriginal band, describes an increasing suspicion of the constraints imposed by an automatic linking of their music with their Aboriginality. Rupert 'Buna' Lawrie formed Coloured Stone in Koonibba, South Australia, in 1978. Through the mid- and late-1980s they released five albums, first through CAAMA/Impartja and then RCA/BMG. Their (and Impartja's) first single 'Black Boy/Kapi Pulka' (1984), typified a concern for traditional themes and Aboriginality, along with participation in the vogue for reggae that marked their early work.

The title song, 'Black Boy', was a hit in the South Pacific but failed to chart in Australia. Perhaps this was one of the experiences behind Coloured Stone's gradual movement away from reggae and specifically black concerns, towards rock and more universal, or at least more generally Australian, themes. Albums entitled *Koonibba Rock* and *Island of Greed* (both 1985) were followed up by 1987's ARIA award-winning *Human Love* and 1989's *Wild Desert Rose*. Buna Lawrie, who avowed an ambition to make Coloured Stone 'the first Aboriginal band to make a number one hit and a gold record' (RCA/BMG press release, 1989), seems well aware of the limitations that overt identification with Aboriginality can impose. The dilemma is an old one. On the one hand the appeal to pan-Aboriginality can be a potent source of initial publicity and a powerful political force within Aboriginal communities, but on the other, the power to name and define the Aborigines as a homogeneous group, according to white interests, also depends on the construction of these collective identities. By the early 1990s, Buna Lawrie and Coloured Stone manager, Russell Guy, seemed to interpret white concentration on the

Aboriginality of their music as a way of keeping them in place, of blocking what should be an 'invisible' movement into the mainstream. On a trip through Sydney in 1990, for instance, they were anxious to distance themselves from the 'Black Boy' era; they shied away from questions about musical Aboriginality. When Guy was approached by the rock magazine, *The Edge*, he expressed the opinion that a story specifically about Aboriginal music only served to 'ghettoize' Aboriginal bands (Hitchings, 1990).

Liminal temporality

Often Aboriginal music expressed its reluctance to resolve itself into either pure tradition (the essential) or pure contemporaneity (the assimilated), by poising itself in a strangely liminal temporality which came to pervade and, in a sense, define it. The urge to cover over the assimilationism of the recent past, to stitch Aboriginality back and forth over the top of it, produces the imperative that the bands must reside simultaneously in an ideal past and future without ever being 'present'. They become nascent, virtual, always already here, but not quite arrived.

Scrap Metal, as their name implies, came to represent the past of the future, or the future of the past. Best known for their 1986 album, *Broken Down Man*, Scrap Metal began, like the Broome band Kuckles with whom they had shared membership, in the CASM-reggae nexus, but their image was soon governed by a balance between rustic isolation and space-age communications technology. Based in Broome, and retaining close links with the local Yawur tribe, they have obtained sponsorship deals with Tandy, OTC and British Telecom which keep them in contact with their manager in Sydney through a laptop modem computer. The National Science and Technology Museum in Canberra even featured an exhibit where you could sit in Scrap Metal's dust-coated combi van and send them a message. This tapped into the McLuhanesque theme of modern technology re-establishing the immediacy of tribal lines of oral/aural communication. (Thus CAAMA sees its role as 'arresting cultural disintegration through the broadcast of educational material and song' (*From The Bush* album liner notes).)

Archie Roach might come from the other side of Aboriginal Australia, both spatially and temporally, but his image at this period was also suffused with a temporal undecidability. If Scrap Metal's starting point determines a leap into the future, Roach's residence there sends him back into the past. In his debut album, *Charcoal Lane* (1990), he sings from the streets of Melbourne in a folk idiom. The songs concentrate on the personal sadnesses engendered by assimilation, the severing of connections with land and community, to which he and others of his generation fell victim. But the album is buoyed by an affirmation of the idea that this severing was never completed (hence the 1991 ARIA award for Best Indigenous Recording). It culminates in the transcendent spatial and temporal return of 'Took The Children Away':

> Back to their people
> Back to their land
> All the children came back
> Yes I came back

There is a sense in these songs not only of Roach's active re-assimilation into a communal past (again rendered through the metaphor of a family's two generations) but also of the realization that he and those around him had never entirely left it. Their alienated later lives had remained muted extensions of the former all along:

> Father, why do you drink your life away
> Father, tell me what you think
> There's so much you can say
> There's so much that you can share
> You've kept it in for far too long
> I don't believe that you don't care
> I've always believed that you were big and strong

This meaning is also suggested on the album's cover, where Roach's face, drawn in charcoal to connect with *Charcoal Lane*, could be on one of those inner city posters coming away in the rain, but reveals itself as more likely inscribed on a stylized ghost-gum (tree) trunk.

What comes across most clearly in all these signs is that the past represents a collective identity and the future an individual one. The musicians ask of their audience that from now on they be treated as individuals (like anybody else), but also as people who have never stopped being part of an ancient community. The difficulty of reconciling the two within a logic which habitually opposes 'the individual' to 'society' produces the feeling of distance.

Culture as rock

Increasingly it is the (often well-meaning) white concentration on a communal past which holds the potential to constrict the flow of Aboriginal music. It produces a reified notion of culture. Culture and tradition become synonymous terms for something solid, self-contained and separated by a definite boundary. Scrap Metal and Kuckles live in Broome, a town that is always described as having 'its own culture'. After their 1990 US tour an SBS (Special Broadcasting Service) interviewer asked a member of Yothu Yindi, 'Did you get a chance to share your culture?'

How does one answer a question like that, without a kind of *material* definition of culture – even as artefacts? These deployments threaten to turn culture back into a biological attribute, an inalienable quality one carries around, rather than a musical process that traverses the borders of body and mind. The imperative becomes that Aborigines must 'have' this 'thing' called culture. Amorphous mainstreamers do fine without it, their dominance allows them to move, not 'stand for'. This creates an environment in which musical contact between black and white is actually discouraged. White listeners come to feel that whatever they attempt to say about the music can only express a grounded bias whose borders they can never cross. Ignoring it altogether becomes a much safer option. Consider this startling passage – with editorial interjection – from a review of Yothu Yindi's first album, *Homeland Movement*, in *RAM* magazine:

> it is possessed of great sadness (or is that just me imposing my own cultural prejudices?) ... the tone is mournful, unsettling, a lament for the buried country. [Surely these songs are a celebration of the living country. They aren't 'original' compositions, as such. They are handed down from a time of cultural purity and serve to again, celebrate, the very abundant (traditional food, culture) landscape that is north-east Arnhem Land, even today.] 'Full credit to Mushroom, incidentally for releasing this: a brave step, not least considering its inevitable commercial failure. Nice to see motives of cultural preservation triumphing (occasionally) over corporate strategies.' (Unattributed, 1989).[3]

Here, in a condensed form, is a major blockage to the reception of Aboriginal music. The pleasure of allowing the music to sink in and take on an ambient meaning in the midst of your own life, on which popular music depends, is immediately intercepted by anxiety about the 'cultural prejudices' of your interpretation. The logic of the majority magnifies the sin. Here, use of the word 'imposing' reveals that the reviewer sees any mistake they might make as more than a simple one-to-one misunderstanding; it becomes an expression of the oppressive weight of the majority he unconsciously feels himself to embody. With so much at stake, any faltering attempt at stringing together a discourse can be undercut at any moment. Someone else is always poised to step in and embarrass you with appeals to 'cultural purity', and so the product is a dead weight to be 'preserved' even before its release.

In these conditions the urge to make contact with Aboriginal Australia is catered for by a recurrent fantasy of *becoming* an Aborigine. In an environment where any truth emerging athwart a border is habitually reduced to an expression of the 'prejudice' of one side or the other without remainder, discovering that you *are* Aboriginal provides the only way for whites to imagine themselves as authors of a valid non-oppressive speech. In Peter Weir's film *The Last Wave* (1977), the white lawyer speaking for Aborigines gradually discovers himself to have always been an integral part of the Aboriginal world. More recently the popularity of world music (and Bruce Chatwin's book, *The Songlines*) seems to stem, at some level, from a common fantasy in which the tired old sand castle of the West subsides into the world-encircling currents of song from which it emerged. The indigenous globalizes itself; there is nothing that does not ultimately flow from it, and so we discover that all of us have always been Aborigines all along. The absurdities this wish produces were affectionately lampooned by Jimmy Chi and Kuckles in the musical *Bran Nue Dae* (first performed at the 1990 Festival of Perth). In it the white hippies head off for Broome singing, in a *doubled* enunciation in which 'I' is 'you' and vice versa, and in which positive and negative are counterbalanced, that *they* are the Aborigines watching their precious land being taken away from them. Later, one of them discovers that he is actually the long-lost offspring of a German missionary and a local woman, an Aborigine in the blood. 'Ich bin ein Aboriginal!' he declares exultantly.

Fusion

Since the mid-1980s, new bands, many of them including non-Aboriginal members, have interpreted themselves, and been interpreted, not so much through the idea that the contemporary *is* the traditional, but rather that their music represents an ideal synthesis of two separate elements. The Warumpi Band opened the way in 1983 by describing themselves to the *National Times* as, 'not black people playing white music but a group of musicians who have synthesised the best of two cultures into one musical form' (Breen, 1989: 60). This theme was then quickly picked up across the country and beyond, from Scrap Metal's adoption of the word 'creole' to describe their music, to the critical reception of Yothu Yindi. In *Rolling Stone* (Australia) they were, 'not another case of black guys trying to sound like white guys and coming off second best, but rather a case of real fusion taking place' (Brown, 1989: 13), and in The *San Diego Union*, 'a revelation, opening with pure tradition and then working it into a pop context' (Mushroom Records press release, 1989).

This synthesis is imagined in two versions. One wishes to retain the specificities of black and white identities at some level. It conceives of the merger not so much as an irreversible fusion but as a joining or articulation, a reaching out. This version governs the naming and structure of the *Building Bridges* (1989) double album, where the artists merge at the level of record and sleeve, intermingling in the red–yellow–black colour code, whilst retaining the specificity of previous identities at the level of the track. Ultimately this layering relies on a deferred meeting derived from Christian notions of transcendence. The soul retains its isolated identity *before* God. The other conception, which seems to approximate tribal ideas more closely, dreams of a comprehensive fusion, an alchemy in which the two original substances lose themselves entirely in the formation of a new state. So, paradoxically, it is tribal Aboriginal thought which sometimes seems 'assimilationist' because it draws on a fundamentally immanent belief system. For it, the other places and beings are not in a separate, higher, later realm; they remain present/absent on this plane (to the chagrin of the mining companies).

So maybe Aboriginal appropriations of C&W or reggae content actually express their own ontology more closely than newer discourses about the 'preservation of cultural identity' would suggest. But, again, the common missionary experience, and hence the integral part Christianity came to play in constructions of pan-Aboriginality, renders futile any attempt to distinguish 'genuine' from 'appropriated' down the black–white line. Still, while Midnight Oil's contribution to the promotion of Aboriginal music in this period is unquestionable (see Steggels, 1992), it is worth stressing here the significance of Midnight Oil lead singer Peter Garrett's belief that he has discovered a 'Christ figure' in Aboriginal culture (Martin, 1989: 17). Midnight's Oil's Christianity and their increasing nationalism led them to sponsor the 'building bridges' version of Aboriginal rock's connection with the outside.

Strict Rules (1988), journalist Andrew McMillan's account of Midnight Oil's 1986 'Blackfella/Whitefella' tour of remote Northern Territory settlements with the Warumpi Band, makes it abundantly clear that Garrett's reassembly as the classic Australian man originating in and withstanding the land is accomplished through a sharp demarcation of urban and tribal Aborigine. Midnight Oil sometimes seemed to preside over a field of meaning which has no place for urban Aboriginal bands, or for women performers, since in Australian nationalist discourse the land is gendered male: 'The Macdonnell Ranges ... crease the desert like the ceremonial scars on an old man's chest' (McMillan, 1988: 3).

The stagescape Midnight Oil dominated also tended to keep tribal bands 'in place' along the collective-past/individual-future divide. Midnight Oil's support bands have exhibited the shy, retiring qualities that have come to signify the 'real' outback Aborigine. Leaving aside questions of aesthetic quality, popular music is about identificatory pairing. Fans use stars as ciphers for the imaginary construction of ideal selves. The British and North American popular music scenes, and the impersonation of stars by unlikely subjects, show that this leap of identification can cross lines of gender and race. But it does need individuals. Typically, the power of band, music and crowd becomes concentrated in the single figure of the lead singer who then becomes the meta-identity everyone momentarily takes on. The seas of outstretched hands at Midnight Oil's gigs testify to the absolutely integral part this process played in their success. But these silhouetting moments were much rarer in the performances of Midnight Oil's Aboriginal support bands. The combination of brief intensive exposure and commercial failure (evoked in the title of the Warumpi

Band's album, *Big Name, No Blankets* (1985)) which seemed to characterize Aboriginal rock at times in the 1980s, might owe more to this blockage than to simple racism.

The significance of Yothu Yindi's breakthrough to commercial success in the early 1990s lay in the fact that their music, lyrics and video images addressed and ·partially overcame these tensions (see Part III of this anthology for further discussion). In their first video, *Mainstream* (1989), paintings of *Wandjinas*, haloed mouthless rain gods from the Kimberleys, alternate with Papunya-style imagery from Central Australia and more traditional bark paintings from Yothu Yindi's own country (see Muecke, 1991 for further discussion). Pan-Aboriginality, as it is being used by Aboriginal groups and art and tourism entrepreneurs, is being evoked here. Mandawuy Yunupingu sings of economic and cultural achievement, of 'building bridges', but the song's central metaphor of fresh and salt water intermingling retains the possibility of immanent fusion. This theme is taken up again in 'Treaty' (version 1) (1991) (written as a collaboration between Yothu Yindi, Paul Kelly and Peter Garrett):

> Now two rivers run their course
> Separated for so long
> I'm dreaming of a brighter day
> When the waters will be one

With this song Yunupingu takes on enough of Garrett's political assertiveness and declarative phrasing to open the way for active identification in suburban living rooms.

For Yothu Yindi, the mainstream is both presence in white society and continuing flow with Aboriginal traditions. Their rhetorical points in the late 1980s and early 1990s tied in more with a post-Bicentenary politics of Aboriginal *renaissance* than with an earlier style of struggle and contestation (compare Gary Foley's dub at a performance of The Clash in 1982, reproduced on CAAMA's tape, *Rebel Voices*, or Kev Carmody's protest songs). Yothu Yindi seem to symbolize more clearly the possibility of avoiding the constrictive tendency of always locating Aboriginal music in a collective past or an ideal future. Perhaps their current success signals the emergence of an aesthetic which allows the maintenance of cultural identity as fusion, thus appealing to both local and broader audiences. In this context 'appropriation' may become a metaphor for affirmative action.

Notes

1. I would like to thank Stephen Muecke for his valuable help in the preparation of this chapter, an earlier version of which originally appeared in P. Hayward (ed.), *From Pop to Punk to Postmodernism: Popular Music and Australian Culture from the 1960s to the 1990s*, Sydney: Allen and Unwin, 1992.
2. K. Teh, *The Age*. Mushroom Records promotional press clipping file, 1989.
3. Reproduced in Mushroom Records press kit.

Discographic note

For a comprehensive discography of contemporary Aboriginal music see Dunbar-Hall (1995)

2

He Waiata Na Aotearoa: Maori and Pacific Islander Music in Aotearoa/New Zealand[1]

Tony Mitchell

In 1991 the popular African-American soul group the Neville Brothers toured New Zealand where they were invited to a *powhiri* (welcome) on a Maori *marae* (courtyard of a community meeting house) in Mangere in South Auckland, a predominantly Polynesian area with a high crime and unemployment rate and poor living conditions. They made a field recording of *Whakaria Mai*, the traditional sung Maori welcome which they were given, and included it as the final track, 'Maori Chant', on their 1992 album, *Family Groove*, singing the English words of the hymn 'How Great Thou Art' over the original Maori recording. The sleeve notes of the album contain a dedication to 'our extended family in Aotearoa (New Zealand): the Te Arawa, Ngati Tuwharetoa, Maniapoto, Ngati Porou and all the Maori people and canoes'. A few months later the Neville Brothers invited the all-woman Maori funk-rap group Moana and the Moahunters, who had taken part in the *marae* welcome, and who won the Best Maori Recording award in the 1992 NZ Music Industry Awards, to perform at the 1992 New Orleans Jazz and Heritage Festival, to support them in a number of gigs, and to assist in a launch of *Family Groove*. After being refused by all the government funding sources and corporate sponsors they approached, the three members of Moana and the Moahunters, together with relatives and a film crew, finally got to New Orleans through the support of family, friends and Maori community groups, as well as $3500 raised from a benefit concert given by Crowded House (Bourke, 1992: 14).

Moana and the Moahunters' New Orleans visit was the first significant international exposure that the hybrid contemporary popular music of Maori artists received. Largely as a result of the interest generated in the US by Moana and the Moahunters and the Maori rap group Upper Hutt

Posse, a feature article on Maori music by Graham Reid appeared in the US music industry weekly, *Billboard*, in May 1992, relating how 'Maori artists have readily assimilated the sounds of the wider world and adapted them as their own' (Reid, 1992a: 1, 34). Moana Maniapoto-Jackson's observations suggested that the wider world may be ready to assimilate the sounds of Maori musicians:

> We've been getting feedback that there's a school of thought overseas that the Pacific is a real fresh source. There's been rumours floating round that Quincy [Jones] and Janet [Jackson] are looking round, y'know. I think there is something unique down here. That was the kind of feedback we got in New Orleans. Though we were doing funk and soul, besides our own indigenous stuff, there was a very Pacific flavour to it that they found distinctive. (Barbie, 1993: 17)

But the Moahunters' struggle to raise funds for their trip to New Orleans illustrates the battle for recognition and autonomy which Maori musicians are still undergoing in Aotearoa, which tongue-in-cheek graffiti on a wall in Auckland once translated as 'the land of the wrong white crowd'.[2]

In 1993, Moana and the Moahunters released the single 'AEIOU'. Its subtitle, 'Akona Te Reo', translates as 'Learn the Language', and was addressed primarily to Maori *rangatahi* (young people), many of whom do not speak Maori, which could be regarded as a dialect of the language spoken throughout Polynesia. (Three per cent of the population of New Zealand is able to speak Maori fluently. This 3,360,000 population is made up of 81.2% Europeans, 9% Maori, and 3% Pacific Islanders, mostly Polynesian migrants from Tonga, Samoa, Fiji and the Cook and Tokelau Islands.) 'AEIOU' is also a plea, mostly in English, to the Maori people of Aotearoa to preserve their native culture (*Maoritanga*), study their history, and take part in the global movement of indigenous peoples for self-preservation. Receiving an NZ Music Industry Award for the song, Moana accused New Zealand radio of racism, commenting that fewer than twenty people present at the awards ceremony would have heard all three finalists in the Best Maori Recording category, as airplay on national radio was still a rarity for Maori popular music groups, especially those who sing in Maori (Reid, 1992b: 36). Four years later, in 1996, a remixed version of 'AEIOU, Akona Te Reo '95', was again nominated for a New Zealand Music Industry Award, in a new category called *Mana Reo* (Maori Language and Culture), which indicated that little had changed as far as mainstream acceptance of Maori music in New Zealand was concerned. (For further discussion of the song and video see Vui-Talitu, 1996.)

The Moahunters had previously released a version of the Sony Charles and Checkmates Limited's song 'Black Pearl' (originally released in 1969), transposed to the context of Maori women, and including a rap segment by Dean Hapeta of Upper Hutt Posse. This was a gold record in 1991, which in New Zealand terms means sales of more than 7500 units. Moana, who was a member of the Maori reggae group Aotearoa before she founded Moana and the Moahunters, indicated then that the group's agenda included producing international, commercially-oriented Maori language music:

> We thought Maori music had a lot of international potential because it's something different. We didn't see much point in just being another funk/soul band with Maori artists because Chaka Khan and co(mpany) do it heaps better than we do. But they can't sing in Maori and do the haka. (Yuzwalk, 1991: 8)

The Moahunters' 1993 single 'Peace, Love and Family', represented a definite move towards the dance music market. It features a ragga-styled rap by group member Teremoana Rapley, who was voted most promising female vocalist in the 1992 NZ Music Industry Awards, together with fragments of a Maori chant. The shift towards an anglophone market within the single's commercial hybridity was offset by its B-side 'Kua Makona' (Satisfied) a more reggae and soul-styled track sung entirely in Maori. The group's first album *Tahi* (One) was released in 1993, and contains a wide spectrum of material, including the group's first three singles, as well as a fourth double-sided single, a version of the Jimmy Cliff reggae song 'Rebel in Me' and a collaboration with Pakeha (foreign/ white) pop composer Andrew Fagan, 'I'll be the One'. Like the work of a number of their Maori peers in contemporary popular music, Moana and the Moahunters combine contemporary pop influences with rap, reggae, funk, soul and aspects of traditional Maori *waiata* (song), with particular emphasis on the latter:

> it's a real exciting challenge to incorporate contemporary styles and the traditional. To mix it up. Using something contemporary and something trad-itional makes it more exciting for youth today that aren't into that traditional kinda thing – it can only be productive because you're bringing in elements young people otherwise wouldn't get access to. (Barbie, 1993: 17)

Musical styles on the album range from Gospel to rock and dance music, while the work of Maori musicologist Hirini Melbourne, who has rediscovered and reconstructed over 100 pre-European Polynesian musical instruments, is also featured, along with traditional Maori instruments like the *purerehua* (bull roarer) and the *poi* (a small ball of flax on a string used in traditional dances).

Pacific hybridization

The project of a hybridization of aspects of traditional Maori *waiata* and imported black American crossover musical forms is one which many

Maori and Polynesian popular groups and performers have pursued in different ways, and to varying degrees, since the Second World War, when touring Maori showbands performed imported British and American popular songs. Hybridization has existed in Maori cultural expression since the earliest contact with the Pakeha (European settlers) and many Maori myths, legends and historical records were obfuscated by the often mystical and self-interested interpretations of 19th-century Christian missionaries to the extent that, as Humphrey McQueen has pointed out:

> Under pressures to assimilate, the Maori lost track of some of their own legends and at the same time absorbed those from the Christian missionaries. The result was that some of today's traditions are partly the by-products of loss and invention. (1993: 52)

In 1989 the American ethnographer Allan Hanson published an article in *American Anthropologist* called 'The Making of the Maori: Culture Invention and Its Logic'. Using post-structuralist rhetorical strategies, Hanson argued that certain key aspects of Maori history and beliefs, such as the Great Fleet migration of the Maori to Aotearoa in canoes in 1350, and the god Io were invented by a combination of Maori storytellers, Pakeha anthropologists and Christian missionaries. This article, which was later rerun in an abbreviated form in the *New Zealand Herald* under the title 'Maori Myths Invented', caused considerable controversy in New Zealand and led to a public debate in the Anthropology Department of Auckland University. Not unsurprisingly, the Maori speakers in this forum challenged Hanson's right to speak about indigenous matters of which he had no first-hand knowledge and stressed the importance of preserving tribal memories for aesthetic, political and moral reasons, as well as acknowledging the need for revaluation of some of the fictions about Maori history which had become current in school curricula. Jonathan Lamb has suggested that the project of constructing (or reconstructing) an indigenous history of New Zealand can be seen as a 'rhetoric' where cognitive notions of knowledge, certainty and authenticity are replaced by

> a figurative discourse whose relation to power is in direct proportion to its capacity to generate belief or astonishment. History's importance is a matter of feeling rather than knowing, of belief rather than certitude. (Lamb, 1990: 671)

Maori popular music could be regarded as an important vehicle for this kind of discourse, and its struggle for recognition as a struggle for cultural power.

Maori reggae and historical rhetoric

A prominent example of the use of history as figurative rhetoric in Maori popular music occurs in the hybrid lore of Auckland-based Maori reggae group the Twelve Tribes of Israel band. The band's name refers not only to the Rastafarian reading of the biblical prophecy of judgement day, but could also be an echo of British colonial governor Samuel Marsden's 1819 proclamation that the Maori were one of the lost tribes of Israel. The band comprises a loose collective of about twenty musicians and orthodox Rastafarians. Their first album, of religious-oriented songs, *Shine On* (1990) was written, sung and produced by Jamaican-born group leader, Hensley Dyer. It features a song entitled 'The Land of the Long White Cloud', which characterizes the Maori as children of *Jah*:

> New Zealand is a group of islands
> The people are brown, from Shem line they have come
> These are Abraham's seed
> The island that was lost has now been found
> The islands down in the South Pacific
> Where Jah children gather to repatriate

The group's second album, *Showcase*, (1991) features twelve different singers performing devotional songs and is co-produced by the group's mentor, Jamaican musician Egbert Evans. Using tapes of musical exercises recorded in Jamaica by Evans, Dyer shaped the group into a professional outfit over a period of seven years. After producing *Showcase*, Evans commented:

> We know that Bob Marley sowed a seed down here, but I wasn't sure how big this tree was. Now getting here and listening to the 12 Tribes of Israel Band, I realise it's really big. It's reached a level where it has to be travelling out of New Zealand, so it can bloom and blossom more. They have the sound, and I think it's international. (Campbell, 1991: 20)

The Twelve Tribes also participated in mainstream New Zealand national projects by recording a single, 'Join Us' (written by Maori musician Toni Foloti), for the 1990 Commonwealth Games. 'Join Us' celebrates international harmony and diplomacy and the unity of nations in competition in the games, specifically mentioning nations from the Caribbean, while a slogan on the record label proclaims, 'He Waiata Na Aotearoa' (Maori Music in New Zealand). The group's reggae becomes an expression in an international idiom of social harmony which positions indigenous Maori concerns in a wider global context.

Although not reaching the national proportions of Jawaiian in Hawai'i, reggae, ragga and dancehall have been important forces in the hybridization of Maori popular music, which contains a number of examples of what Andrew Weintraub describes as 'the way reggae and its associated images and ideas, when transported to a different social system, take on a different symbolic meaning' (1993: 78). This is evident in the computer-driven South Pacific reggae of Dub Congress, a Sydney-based Maori duo; as well as two Twelve Tribes members who have made solo recordings on the Deepgroves label – the toaster The Mighty Asterix, and Maori female singer and DJ Jules Issa. Issa has expressed that she finds no difficulty in juggling her subordinate status as a woman within orthodox Rastafarianism, her Israelite identity and belief in repatriation to Africa, with her Maori warrior status:

> In my tribe, Ngati Porou, women are allowed to speak on the marae, there are a lot of maraes there that are named after women. Women are very much like warriors, like the men. It's the only tribe in New Zealand that's like that and being of that tribe I'm not afraid to attack an area where there's strictly men involved, like DJing. (Campbell, 1993: 51)

The hybrid contemporary popular forms of Maori and Polynesian music could be regarded as an important aspect of biculturalism in Aotearoa, as could the respectful incorporation by Split Enz of aspects of *waiata* (the title of their 1981 album) into their music and performances. Given the implausibility of entertaining strict notions of authenticity and purity in relation to Maori cultural traditions (or to any contemporary indigenous musical forms), the combination of traditional *waiata* and Anglo-American popular musical forms could be seen as part of a cultural project of self-assertion and self-preservation which links itself with a global diaspora of expressions of indigenous and black social struggles through music. But the use by some Maori musicians of a range of (white) Anglo-American musical influences can also be regarded as part of a bicultural project of interracial harmony, tolerance and respect which has also been expressed through Maori popular music.

Biculturalism and its discontents

The modest but distinctive success of Moana and the Moahunters (and of a growing number of other Maori groups and performers in Aotearoa) amongst both Maori and Pakeha reflects a clear, but often contested, shift towards biculturalism in the New Zealand national identity which has occurred since 1980 and intensified since the 1990 sesquicentennial of the Treaty of Waitangi, signed by Maori tribal chiefs and British colonial governors in 1840 and still the basis of land negotiations between Maori and Pakeha.

'Over the last ten years ... it's gone the other way and everybody wants a marae ... Maori culture's becoming quite an in thing.' This was the

observation of a slightly disgruntled Pakeha former employee in Maori
Affairs, cited in British sociologists Margaret Wetherell's and Jonathan
Potter's discourse analysis of middle-class Pakeha attitudes to the Maori,
Mapping the Language of Racism (1992: 146). Wetherell and Potter argue
that articulations of a pan-Maori culture as a site for resistance and
struggle for social change have frequently been co-opted and nuanced by
Pakeha New Zealanders (*ibid.*: 129). Framed by liberal Pakeha discourse,
Maori culture is seen as 'heritage' and 'therapy'. The responsibility for
preserving a heritage of language, traditions, customs and cultural
practices, some of them lost since colonization, is placed firmly on the
Maori. This duty of cultural preservation, Wetherell and Potter argue, is
also seen by Pakehas as a panacea for the Maori's displacement,
fragmentation, identity loss and urban alienation – which is sometimes
expressed in violence and crime. For the Pakeha, on the other hand, Maori
language and culture become a rich resource for appropriation: learning
Te reo Maori or aspects of *Maoritanga* are seen as options Pakehas can
toy with, depending on how 'bicultural' they wish to become.

There is a marked difference, however, between the increasing
tendency of many Pakeha journalists to 'spice up' their writing with
smatterings of Maori terms as a gesture of political correctness, and the
refusal to translate what are often literally untranslatable Maori terms by
a number of Maori writers. The Maori poet, artist, playwright and theatre
director, Roma Potiki, for example, writes of

> a driving force in Maori theatre to re-establish cultural identity, to work with
> our own stories and people and to reassert the *mana* of the *tangata whenua*. I
> see Maori theatre as *Tino Rangatiratanga* in action. (1991: 57)
> [*mana* = authority, *tangata whenua* = native inhabitants, *Tino Rangatiratan-*
> *ga* = sovereignty and autonomy.]

Given that Maori cultural formations do not demarcate between music,
dance and theatrical representation, Potiki's statement could equally
apply to aspects of Maori popular music. Potiki also expresses
exasperation at 'Pakeha people coming to Maori theatre looking for a
lost spiritual element in their own personalities, and expecting us to
provide it' (*ibid.*: 60), which points to the pressures sometimes exerted on
Maori cultural activists by liberal Pakehas anxious to discover and
appropriate what they see as authentic and indigenous spiritual traditions
of Maori culture.

As Wetherell and Potter (1992) point out, the word 'Maori' means
'people who live in this land', while 'Pakeha' means 'foreigner', a frame of
reference forcibly reversed after colonialism. As they also note, while
many Pakeha continue to regard Maori culture as exotic, '[if] the Pakeha
have a culture at all, it is the "high" culture of operas, novels and art'
(*ibid.*: 136). Some of the differences between Maori and Pakeha cultural

frames of reference were aptly illustrated in controversies over the 1985 *Penguin Book of New Zealand Verse*, edited by the Pakeha poet Ian Wedde, which included, for the first time in such an anthology, a number of Maori poems translated into English. The English versions of some of these poems, which seem banal to Pakeha readers nurtured on English and American canons and poetic traditions, were explained by Maori novelist Keri Hulme:

> Maori is a word-of-mouth language; it has only recently been turned to print, and a great deal of its *mana* and strength still lie outside the blackened word. If you speak Maori, understand Maori, even what you read is fraught with sound – and not sound alone. (1985: 303)

A further consideration is that Maori poetry, as Michael King (1993) has pointed out, is more properly seen in the context of cultural representations such as *waiata, patere* (abusive songs or grotesque dances) and *tauparapara* (an incantation for moving a canoe or other purposes) in which European distinctions between high culture and popular culture are irrelevant (*ibid.*: 133). But prominent Pakeha novelist, poet and former Auckland University English professor, C. K. Stead, whose work was also represented in the anthology, launched an attack in the prominent literary quarterly, *Landfall,* in 1985, on what he saw as a token gesture of liberal orthodoxy and political correctness on the editor's part in including the Maori poems:

> the poems in English were chosen because they were good of their kind while the poems in Maori were chosen because they were poems in Maori... Between the English language poems in this anthology a continual dialogue has gone on, involving influence, reaction, interaction, rejection. No such dialogue has occurred between the poems in Maori and those in English. To represent Maori poetry as part of a lively New Zealand literary scene is simply dishonest. (*ibid.*: 299)

Stead went on to support his argument for the primacy of English literary principles in New Zealand by claiming that English had become 'the language of the land', and that British and European culture was also 'a part of the inheritance of most who are of Maori blood' (*ibid.*: 301).

It is perhaps not surprising that such neo-colonialist assertions of the *mana,* and superiority of anglophone high culture and poetic traditions to what is an *a priori* characterization of impoverishment in Maori culture, were expressed so openly in the mid-1980s. What is more surprising is that a significant number of intellectuals and academics expressed agreement with Stead's argument. Revisiting the controversy in 1992, in the light of subsequent attacks by Stead on the increasing biculturalization of New Zealand institutions, Michael King described Stead's position as an 'anti-anti-racist' espousal of 'ethnic cleansing' which refuses to accept that a knowledge of Maori language and culture is 'a necessary prerequisite for making Olympian judgments about the nature of New Zealand literature as a whole' (1993: 135).

Although Maori popular music has not had to contend directly with the prescriptions of gatekeepers of high culture such as Stead, it has frequently been regarded by Pakeha liberals as either a sell-out or an obliteration of traditional 'authentic' Maori cultural forms of expression in favour of an unquestioning appropriation of the most commercial and sentimental Anglo-American idioms of pop music. In the 1960s, for example, Maori ballad singers like Howard Morrison, Toni Williams, Ricky May and John Rowles, and comedians like Lou and Simon, whose repertoires consisted of a high proportion of cover versions of American middle-of-the-road songs, were regarded with disdain as purveyors of low-brow clichés by most Pakeha intellectuals (including myself). The following historical overview of Maori popular music from the Second World War to the early 1990s is an attempt to contextualize the appropriation of both black and white Anglo-American musical forms by Maori performers and musicians, and to trace the growing prominence of indigenous Maori musical elements within these forms. (NB. A detailed discussion of Maori and Polynesian music in the period 1992–97 follows in Chapter 11 of this anthology.)

From pop to rock to rap

Since Victorian times Maori concert parties, featuring the polyphonic harmonies of traditional songs and dances of Maori folklore like the *poi* dance, the *haka* and the *karanga* (call to ancestors), have been performed in various colonial contexts, often touring outside New Zealand or performing for overseas tourists. In the 1950s Maori showbands began performing repertoires of largely Anglo-American music on cabaret circuits, sharing the indigenous popular music scene with Hawaiian-styled combos and US-influenced Country and Western singers. As Graham Reid has pointed out, the first song to be recorded and pressed in New Zealand (in 1948) was the strongly Hawaiian-influenced 'Blue Smoke' by the Ruru Karaitiana Quartet, who preserved few traces of traditional Maori *waiata* (Reid, 1992a: 1).

In 1955, a Maori country music artist, Johnny Cooper, known as 'the Maori Cowboy', was prevailed upon to record a cover version of Bill Haley's 'Rock Around the Clock' (1955) in an unsuccessful attempt to launch an indigenous rock and roll scene. John Dix has claimed that this was 'probably the first rock and roll recording made outside the USA' (1988: 16) but it failed to have much impact on the local charts, and it was not until the film featuring Haley's original version was released that New Zealand youth of the 1950s discovered rock and roll. Cooper made significant contributions to the local rock and roll scene by recording his own composition, 'Pie Cart Rock and Roll' (1956) and tutoring the Pakeha singer Johnny Devlin, who became a local legend in 1958. He also set a precedent for Maori musicians playing rock and roll, to the extent that, as Dix has pointed out, any discussion of New Zealand rock and roll 'cannot bypass the Maori contribution' (ibid.: 330).

The influence of Hawaiian music continued into the 1950s and 1960s, and was prominent in 'Haka Boogie' (1955), a composition by Lee Westbrook sung by Morgan Clarke with Benny's Five, which announced a hybridization of traditional Maori waiata and popular dance music (as did Rim D. Paul's 'Poi Poi Twist' in 1962). In 1990 a seven-part television programme, When the Haka became Boogie, featured Maori popular entertainment from the 1950s to the 1970s, and proved to be so popular that it expanded into 25 episodes, and two albums of its 'Greatest Bits' were released by Tangata Records in 1992. Featuring cover versions of songs made famous by Frank Sinatra, Bobby Darin, Elvis Presley, Dean Martin and others, the first album, Nga matua (The Stem), focused on the 'golden age' of Maori entertainment in the 1950s and 1960s. The second album, Te Rangatahi (Modern Youth), featured Maori artists of the 1980s and 1990s, both albums establishing an historical continuity of appropriation of US influences combined with elements of traditional Maori language waiata.

In 1968 the popular Maori ballad singer John Rowles illustrated prevailing cabaret tendencies and influences in mainstream Maori music with his British Top 20 hits 'If I Only Had Time' and 'Hush, Not a Word to Mary', while his song about his cousin, 'Cheryl Moana Marie', remained in the Top 20 throughout Australasia for several weeks in 1970. All three hits typified the strong influence on popular Maori singers of popular ballad singers like Pat Boone, Tom Jones and Engelbert Humperdinck. Humperdinck's hits 'Release Me' and 'Ten Guitars' (both 1967) became synonymous with impromptu Maori singalongs at parties throughout the late 1960s and the 1970s.

Sir Howard Morrison, who received an OBE[3] and a knighthood for his eponymous quartet's 40-year services to New Zealand popular entertainment, was the most successful Maori singer of the 1950s and 1960s. Although he never gained European or North American recognition, he was acclaimed in Hawai'i and in the Philippines under the Marcos regime, performing a repertoire of mostly sentimental ballads which expressed little Maoritanga but nonetheless contained identifiably Maori inflections in their smooth harmonies. Morrison also performed songs expressing militant Maori perspectives: his adaptation of Lonnie Donnegan's skiffle hit 'My Old Man's a Dustman' (1960) renamed 'My Old Man's an All Black', was released in 1960 in protest at the exclusion of Maori players from the 1960 New Zealand national rugby team tour of South Africa, and his version of Johnny Horton's 'The Battle of New Orleans' (1959),

'The Battle of Waikato' (1960), was a celebration of one of the many successful wars the Maori fought against British colonial settlers. His adaptation of Ray Stevens' ethnic caricature 'Ahab the Arab' (1971) into 'Mori the Hori' however, was less well received by some of his Maori listeners. ('Hori' is a colloquial term for 'Maori'.) Dix's characterization of the Howard Morrison Quartet as 'basically a comedy act ... indiscriminate in choice and arrangement of material ... [who] did no actual harm to Kiwi Rock – they simply operated outside of it' (1988: 37) does not account for Morrison's importance as a Maori entertainer.

Morrison's friend, Billy T. James, a noted Maori ballad singer and comedian, was a more controversial figure, up to his death in 1991, for his portrayal of Maori and other ethnic minorities in an often self-deprecating way. Many Pakeha found the occasionally homophobic and even quasi-racist aspects of his humour offensive, and other jokes belittling towards Maori self-esteem. However, many Maori people saw James's humour as conveying an important Maori underdog perspective. As a singer, he operated strictly in a middle-of-the-road cabaret context, performing cover versions of songs like 'The Way We Were' and 'When a Child is Born' (in Maori). Some of James's repertoire, like his jokes about the division of New Zealand society into 'Caucasians' and 'Other People' on election ballot forms, was closer to Pakeha notions of Maori militancy, but he remained a contentious figure up to his death, transgressing Pakeha liberal notions of politically correct humour, but expressing an important Maori comic perspective.

In the 1970s the pyrotechnical blues and acid rock of black American guitarists Jimi Hendrix and Carlos Santana were an important influence on Maori guitarists like Billy Tekahika (aka Billy TK), who combined Hendrix-like inflections with aspects of *waiata* and Polynesian guitar rhythms, before shifting to a more John McLaughlin-influenced style of 'spiritual' rock.[4] Dix (1992) has indicated that there have been apocryphal claims that Hendrix was of partial Maori descent, in which Wi Wharekura, a member of the Aorangi Maori Concert Party which toured to New Orleans in 1929, has been identified as Hendrix's grandfather. Guitarist Tama (Tama Renata), who toured Sydney in May 1993 with separate shows billed as tributes to Hendrix and Santana, combined Hendrix-like lead guitar with reggae, soul, blues and funk rhythms on his 1989 album, *Workshop*, which he recorded and mixed on his own '3 and a half track' and released on the independent Te Aroha label (see Shuker, 1994: 17) through Jayrem, with the slogan 'He Waiata na Aotearoa'. Tama was billed in the Sydney weekly music paper, *On the Street*, in Maori warrior-like terms, issuing a challenge to all-comers: 'The legendary Maori Acid Rock Guitarist – He blew out Jeff Beck and Frank Zappa, now he'll blow out anyone that's game to turn up with their axe' (19 April 1993: 39). But, in performance, he produces a distinctively lithe, laid-back and Pacific-inflected style of guitar playing which expresses little of the aggressive intensity of the archetypical acid rock guitarists. But apart from Tekahika's various groups, Renata, and the Rotorua group, Butler, Dix (1988) has observed that there were few all-Maori rock bands in the 1970s and 1980s.

Although Dix claims that soul music as a genre 'has little in common with traditional South Pacific music' (ibid.: 332), the 1980s also saw the emergence of a Maori soul scene in Auckland spearheaded by Ardijah, who continue to perform and record a mixture of soul, funk and dance music. But the most distinctive figure in Maori popular music of the 1980s was Dalvanius Prime, who produced 'E Ipo' for the middle-of-the-road singer Prince Tui Teka, a song which won two Record Industry Awards in 1982. This was followed by 'Poi E', written and produced by Dalvanius on his Maui label and performed by the Patea Maori Club, which reached number one in the New Zealand charts in 1984. 'Poi E' combined traditional Maori vocals and showband and concert party forms with funk and break dancing, and eventually won the 1988 New Zealand Recording Industry Best Polynesian Record Award. The Patea Maori Club, whom Geoff Lealand describes as 'the group that comes closest to capturing some of the unique nuances of life here ... due to its unique coupling of two unmatched musical traditions' (1988: 76) also won Best Polynesian Record in 1984 for their second single, 'Aku Raukura'. The tradition of the Patea Maori Club was maintained in 1992 when Dalvanius and Maui Music produced 'Harmonic Reggae', a four-track reggae-funk release by the young Maori singer Jay Rei.

After Bob Marley performed in New Zealand in 1979, reggae music and Rastafarian philosophy were adopted and adapted by Aotearoa and Dread Beat and Blood (later Dread Beat, who were associated with another Maori reggae group, Sticks and Shanty), both forming in 1985 and disbanding in 1988, and combining mellifluous Maori vocal harmonies with Jamaican rhythms. These groups also used reggae rhythms to express Maori militancy in their lyrics, and Aotearoa's 1985 single 'Maranga Ake Ai' (Wake Up People) was a plea to young Maori to become politically aware and 'take up the cause'. It became one of Jayrem's biggest-selling records, despite being banned by local radio stations because of its militant Maori activist content. As Ngahiwi Apanui, former Aotearoa singer-songwriter and founder of Tai E, a new Maori music recording label, said of Aotearoa:

We wanted to say, 'here we are, we are Maori and we don't give a shit about what you think. You disagree with us and you're in for trouble.' It was the feeling of the youth at the time. It was a political 'hot potato' but it gave us a high profile. (Reedy, 1993: 67)

Graham Reid has described Ngahiwi Apanui's 1989 solo album *Te Hene Ki Te Kainga* (The Link with the Homeland) as 'an ambitious and largely successful attempt at blending traditional Maori instruments like the *koauau* (nose flute) and *purerehua* (bull roarer) within the rock context' (1992a: 34).

Dread Beat's repertoire included songs like 'Colonial Law', 'No More War' and 'One People'. According to Duncan Campbell, they

> displayed fine melody and harmony in the true Polynesian tradition and a rhythm section that had bite without the metallic overkill that spoiled too much local reggae. At their best, Dread Beat could be compared to UK champions like Aswad, Misty in Roots and Matumbi. (1993: 48)

But the most prominent and longest-surviving Maori reggae group is Herbs, who were formed in 1980 and continue to perform. Herbs' first single, 'French Letter', which referred to the French as 'unwelcome guests making nuclear tests' in the Pacific, went to number eleven in the national charts in 1982, but received little radio play. Campbell (1993) claims that Herbs 'epitomized the common purpose of Maori and Islander at a time when the youth of the two communities were more intent on gang warfare'; and that their 1981 debut EP, 'What's Be Happen?' 'set a standard for Pacific reggae which has arguably never been surpassed' (*ibid.*). Their album *Sensitive to a Smile* won the Recording Industry Album of the Year Award in 1989 and two cuts from it also won Best Polynesian record and Video of the Year. Herbs' soft brand of politically-oriented Polynesian reggae, which includes the occasional song in Maori, became highly successful throughout the Pacific Island region, where they toured extensively, and in 1986, US blues artist Taj Mahal recorded two of their songs, 'Light of the Pacific' and 'French Letter', on his Pacific-oriented album *Taj*. As Reid (1992a) has commented, Herbs 'were always more influential than their sometimes modest record sales indicated' (*ibid.*: 31). Moana Maniapoto Jackson has also acknowledged Aotearoa and Herbs as 'people who laid the groundwork for us' (Barbie, 1993: 17). After Toni Foloti left Herbs to join the Twelve Tribes of Israel, they also played on Dave Dobbyn's Australasian number one hit 'Slice of Heaven' (1987), which went on to become the theme song of Australian television commercials for the New Zealand Tourist Board in 1993. Herbs' last album *Homegrown* was produced by Joe Walsh and consequently sounds uncharacteristically similar to the Californian country rock of the Eagles, but nonetheless won Best Polynesian Record in the 1991 New Zealand Music Industry Awards.

Members of Herbs collaborated with Rarotongan pop-soul singer Annie Crummer, a former backing singer with Jimmy Barnes, in 1993. Crummer's single 'See What Love Can Do', from her debut album *Language*, was the second highest-placed local single in the Top 100 in New Zealand for 1992, and the album was subsequently voted Polynesian record of the year in the 1992 NZ Music Industry Awards. The album's title track, which is about learning to speak Maori, contains a robust chorus sung by a Polynesian choir, and Crummer attributes some of her pop-oriented style of music to the influence of her father, whom she has described as 'the Pat Boone of the Cook Islands' (Rae, 1992: 5). Before recording as a solo artist, Crummer was a member of the all-girl group When The Cat's Away, which also included Margaret Urlich, perhaps the most internationally successful Maori popular singer of the 1990s. Urlich, whose first album, *Safety in Numbers*, sold nearly a quarter of a million copies in Australia, has indicated that success across the Tasman involves both a denial of her Maori and Pacific roots and overcoming Australian antipathy towards soul music:

> There's no Pacific Islanders there and I think that's quite strange because my dad's half Maori and I've always had that influence. It's totally whitesville there and that's reflected in the music as well. There's no soul music, it's very much rock and roll. There's people who want soul music but the radio stations won't play it, it's such a male rock tradition there. (Yuzwalk 1992a: 6)

Urlich's increasing tendency to move into a jazz and cabaret idiom is one which many Maori artists before her have shown, but the music of other Maori and Polynesian women singers in the 1990s has often tended to incorporate the influences of the African-American dance music performed by Paula Abdul and Janet Jackson, or Afro-Carribean British groups like Soul II Soul. The disco-soul singer Ngaire (Ngaire Fuata), who is from Ratuma near Fiji, made some impact on the local dance scene with her eponymous album in 1991. Like her backing group, D-Faction, who released an album in 1992, Ngaire tends to operate in a dance-disco medium where there is little room for expressing Maoritanga through the music, but where she nonetheless operates as a role model for Maori young people. Maree Sheehan, on the other hand, who records on the Tangata label, combines soul, funk and rap with Maori percussive instruments like the *poi* and sticks, and stresses the importance of using aspects of *waiata* in her music in order to make it distinctively local:

> I want to see Maori people be international. But at the same time I went overseas this year and I did notice there's so many rap and dance artists. I think it's important to use the elements of our culture in our music so it is something that is really unique to the world. (Yuzwalk 1992b: 4)

The thirteen music videos by Maori and Polynesian singers and groups included in *Blurring the Boundaries,* George Hubbard and Timothy Moon's compilation for the Sydney Museum of Contemporary Art's 1992 New Zealand exhibition 'Headlands', indicates a predominance of Maori women performers and singers of contemporary pop in Aotearoa. One artist who stands out in particular in *Blurring the Boundaries* is Merenia, a talented singer and keyboard player in a blues and jazz idiom. Her 1991 debut album *Maiden Voyage* features an unaccompanied version of the Billie Holiday song 'Strange Fruit' along with songs written with her father, Rob Gillies, who plays bass with Merenia's backing group, Where's Billie? Margie Thomson has commented that the picture of Merenia featured on the album's cover 'looks as glossy and sultry as any Black American pop-industry siren' (1991: 23) but she remains a relatively undiscovered and undersold figure in the New Zealand pop landscape, a factor compounded by her move to Sydney in 1993. While sounding similar to Joan Armatrading and Tracy Chapman at times, Merenia developed a distinctive, blues-oriented soul music, which her 1991 dancefloor version of the Phil Judd song 'One Good Reason' with the Straw People and her 1992 single 'When You Leave' display to good effect.

The dominance of African-American influences over aspects of Maoritanga in the music of Merenia and Ngaire has brought criticism from Mahinarangi Tocker, a respected but commercially unrecognized Maori folk singer-songwriter who is a veteran of the New Zealand music industry:

> They shouldn't need to pretend to be a Whitney Houston. I feel very sad when I see Maori singers influenced by black singers from America. We're unique, and we have our own style, our own rhythms – we don't need to import a style to copy. Anyway, we're relating to the wrong people: we have far more in common with the indigenous people of America in terms of trying to preserve our culture, than we do with American Blacks. (Thomson, 1991: 23)

But the musical paths taken by these young Maori and Polynesian women are dictated more by musical preferences and the need for a marketable image in the industry than by indigenous ideological choices. Their use of African-American idioms is also a response to a global musical culture of sounds and images which relate to a shared black aesthetic, against which local notions of blackness can be defined.

Breakdancing was a prominent and prototypical example of a black American import culture being adopted widely by Maori youth in the 1980s, as a study of breakdance as an identity marker in Palmerston North by Tania Kopytko (1986) indicates. According to Kopytko, breakdance first arrived in New Zealand in 1983 via Western Samoa, and by 1994 local breakdance teams, consisting mostly of young Maori and Pacific Islanders, were appearing on local television programmes. Television New Zealand even sponsored a national breakdance competition. Kopytko argues that for Maori and Pacific Islander young people with little chance of achieving recognition through conventional channels such as school, sport and social position, 'breakdance provided a very strong and positive identity that did much to raise their self esteem and realise their capabilities' (*ibid.*: 21–2). She also claims that, despite the local mass media's association of break dancing with street gangs, glue sniffing and petty crime, which gave it pejorative associations and contributed to its decline by 1985, it provided Maori youth in particular with a substitute for their own culture:

> Amongst Maori youth the association with an international Black identity compensates in part for the lack of a thorough knowledge of Maori culture. Also, popular culture movements are more readily accessible without the commitment and effort necessary for a knowledge of Maoritanga. (*ibid.*: 26)

Following the adoption of breakdancing by Maori and Pacific Islander youth, rap music and hip hop culture became an inevitable medium for musical expressions of Maori militancy. The most prominent Maori rap group in the late 1980s and early 1990s was Upper Hutt Posse, whose Public Enemy-influenced hardcore rap, featuring Teremoana Rapley (who later joined the Moahunters, before becoming a solo artist), had some impact in both New Zealand and Australia, despite group leader Dean Hapeta's espousal of some of Public Enemy's anti-Semitic tendencies and his association with Nation of Islam leader Louis Farrakhan. In 1990 the group toured *maraes* to 'show them there's more to Maori music than just guitars' (Gee, 1990: 16), supported Public Enemy on their New Zealand tour, and played with Macca B. and the Bhundu Boys in Australia.

Upper Hutt Posse released the first hip hop record in New Zealand, 'E Tu' (Be Strong) in 1988, combining black American revolutionary rhetoric with an explicitly Maori frame of reference. 'E Tu' pays homage to the rebel Maori warrior kings of Aotearoa's colonial history, Hone Heke, Te Kooti and Te Rauparaha. It also praises the 28th Maori Battalion, a celebrated volunteer force in the Second World War who suffered high casualty rates which caused the loss of most of a generation of Maori men: 'Yes yes the Maori was a strong warrior/Strike fear in the heart of a Babylon soldier.' 'Intervention' targets British colonialism and the French government-sanctioned bombing of the Greenpeace ship *Rainbow Warrior* in Auckland harbour, while 'Hardcore' celebrates Malcolm X. In an article on the group, Kerry Buchanan commented on their US–NZ hybridity:

> Upper Hutt Posse is modern Maori music with links to the spirit of hardcore black American hip hop, as in the reference in the rap *Hardcore* – 'Like Malcolm X him preach the hard truth/And we'll remember him and what he did contribute'. In the Posse's rap Hone Heke and Malcolm X can exist side by side because they represent the spirit of resistance against the dominant power structure. (1988: 35)

But the group's 1989 album, *Against the Flow*, delivered in a mixture of New Zealand and American accents, and including a paean to American basketball, combined some rather inchoate political rhetoric with an overriding concern with American hip hop styles. While the singles taken from the album, 'Do It Like This' and 'Stormy Weather', achieved some degree of popularity in New Zealand and Australia, there was a notable absence of any of the specific Maori references or use of the Maori language that distinguished the early recordings, as if the group had decided to de-localize their songs in the interests of a broader international appeal, while maintaining a militant rhetorical pose.

Of the eleven tracks on *Against the Flow*, only the title track, which begins with a reference to the Sesquicentenary of white settlement, has any local frame of reference, but is otherwise a vague and non-specific tirade against generalized oppression. Together with 'Stormy Weather', which contains references to Jews and Nazis and Central America, but does not mention New Zealand, these are the only two tracks which have any specifically political address. The video clip of 'Stormy Weather' uses footage of 1977 Maori land rights demonstrations at Bastion Point, protests against the 1981 South African rugby tour of New Zealand and opposition to French nuclear tests in the Pacific together with scenes of a Kanaka labourers' strike in Queensland and demonstrations in South African townships. This attempt to contextualize the song's claim that 'people's culture's not respected ... madness rules the world' remains an unconvincing domination of hardcore rap style and rhetoric over content, as does the fist-pumping but context-free dance track 'Do It Like This'. While Dean Hapeta continued to be an outspoken figure on racism and local political issues in the local mass media, Upper Hutt Posse's music and lyrics seemed to becoming more homogenized into a mode of black music which was losing its local features, reflecting the group's ambition to move into the overseas market, and Hapeta's visits to the US. As Hapeta has claimed: 'there used to be a lot of diversity to Maori bands, they used horn sections, the whole lot. That all seems to be lost now' (Gee, 1990: 16). The group's contribution to this loss of diversity is perhaps indicated in DJ Darryl Thompson's statement about their responses to overseas influences:

> We're not copying overseas sounds, but we're relating to them. It's the same with the reggae, it's about something that we've experienced, being ripped off or whatever, something we see. I can relate better to what Public Enemy or Gregory Isaacs have to say than I can to John Farnham. (*ibid.*)

In 1992 Upper Hutt Posse returned to its reggae origins, releasing four different mixes of 'Ragga Girl', a ragga/dancehall single which rose in the local charts, and was subsequently included on the soundtrack to Lee Tamahori's highly successful 1994 film, *Once Were Warriors* (discussed in detail in Mitchell, 1995: 1–8). Despite this success, the early 1990s witnessed a new development in Maori and Polynesian popular music, one which – as discussed in Chapter 11 of this anthology – was identified with the South Auckland suburb of Otara, and represented a form of 'New Urban Polynesian' cultural identity and expression.

Notes

1. Aotearoa is the Maori name for New Zealand, and is now officially recognized. Throughout this chapter the two names are used interchangeably.

   An earlier version of this chapter originally appeared in P. Hayward, *et al.* (eds), *North Meets South: Popular Music in Aotearoa/New Zealand* (Umina, NSW: Perfect Beat Publications, 1994).

2. NB. Aotearoa translates into English as 'land of the long white cloud'.
3. OBE: Order of the British Empire, an honour awarded to British colonial subjects by the Queen, on recommendation of the British Government.
4. Moana and the Moahunters have paid homage to Billy TK by including his song 'Prisoner' on their 1993 single 'I'll be the One', which features Billy TK's son on guitar.

Discography

Aotearoa, *He Waiata Mo Te Iwi*, Jayrem, 1986.
Hgahiwi Apanui, *Te Hene Ki Te Kainga*, Jayrem, 1989.
Ardijah,'Take a Chance', WEA, 1987.
Annie Crummer, 'Language', East West, 1992.
Double J and Twice the T, 'All Wrapped Up', Definitive Records, 1989.
—'Def to be Green', EMI, 1990.
Dread Beat, *All Our Lives*, Jayrem, 1988.
Dread Beat and Blood, *No More War*, Jayrem, 1987.
E Tu, 'Whakakotahi', Tangata Records, 1993.
Herbs, *What's Be Happen?* Warrior, 1981.
—*Sensitive to a Smile*, Jayrem, 1988.
—*Homegrown*, Tribal Records/WEA, 1990.
Billy T. James with the Hot Band, *Billy T Live! at 'Pips'*, Pagan, 1985.
Taj Mahal, *Taj*, Ode, 1986.
Merenia, *Maiden Voyage*, Pagan, 1991.
—*When You Leave*, Pagan, 1992.
Moana and the Moahunters, *'AEIOU' (Akona Te Reo)*, Southside, 1992.
—*Tahi*, Southside Records, 1993.
—'I'll Be the One/Rebel in Me', Southside, 1993.
—'Peace, Love and Family/Kua Makona', Southside 1993.
The Neville Brothers, *Family Groove*, A&M, 1992.
Ngaire, *Ngaire*, Southside, 1991.
Jay Rei, *Harmonic Reggae*, Maui Records, 1992.
Maree Sheehan, *Make U My Own*, Tangata, 1992.
—*Dare to be Different*, Tangata 1992.
Tama, *Workshop*, Te Aroha, 1989.
The Twelve Tribes of Israel Band featuring Hensley Dyer, 'Join Us', Jayrem, 1989.
—*Shine On*, Twelve Tribes of Israel, 1990.
—*Showcase*, Twelve Tribes of Israel, 1991.
Upper Hutt Posse, 'E Tu', Jayrem, 1987.

—*Against the Flow*, Southside, 1989.
—'Whakamutungia Tebei mahi Te Patupatu Tangata', Alcoholic Liquor Advisory Council, 1992.
—'Ragga Girl', Tangata, 1992.
Margaret Urlich, *Safety in Numbers*, CBS, 1989.
Various, *AK 89: In Love with These Rhymz*, BFM Rap.
—*Trax*, BFM Music 1989.
—*1991 Compilation*, Tangata Records, 1991.
—*Reggae Blasters 1 and 4*, Far I Records/Jayrem, 1991.
—*Tribal Stomp*, Tangata Records, 1992.

3

Indigenization and Socio-political Identity in the *Kaneka* Music of New Caledonia[1]

Dedicated to the memory of Alexis Poindipenda, lead singer of Jémââ, who died in a tragic accident in 1994

David Goldsworthy

Introduction

Kaneka is a style of popular music in New Caledonia which developed in the 1980s, fusing indigenous elements with melodic, harmonic and rhythmic features of Western popular music. The word *kaneka* was fabricated from a play on the words *kanak* , *kanaki* and *kanaké*.[2] The very name by which this music is known has both political and musical resonance. Its use in this context is simultaneously a statement of socio-political affiliation to an indigenous movement for independence, and an onomatopoeic reflection of the basic percussion beat which serves to generically define this type of music. The development of *kaneka* has created a distinctively regional brand of popular music in New Caledonia, and is the result of a conscious, deliberate attempt to achieve Kanak cultural identity through a popular music medium. The strong socio-political dimension of many *kaneka* song texts, combined with the heavy reliance of some bands on indigenous musical instruments and rhythms, sets this style apart from both other previous (and still current) styles of popular music in New Caledonia and also much popular music in the Pacific. This conscious process of infusing a tradition with indigenous elements in order to make it more regionally specific and representative may be termed 'indigenization'.

This chapter consists of four sections. The first examines the process of indigenization. The second traces the historical development of *kaneka* music in New Caledonia, relating this to both socio-political and musical factors. In the third section, the *kaneka* band Jémââ is selected for scrutiny as a case study. The chapter concludes with a brief discussion of *kaneka* as an example of indigenization within the broader context of cultural construction.

Indigenization

Indigenization is not a new term nor a new process; it has been observed in many places and periods. Carol Babiracki has compared the different ways in which indigenization of Christian ritual music in India and Africa has been achieved, and relates this process to a 'larger movement of indigenization of Christian ritual and music throughout the non-Western world' (1985: 97).[3] Indigenized idioms of Christian music which emerged by the late nineteenth century in the Pacific have been discussed by Amy Stillman, who posits five broad stages or processes of indigenization: survival and resurgence, coexistence, appropriation, emergence (of new idioms) and absorption (of old/new idioms into indigenous conceptual frameworks) (1993: 93). In the area of secular popular music, indigenization has been noted in several cultures, for example, in Indonesia with the injection of Javanese elements into *kroncong* music in the early twentieth century (see Kornhauser, 1978: 133–4).

A particularly close parallel to the indigenization of *kaneka* music in New Caledonia has been documented by Gage Averill (1994) in his study of Haitian music. He discusses the emergence of voodoo-jazz groups in the 1940s and 1950s and *mizik rasin* ('roots music') groups in the late 1970s as 'neo-traditional' movements which sought to establish new Haitian musical identities through a process of indigenization (and external appropriation of Jamaican reggae). As with *kaneka* groups, voodoo-jazz bands actively incorporated traditional peasant rhythms and instruments (bamboo trumpets) into their music. Describing the process, Averill quotes Tit Pascal, a *mizik rasin* performer, describing his 'difficult apprenticeship in traditional musics, exploring tradition-specific compositional principles' (*ibid.*: 173). He distinguishes *mizik rasin* groups from other Haitian groups belonging to the *nouvel jenerasyon* movement which is more closely oriented to commercial Euro-pop (*ibid.*: 175). In particular, Averill identifies three aspects which differentiate these two music movements – size of group, dependence on technology, and length of compositions. These three aspects also distinguish *kaneka* groups from other types of popular music in New Caledonia. As with neo-traditional groups in Haiti, *kaneka* bands tend to be larger, have access to less sophisticated technology (at least in the early days of the movement) and produce longer and more elaborate compositions (in comparison with other types of bands in New Caledonia). Other differences were highlighted by Jean Oedin in a 1991 report to the Director of Cultural Affairs in New Caledonian. Oedin divides live bands in New Caledonia into two types. The first of these he identifies as 'European'-type groups, who have regular practices in rehearsal rooms, invest in good quality equipment, have an elaborate repertoire which they play in regular fortnightly gigs at night clubs, and whose members may have done music courses at an institution. The second he identifies as *kaneka* groups – ensembles who have less regular rehearsals in makeshift areas, usually possess inadequate equipment, hold performances less frequently, and whose musicians all work in the oral mode. (Oedin also adds that the *kaneka* groups are attracting a greater percentage of the youth.)

Indigenization is one of many processes at work in culture contact situations. The processes and products of 'acculturation' or 'transcultura-tion' in the musical sphere have been discussed at length in the ethnomusicological literature (see, for example, Kartomi, 1981). At one level, the terms 'indigenization' or 'indigenized' may refer simply to the inclusion or combination of indigenous elements with foreign or introduced elements in genres or idioms of the non-Western world. (Stillman, 1993, for example, seems to use the term in this way.) This musical syncretism is, of course, a common feature of many popular music styles and develops as a result of conscious selective and adaptive strategies of musicians from one or more cultures. My use of the term indigenization in this chapter, however, refers to a process of an even more conscious and deliberate nature whereby an already acculturated style is *re-infused* with indigenous elements to give it a more 'authentic' (and less Western) sound, and, more significantly, to embody a specific socio-political and musical identity for the practitioners and consumers of the newly constructed tradition. As Martin Stokes points out, music and dance often symbolize social boundaries and 'provide the means by which the hierarchies of time and place are negotiated and transformed' (1994: 4). Although some writers have rightly stressed that even so-called 'traditional' genres entail continual re-creation and are always in some measure self-conscious about this process (Handler and Linnekin, 1984), postmodernists/deconstructionists do admit that self-conscious reflection (and action) in cultural construction is more intense when perceived cultural/ethnic differences are politicized (Linnekin, 1992: 253), as is the case in New Caledonia. Miller (1994) suggests that this greater degree of self-consciousness derives from a shift in temporal consciousness brought about by the onset of 'modernity', which he discusses according to a structural model derived from Hegel and Habermas.

In New Caledonia, *kaneka* music has been created consciously by musicians to forge a musical identity with a specific socio-political orientation. Aspects of this affiliation to Kanak social and political independence are clearly encoded in the musical sound, style, texts, performance practice, dress and behaviour, as they are in Haiti (Averill, 1994: 179). In the process of creating a pan-Kanak socio-musical identity, certain *region*-specific features have been reshaped or homogenized, a common procedure in national *kastom* (custom) construction in the Pacific (See Babadzan, 1988).

Socio-political and musical factors in the development of *kaneka*

The origins of *kaneka* are rooted in the quest for a viable Kanak identity in the post-World War Two period and, in particular, the political struggle for independence from the colonial French regime. Fraser has argued that

> The general post-war mood of emancipation, combined with the Kanak experience of paid employment ... weakened the French suppression of the Kanaks and led to the abolition of the code of native regulations in 1946. (1988: 4)

The formation of several Kanak men's associations helped to socially restructure and unify Kanak people and prepared the way for the growth of political movements. The conferral of voting rights on Kanaks in 1951, and the establishment of the Union Caledonienne (UC) party in 1953 by a French radical and a Kanak chief, were early landmarks in the Kanak quest for liberation. Kanak radicalism accelerated in the 1970s with the staging of demonstrations and protests, culminating in the formation of the Front Independantiste (FI), a coalition of independence parties, in 1979.

The 1970s also proved to be a formative period for Kanak *cultural* liberation from French colonial dominance in New Caledonia. In 1971, a women's association, the 'Smiling Melanesian Village Women's Groups' was formed and put forward the idea of a cultural festival to promote indigenous Kanak arts. This initiative resulted in the first festival of Melanesian arts, 'Melanesia 2000', held in Noumea in September 1975. This festival was not only a celebration of the diversity and calibre of indigenous Melanesian arts, but a pan-Kanak exercise in identity-seeking and formation. That this was a motivating factor behind the festival is clearly confirmed by the report of the president of the organizing committee to the territorial and national authorities (as reported by Tjibaou, 1978).

The years 1975–6 also saw the release of the first music cassette recordings by Kanak musicians. The group Bethela is credited with this initiative (Tein *et al.*, 1993: 15). From this time, the nexus between musical and political developments becomes clear, and the groundwork for the subsequent formation of the *kaneka* style proper is laid. Kaloonbat Tein, from Hienghène on the north-east coast of the main island, describes how he was directly encouraged in his composing and recording endeavours by the great political figure, Jean-Marie Tjibaou, whom he quotes as saying:

'one must plant many trees for independence, one must compose many songs for independence' (Tein, 1993: 12). Encouraged by Tjibaou, the albino Kaloonbat Tein, one of the major figures of the subsequent *kaneka* music movement, formed his first (unnamed) band in 1977, and produced his first cassette in 1978 (called *Maxa* by Tjibaou himself after his political group which ran for the 1977–78 territorial elections). According to Tein, Tjibaou actually helped negotiate with the studio (Horizon) on their behalf, with Tjibaou contributing the lyrics to one of the eight songs on the album. This group produced a second cassette, also called *Maxa*, in another studio. By now the group had a name – The Adventurers of the Mainland, Hienghène. This 1978 release represents the first recording of a mainland group to sing in their own language (Nemi).

One factor in the development of *kaneka* in the late 1970s and early 1980s may have been a policy of the French government which deliberately encouraged massive migration of French people to New Caledonia throughout the 1970s to improve 'the numerical balance of the races' (Fraser, 1988: 6), and which resulted in the reduction of the Kanak population to a minority of 43 per cent by the 1983 census. 'Ethnicity' often emerges as a significant concept for indigenous people precisely in population centres of an overseas diaspora where such groups are in the minority or, in countries such as Malaysia and Fiji where the population of indigenous peoples has been equalled or outnumbered by other ethnic groups through immigration. In New Caledonia, the rapidly growing population imbalance combined with the inequity of the political system and obvious disparity with Pacific neighbours who had already achieved independence from their colonial masters,[4] provided a ripe breeding ground for political dissension and a stronger impetus for movements such as *kaneka* which would help facilitate and foster group solidarity and Kanak ethnic identity.

The late 1970s and early 1980s witnessed the formation of several groups which were to become the vanguard of the *kaneka* music style, including Kirikitr, Jémââ and Bwanjep (Kaloonbat Tein's new group). From this period dates experimentation with the incorporation of traditional instruments and rhythms in popular music. Groups began to look to indigenous Kanak ceremonial music and dance traditions (generically called *pilou*) for their inspiration.

The texts of early *kaneka* songs were not only in local languages, but began to reflect religious, moral and political issues of the time. Some songs had humorous texts (for example, songs by the group, Bwanjep) and love themes were still important but no longer dominant. Specifically musical developments, however, were overshadowed, and, to some extent, postponed (see Tein, 1993: 13), in the face of increased political activity from both independence and anti-independence forces, culminating in the assassinations, armed resistance and violent struggles of the 1984–88 period. Several *kaneka* musicians were directly involved in this violent struggle. According to Jacques ('Kiki') Kare, leader of Jémââ, band members of his group waged political protests as well as burning French farm houses (interview with the author, 1994). Some Jémââ members were jailed as political prisoners. Musical and political spheres are thus clearly linked at this time. The impetus for the further development of *kaneka* was provided by these turbulent events.

The official date for the birth of *kaneka* is usually given as February 1986. On the 13th and 14th of that month, an historic meeting took place in the Cultural Office at Nouville in old Noumea (Tein *et al.*, 1993: 15). Several major musical figures were present at that meeting which addressed various cultural issues and new developments in Kanak music. Kanak musicians began, in earnest, to research their own traditional music and dance in order to discover a firm basis on which to build a popular music which, although rooted in Kanak tradition, would still be meaningful to the youth of the day. The meeting in February 1986 facilitated dialogue between like-minded musicians and set the scene for the subsequent development of the *kaneka* style.

Prior to the development of *kaneka*, most popular music in New Caledonia was basically European or American-style music with a Kanak 'flavour'. Song texts were often in French. Some songs mixed French and Kanak and a few used a local language. English language songs also became common. Love themes dominated and a basic voice, guitar and drums set-up was employed with little use of keyboard or percussion, and no brass. The most important influences on popular music in New Caledonia were North American folk rock and blues, and more recently, reggae.

Some pre-*kaneka* bands, however, from both the main island and the Loyalty Islands, developed regionally-specific styles, reflecting distinctive musical aspects (such as vocal production and harmonies) as well as employing vernacular languages in their songs. One Loyalty Island band which achieved great popularity throughout New Caledonia was Black Brothers,[5] one of only a few pre-*kaneka* bands inclined to use local languages in their songs (Tein, 1993: 15). This band is also credited with the first appearance of organ and solo guitar on a Kanak recording (1982).

Pre-*kaneka* acoustic and electric bands, however, did not provide the primary basis for the *kaneka* initiative. Kanak musicians turned to other internal and external sources for their inspiration. Indigenous Kanak ceremonial music and dance traditions have provided instruments, rhythms and, in some cases, melodic chants for *kaneka* songs. Although many regional *pilou* rhythms exist, one common rhythm — ♩ ♪ — has become the pan-Kanak rhythmic base for *kaneka*. Some Kanak musicians have described this rhythm in metaphorical terms as the two overlaid sounds of water falling over rocks in a river.[6] According to these Kanak musicians, the basic rhythm of *pilou* was derived from this natural phenomenon. In modern *kaneka* a battery of percussion instruments may be used to realize this rhythmic base. Indigenous Kanak instruments include bamboo stamping tubes (*bwanjep* or *jö*) and concussion bark bundles (*jêpak*). Congas, bongos, maracas and the drum kit from Latin/Western popular music are also used. Apart from instruments and rhythms, actual Kanak chant melodies have occasionally been used as the basis of some *kaneka* songs (Tein *et al.*, 1993: 16).

A major *external* source of inspiration for Kanak musicians in their quest for cultural identity through music has been reggae. From the late 1970s, reggae and its associated cultural baggage has been a formative influence on popular music in New Caledonia. The New Zealand Maori band Herbs, who play reggae-based music, achieved great success and popularity throughout the Pacific Island region and have had a particularly strong impact on *kaneka* bands. While reggae is popular amongst many Pacific peoples in New Caledonia, many of the younger male generation (including several *kaneka* musicians) also cultivate dreadlocks and some smoke marijuana in addition to performing and consuming reggae music, both imported and local. This does not seem to be a common trend in Pacific cultures (apart from New Zealand). Rastafarian religious practices, however, have not penetrated the New Caledonian cultural scene.

Kanak culture is not alone in the Pacific in its enthusiastic embrace of reggae. Reggae has formed the basic musical style of several Australian Aboriginal bands, starting with No Fixed Address and bands such as Herbs in New Zealand and Exodus in Fiji. Nor, of course, is this phenomenon restricted to the Australia-Pacific area, but is evident in the Americas, Africa and elsewhere in the world. Averill (1994) describes the development of *mizik rasin* groups in Haiti which looked to Jamaican Rastafarian practices and reggae in the late 1970s for musical models and links such 'Afro-centric' musical movements to broader global perspectives of black identity:

> These movements foster oppressed group solidarity, link local exploitation to larger struggles of black peoples, and create a cultural space to articulate anti-hegemonic counter-narratives, tales told *about* the oppressed *by* the oppressed. (*ibid.*: 159).

In New Caledonia, Kanak musicians have also strongly identified with this larger picture of black solidarity and anti-hegemonic activity in their pursuit of their own specific goals, for which the reggae musical style provides an appropriate expressive framework and outlet. There is also, perhaps, a musical explanation for the popularity of reggae amongst *kaneka* groups. The pan-Kanak rhythmic base of *kaneka* mentioned above (derived from *pilou*) is itself very close to a reggae rhythmic feel. The musical influence of reggae on *kaneka* has persisted to this day. Some bands (for example, Mexem) base their style primarily on reggae.

The development of *kaneka* in New Caledonia is possibly related to a parallel phenomenon in Papua New Guinea – the career of the band Sanguma, which may have provided a more specific external model for Kanak musicians. Like Jémââ and some other *kaneka* groups, Sanguma consciously incorporated indigenous instruments, rhythms and even chants in their songs to produce their own fusion style. As Kiki Kare admits in an interview reported in the Cook Island News, 'Sanguma was a kind of daddy to us, because they started [doing things] about ten years ago' (Sword, 1992: 5). It is not clear to what extent Sanguma actually influenced the Kanak initiative, but the existence, acceptance and eventual popularity of a band with similar goals of indigenization in another Pacific culture has no doubt provided support for *kaneka* musicians in their endeavours. Festivals such as that held annually in New Caledonia (starting in Poindimie in 1989) and the Pacific Arts Festivals (for example, the 1992 Festival in Rarotonga) have brought together both 'traditional' and 'popular' groups from all over the Pacific. This has provided a stimulating forum for sharing of musical styles and, in some cases, facilitated the cross-fertilization of ideas, techniques and styles.

The long period of political turmoil in New Caledonia finally ended in 1988 with the signing of the Matignon Accord by both French and Kanak parties. It set out a ten-year plan for the territory's future, which would culminate in a vote on independence in 1998. The years of relative peace and stability in New Caledonia since 1988 and the terms of the accord itself, some of which directly refer to encouraging and ensuring Kanak-based initiatives in the arts, have provided a positive context for various cultural developments, including *kaneka* which has flourished during this period. *Kaneka* has continued to function as a mechanism for establishing and consolidating pan-Kanak identity and a means of achieving social cohesion between various Kanak groups. The last eight years have been marked by several musical and technological developments in *kaneka*. The recording and release of *kaneka* albums has increased significantly. The first live *kaneka* recording (of the group Kiriktr) was released by Mangrove Studios in 1991. Festivals and tours by *kaneka* bands (such as that by Vamaley to New Zealand in the early 1990s), have secured some international recognition for this tradition, although *kaneka* is still not widely known outside New Caledonia.

The rapid development of *kaneka* since 1988 has been assisted by various institutional agencies. The Agency for the Development of Kanak Culture (ADCK), itself a child of the 1988 agreement, has been working since 1990 to document and promote Kanak culture, and has thereby encouraged the push towards indigenization of Kanak arts. The Kanak broadcasting station, Radio Djido, also focuses on playing popular music from the Pacific as well as Western popular music and reggae. Its music programmes include *kaneka*, although little traditional (*pilou*) Kanak music is broadcast. Recording studios such as Mangrove, and its manager, Alain Lecante, who is sympathetic to *kaneka* musicians, have also encouraged the recording and dissemination of this genre. As one of the largest cities in the Pacific, Noumea certainly has the technical know-how and facilities, the appropriate infrastructure, and a ready market for products of the recording music industry. Ironically, perhaps, it is Western technology which has accelerated the development of *kaneka* in the last decade. As Carol Babiracki notes in relation to Christian music in Africa and India: 'indigenization ... probably could not have achieved the momentum that it now has without the modernization and secularization tendencies of post-colonialism' (1985: 99).

Jémââ: a case study

There are currently over 40 active *kaneka* bands in New Caledonia, located in Noumea, the interior of the main island, and in the Loyalty Islands. Of all these bands Jémââ has been most rigorous in its attempts to create a fusion of Western and indigenous elements, and is the band which most heavily relies on Kanak-derived features. Jémââ is one of the oldest *kaneka* bands in New Caledonia, but only produced its first album in 1994. Jémââ exemplifies the indigenization process at several levels, including that of the music industry, and is therefore an excellent focus for the study of *kaneka* music in New Caledonia.

Jémââ is a cultural association, with a defined organizational structure and affiliations to other such Kanak associations. It is a rather large, all-male band with between 16 and 20 performing members (depending on the number of percussionists required). The band is based in Tiéti, a Catholic village near the town of Poindimie on the east coast of the main island. Four members of the band belong to the same family. Jean-Ives Poindipenda, the lead guitarist, is the recognized musical leader of the group, while Kiki Kare, a charismatic political figure who has lived in France and Australia, acts as producer and functions as the group's main link with the modern commercial world. Because Kare comes from a different region of the island (Houaïlou), the members of Jémââ often communicate in French.

Early in 1994, Jémââ embarked on an ambitious project – a self-produced album. To achieve this goal, they drew up a rigorous four-week rehearsal schedule to fine-tune eight songs (which they had been performing live for several years). The group met at about 4 p.m. after work each day and practised for seven hours. Jémââ is a rather unusual *kaneka* band in that under normal circumstances it usually rehearses three times a week for two hours. The group take a serious and professional attitude to rehearsal with much self-criticism (encouraged by Kare and Poindipenda) in order to achieve a higher standard of performance. The four-week rehearsal schedule was designed to shorten and arrange already-composed songs for the recorded album format and to work on finer aspects of performance, especially dynamics, attacks and harmonies.

In February 1994 I was fortunate to be able to spend three days with Jémââ in Tiéti while they rehearsed for their album recording, and was able to observe the way in which they synthesized indigenous and western elements in their individual brand of *kaneka* music. Jémââ usually employ a large battery of traditional and western percussion instruments for their music. Indigenous percussion used at these rehearsals consisted of two bamboo poles stamped on a pillow on the ground by one man, pairs of bark bundles beaten against each other by two men, and one or two dried leaf bundle scrapers. Western/Latin instruments included a drum kit, a separate floor tom played with two sticks, maracas, bongos, congas (tam-tam) and a single cow-bell. The percussion instruments were all located together at one end of the kindergarten hall in which the group rehearsed, while the other instruments were at the other end, with a recording and mixing desk in the middle. These other instruments were three electric guitars, a bass guitar, keyboard and harmonica. Two other wind instruments were used sporadically (usually for rhythmic/percussive purposes) – a conch shell and an eight-piece raft panpipe. A lead singer and a chorus of three men providing harmonies completed the group.

The percussion battery was not only physically separated from the other electronic instruments, but often practised on its own (before joining the whole group) working as an independent unit to achieve precise attacks and rhythmic co-ordination. In Jémââ songs, the percussion often has the important role of commencing items and setting the subsequent rhythmic base of the whole piece. Jémââ and some other *kaneka* bands regard the battery as the most important, central part of their music and request a boost in volume for studio recordings. This is probably to make the percussion of their *kaneka* items more closely resemble the powerful, deep sounds of the traditional *pilou* dance percussion ensemble which includes a large number of bamboos and bark bundles, thereby achieving its high volume by natural means.[7]

The rhythmic patterns played by the percussion instruments tend to reinforce the pan-Kanak rhythm mentioned above. The repeated patterns for a Jémââ song, 'Tö Jö' (which they rehearsed at these sessions and which is included on their first album), are reproduced below and may be considered fairly typical.

The single floor tom and the hi hat of the kit both play the basic crotchet-quaver rhythm, while the four men who play the scrapers and bark bundles also produce this rhythm between them by interlocking (one performer of each pair playing on the beat and the other pair playing off the beat in alternation). The use of rhythmic interlocking is a feature derived from indigenous Kanak music. *Cada* historical chants, for example, are accompanied by both bamboo stamping tubes and bark bundles which are divided into two equal groups which interlock. (See

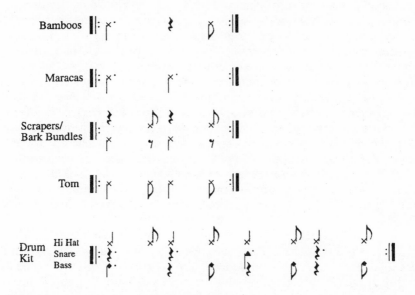

Figure 3.1 *Percussion patterns for 'Tö Jö'*

Cada et Ayoii). The dualistic principle involving pairing of instruments and interlocking is common throughout Melanesia, for example, the *au ni mako* of the Solomon Islands, and the flute music of the Sepik area of Papua New Guinea (see, for example, Zemp, 1978 and Spearritt, 1982). The bamboos, maracas, scrapers, bark bundles and single floor tom usually repeat their patterns with very little or no variation throughout a song. The drum kit repeats its two-bar cycle also, but the drummer usually provides drum fills at various structural points in a song.

The other percussion instruments in the ensemble – cow-bell, bongos and congas – do not usually play ostinati, but play intermittently and often in a Latin or reggae rhythmic style. They provide rhythmic interest and variety and may be used to highlight structural points in the song.

The tight circular seating arrangement of the percussionists in *kaneka* rehearsals may be regarded as a traditional Melanesian feature. Circular and centric performance arrangements are common for vocalists and/or instrumentalists in some parts of Melanesia (for example, Fiji).

Other Kanak aspects of *kaneka* emerge from a consideration of bands operating in a live performance context. *Kaneka* bands rarely play in the bars and clubs of Noumea; these venues are usually played by European-type bands (and Tahitian dance shows). Large-scale concerts and festivals are the main performance contexts for *kaneka* bands. Concerts are infrequent, once or twice every six months, and are often long, drawn-out, multi-stranded events which may last all night (and over a two-day period). They are often organized in conjunction with some fund-raising purpose, for example, for a football club. These infrequent and lengthy performance events linked to modern cultural institutions assume a ceremonial dimension, not unlike that of traditional *pilou* performances and quite unlike performances of other popular music in New Caledonia. Therefore, the social context and function of *kaneka* would also appear to be related to pre-European traditions. The dress, movements and song arrangements at live gigs also tend to reflect the operation of the indigenization process. Jémââ musicians often dress in traditional costume and 'dance' while playing on stage. Their song arrangements at these concerts bear little relation to the short, standard popular song format. Lengthy versions of songs with percussion breaks, improvised sections and, in many cases, links between songs, predominate in their performances, again suggesting similarities to traditional *pilou* performances.

Of course, the songs of Jémââ and other *kaneka* bands include many obvious western aspects. The instrumentation of guitars, keyboard and drum kit has already been mentioned. The functions of these instruments and the patterns they play are also derived from Western popular music on the whole. The Jémââ group use popular terminology in discussing their songs – 'lead' guitar, 'solo', 'verse', 'chorus', etc. Songs are usually set in standard Western keys (major or minor) and their melodies and harmonies clearly follow the patterns of Western popular music. These features can be observed in the transcription of the melody and chords of 'Tö Jö', a song from Jémââ's first album:

Figure 3.2: *Basic melody and chords of 'Tö Jö'*

Note the triadic basis of the vocal melody, symmetrical phrasing and the simple, three-chord harmonic format. Many *kaneka* songs follow the common verse–chorus form of western pop songs, but 'Tö Jö' has a single eight-bar verse repeated throughout (with instrumental breaks).

The first Jémââ album, entitled *Kèpunê Ge Cagötü*, was released in March 1994 and contains eight songs. All eight songs are concerned with issues of French oppression or indigenous Kanak identity and liberation. As Kare said to me, 'There is time enough for love after independence!' (interview with the author, 1994). Most songs are sung in Kanak languages, but two are macaronic ('L'Aube se Lève' and 'Prestation'), and one has a French title ('Vingt-Quatre Septembre'). 'L'Aube se Lève' ('Dawn Breaks') has both French and Kanak sections, while 'Prestation' has verses in Baîti and a French chorus – 'Prestation, travaux forcées' – which refers to the much-hated practice of 'forced labour'.[8] The song, 'Tö Jö' (see above) has a simple text about playing, singing and dancing *kaneka* music, which is, of course, a musical symbol of Kanak identity. The words (and title), 'Tö Jö', which mean 'strike the club', could easily be a veiled reference to armed insurrection.

According to Kare, *Kèpunê Ge Cagötü* is the first self-produced, self-funded and self-distributed Kanak album in New Caledonia.[9] Most albums are produced by a studio which pays for production costs and returns 20 per cent of sales to the artists (compared with 8–15 per cent in Europe).[10] Artists do not get royalties (for radio broadcast, etc.) because there is no collecting agency for copyright in New Caledonia.[11] In Jémââ's case, the association financed all production costs (including the studio recording itself for which Mangrove Studios were paid an arranged recording fee) and did its own distribution, but receives all monies accruing from the sale of the cassette.

The first Jémââ album project reflects an important stage in the indigenization process of *kaneka* music in New Caledonia. The project was not 'Top 10'-driven, but rather intended as a political statement of Kanak self-reliance and independence in musical terms. According to Kare, Jémââ want to work *with* the music industry but at the same time have no desire to 'sell their souls' (his words) in the process (interview with the author, 1994). Their project is part of an overall trend to establish self-driven and self-funded Kanak initiatives which includes other such projects in the arts (e.g. painting and sculpture). By successfully completing its own project, Jémââ hopes to help other bands and cultural groups who wish to take the independent path. Kare and Poindipenda have kept a detailed dossier on their album project for other groups to consult if they require.

In addition to their aim to operate within a financially independent framework, Jémââ demonstrate an indigenized musical approach in several other ways. Jémââ have three capable songwriters in the band and stress originality of composition. Almost all the songs they perform are their own, and the band aims to avoid imitation and pastiche of other bands' styles. Jémââ also exhibit a fiercely independent Kanak emphasis in their songs which tend to be aggressively anti-establishment and pro-liberation in spirit (compared with other bands who have moderated their extreme political positions since the late 1980s). Most Jémââ members were political prisoners of the French regime at one time or other and still maintain a critical attitude towards those in power. Jémââ meetings and rehearsals are marked by a collective, democratic decision-making process and include formal occasions (such as the official signing of the first album contract with Mangrove Studios) reminiscent of traditional Kanak rites.

Indigenization as cultural construction

Kaneka not only represents an instantiation of the process of indigenization in Pacific music, but is also part of a broader process of cultural construction[12] as articulated by those social science scholars who adopt a 'constructionist' approach, in opposition to the 'narrative' tradition of anthropology with its more pronounced essentialist and objectivist perspectives. According to the cultural constructionist approach, 'culture' or 'tradition' (*kastom* or *coutume*, as it is often called in the Pacific) is viewed 'as a symbolic construction, a contemporary human product rather than a passively inherited legacy' (Linnekin, 1992: 249). Many constructionists warn of the danger of oversimplification in the polarized 'traditional–modern' view of culture, with degrees of self-consciousness, authority and authenticity as central dividing concepts (see, for example, Jolly, 1992 and Miller, 1994). All 'traditions', whether old or new, are said to involve continual re-creation rather than passive perpetuation (Handler and Linnekin, 1984: 281–5). Cultural constructionists and postmodernist theory assume a 'plurality of histories that are told and retold according to interests, perspectives and circumstances' (Jolly and Thomas, 1992: 244). Ethnicities and identities can therefore be actively created or constructed according to historical circumstances and social context. Identity can also be reconstructed according to changing circumstances (Averill, 1994: 159 and Stokes, 1994).

Many scholars emphasize the *active* role of the cultural players themselves in constructing or reconstructing identity, rather than perpetuating a view which emphasizes passive response to internal or external pressures (see, for example, Stillman, 1993; Stokes, 1994; and Jolly, 1992). Moreover, music often has an active role to play in such identity construction/reconstruction, and is not simply reflective of general cultural tendencies. Music can, in fact, *directly* activate cultural innovation, changes in identity, and political processes (see, for example, Stokes, 1994: 10 and Averill, 1994: 178).

Kaneka is a clear example of the conscious construction of cultural identity through music. The creation of a self-reliant Kanak musical identity with definite socio-political affiliations is particularly clear in the case of the band Jêmââ with the direct involvement of its members in the political process, and the obvious socio-political messages embodied in their songs and in the very process of production of their first album. This pan-Kanak socio-musical identity has been fashioned from existing resources and structures (both foreign and indigenous); Kanak musicians have deliberately invoked 'tradition', that is, indigenous elements of pre-European Kanak music, which, in combination with introduced musical features, represent this emergent identity. Unlike some other Pacific cultures, this modern Kanak music has not experienced major conflict between micro and macro constructs of tradition, perhaps because of a common and persistent foe, the French regime, which has continued to dispossess and outnumber indigenous Kanaks. Nevertheless, some Kanak radicals have strongly protested against the 'folklorization' of Kanak music at festivals, which they describe as 'a prostitution of Kanak culture' (Babadzan, 1988: 215). Although *kaneka* undeniably smooths over distinctive regional (micro) features in its attempt to create a modern Kanak supra-regional identity (for example, in its adoption of a single, standard rhythm from the many regional possibilities in pre-European Kanak music), *kaneka* has managed on the whole to avoid such criticism.

The main motivation for indigenization and cultural construction of *kaneka* in New Caledonia has been the specific socio-political situation of Kanak people within a French regime, combined with the drive to create a distinctive form of modern Kanak music which clearly represents Kanak culture. In many ways this Kanak phenomenon is not unique, and indigenization is part of a global tendency. *Kaneka* has, for example, parallels in Papua New Guinea and in Haiti. As Simon Frith (1991) points out, celebration of local music in terms of 'self-production' rather than reliance upon the centralized recording industry is a common feature of discourse amongst musicians of the world music scene (or, at least, as he cynically points out, amongst scholarly interviewers of such musicians), and also in the West, where performers 'want to be successful internationally while remaining true to their roots' (*ibid.*: 284–6). In New Caledonia, Jêmââ and some other *kaneka* bands also have similar aims and concerns. Carol Babiracki (1985: 97) has also noted the global tendencies of indigenization in Christian music and points out the economic and social advantages of being 'traditional' or 'tribal' as a major motivation for this process. This also applies to the New Caledonian situation in that *kaneka* is viewed by many Kanak people as more ideologically correct than other forms of popular music. Since the Matignon Accord of 1988 this view has been encouraged by the French (through, for example, the ADCK, by way of policies and grants).

The growing acceptance and popularity of *kaneka* music over the last eight years has possibly led, in some cases, to a dilution of its more obvious antagonistic elements as it becomes subsumed by commercial mainstream culture (as, for example, has happened on several occasions in the history of Western rock). In fact, a cynical commentator might point out that in some cases, *kaneka* has functioned as a palliative device in the post-accord period, to rally feelings of pan-Kanak identity on the one hand, but also to divert attention from divisive social and political issues which still remain despite the proclamation of 'peace'. At any rate, the differences between *kaneka* and other forms of popular music in New Caledonia should not be overemphasized. Some *kaneka* tracks released in recent years make only limited or tokenistic use of Kanak rhythms and instruments and may sound little different from other non-*kaneka* popular music. As Averill points out in relation to *mizik rasin* and *nouvel jenerasyon* groups in Haiti, 'the two musical movements ... have a considerable amount in common' (1994: 179) and both owe a debt to 'international pop aesthetics' (*ibid.*). This is also true of some sections of the *kaneka* movement in New Caledonia today. The band Jémââ, however, is exceptional in some ways. It has rigorously maintained its anti-establishment political and musical stance and quite self-consciously invoked 'tradition' to construct a distinctive socio-musical space for its own style of *kaneka* music.

Notes

1. This chapter originally appeared in *Perfect Beat* vol. 3, no.2 (January 1997).
2. The word 'Kanak' is used to refer to indigenous Melanesians in New Caledonia. Originally a perjorative label used by Europeans, it was adopted by radical groups whose leaders encouraged their people to use the term proudly as a positive statement of their identity (Fraser, 1988: 5).
3. The term 'inculturation' also occurs in publications of the Catholic Church to describe the deliberate policy of adapting Christian liturgy and music to its local context. (See, for example, Karecki, 1993). This term, however, does not generally occur in the standard ethnomusicological literature.
4. Six Pacific countries achieved independence in the 1970s, starting with Tonga and Fiji in 1970.
5. Not to be confused with the West Papuan band, The Black Brothers.
6. See Steven Feld's work on the Kaluli people of Papua New Guinea (1981). The Kaluli also have water-based metaphors for musical features and techniques.
7. Some bands actually record the percussion track for their songs in the bush and then add the other instrumental and vocal tracks in the studio. This serves two purposes: it produces a more naturalistic and ambient sound and also avoids taking so many people to the studio.
8. The statute permitting the practice of forced labour was finally repealed after the Second World War.
9. The European band, Pas Possible, was the first band in New Caledonia to put out a self-produced album in 1984.
10. In 1994, cassette albums sold for 1800CFP of which the studio would normally get 1100 (wholesale) or 1300 (retail).
11. As reported by Ward (1993), the French copyright law of 1957 was reviewed and reaffirmed in New Caledonia in 1993 but is ineffective due to the absence of any collecting agency.
12. See Linnekin (1992) for a discussion of this and other terms in relation to recent socio-cultural studies of Pacific cultures.

Videography

Kaneka Live, PKY Productions, 1993.
Nîärî ma Côô, ADCK, 1992.

Discography

Bethela, *Souvenirs*, Mangrove, 1993.
Bwanjep, *Percussions*, Mangrove, 1992.
Jémââ, *Kèpûnê Ge Cagötü*, Thoo-Gaom Productions, 1994.
Kirikitr, *En Concert Au Liberty*, Mangrove, 1992.
Mexem, *Indigène*, Mangrove, 1993.
Vamaley, *Echos du Passé*, Mangrove, 1993.
Unattributed, *Cada et Ayoii, Chants de Hienghène*, ADCK, 1986/1992.

4

Koori Music in Melbourne: Culture, Politics and Certainty[1]

Robin Ryan

Introduction

The cultural production of contemporary Koori[2] music in Melbourne has maintained the political thrust it first established in the mid-1980s even as political and social conditions have changed. 'Bash Against Bicentenary' may have been the in-phrase amongst Melbourne's Koori community musicians in 1988, but in 1993 it was 'Mabo Mambo' – the title of a major gig held at the Sarah Sands Hotel, Brunswick on 9 July. This featured six local Koori acts, and was staged during the most concerted push for Native Title since white settlement. Throughout the International Year of the World's Indigenous People, the heated political debate around Aboriginal land rights was strengthened by the continued efforts of Aboriginal artists to assert their presence and their culture. Since the bicentennial year of 1988, several Aboriginal acts (most notably Yothu Yindi) have achieved passing waves of recognition in the commercial arena of what Kev Carmody calls 'CCAM' (Consumer Con Advertising Music). Despite a rapid rise in the general awareness of Koori music in Melbourne since 1988 however, little attention was given to the unique problems and issues confronted by Koori musicians themselves until 1993. In February 1993, Ausmusic offered an educational kit on Koori music, entitled 'Urban Songlines', to schools. Other notable initiatives included the workshop on entertainment law, sponsored by the Victorian Rock Foundation; and the establishment of music industry training initiatives directed specifically at Kooris. These are, however, only the beginning of the support needed to bring Koori music into the mainstream, and represent an overdue attempt by the Australian cultural establishment to redress a long-standing neglect since, as Kelli McGuinness and Brad Brown argued, a community which is denied its ability to create, due to a denial of resources is an unhealthy community. A society which denies a community its creativity by denial of these resources is a sick society. (1985: 20)

Fortunately, the Songlines project has fared well in the face of various government cutbacks since 1993, including those to Ausmusic itself. Indeed, the project has subsequently consolidated and a Songlines compilation CD has been released.

This chapter presents a social history of some of the Koori bands and individuals who actually manifest the 'urban songlines'[3] by producing contemporary Koori music in Melbourne. The various musical styles and genres which they employ have been shaped by the experiences of their songwriters, for music has acted, and still acts, as a barometer of the social mood or feelings of each generation. Ever since Koori families moved to the Melbourne suburb of Fitzroy between World War One and World War Two, their creative endeavours, mainly in non-tribal musical modes, have undergirded their social identity and communal solidarity. This fact adds local credence to Sullivan's description of Aboriginal creative endeavour in non-tribal modes:

Research to date has uncovered considerable evidence of what was once a vibrant, creative and unique tradition of social music, in many ways paralleling the white traditions but in itself a separate entity with its own creative thrust. While most people would be aware of the existence of Aboriginal rock bands and Country music few know that there has been a musical continuum from pre-contact times until the present. Most, if not all, contemporary Aboriginal musicians have grown out of these older traditions and reflect their influences strongly, e.g. Harry Williams and Jimmy Little. (1988: 64–5)

The roots of contemporary urban Koori music began in Melbourne in the 1940s, with the singing of hymns and wartime songs at the Gore St Mission, Fitzroy, from 1943, and the 'Corroboree' season of vaudeville acts staged in 1949 at Wirth's Olympia. The 1950s saw further initiatives, such as various entertainments held at the Melbourne Aboriginal Moombas (carnivals) and at the Belgrave indigenous art shop; and performances by the Harold Blair Choir. Along with annual Aboriginal balls (held since 1949) and regular socials, dances and fund-raisers sponsored by the Aboriginal Advancement League since the 1960s, these early contexts and venues for Koori music-making in Melbourne provided cultural escapes from, and compensations for, the social and economic problems associated with rural–urban drift.[4]

The Koori music network

The Koori music network in Melbourne comprises a complex, interlinked social and cultural matrix within which musical activity is enabled, nurtured and expressed. Analysis of the network shows that it operates within the boundaries of its own support structure, goals, needs, resources and personalities. A strong infrastructure of Koori service organizations undergirds the Koori socio-musical system. This infrastructure manifests itself in various ways and through various agencies. For example, organizations such as the community-based Victorian Aboriginal Health Centre are significant for providing a youth club gymnasium with a stage for plays and a practice space for Koori community bands and music recording. Similarly, the Koori Kollij in Collingwood, a community-controlled health worker's school, offers musical activities as part of its programme and houses the Aboriginal Elders' History Program, which includes the study of traditional art and music. The Aboriginal Rights Solidarity Group which developed alongside the Koori Information Centre (KIC), has also supported musical projects, such as a series of 'Rock Against Racism' fund-raising concerts and the 'Don't Celebrate '88' campaign. However, the most effective organization propagating Koori music in Melbourne is radio station 3CR. The station features Koori-run music programmes (featuring commercially-recorded, taped and live music) and also includes Koori music on other, talk-oriented Koori shows. 3CR's Koori radio projects have now been operating for over twenty years. Another Melbourne radio station, 3EA, wholly established for the benefit of the multicultural community, runs an Aboriginal Program Exchange (TAPE). Its Koori co-ordinator, Cheryl Vickery, collates material and exchanges tapes with Aboriginal broadcasters all around Australia.

As ethnicity-reinforcing structures these core groups and projects provide a framework to sustain and develop the Koori socio-musical system, for they build up confidence and pride in the cultural group via internal sponsorship. They provide 'territory' – places in which Kooris can exert the right to do things their way – and, arguably, reflect the growing sense of the specific Aboriginal identity which the urban environment has forced upon their members.

Many Melbourne Kooris believe that the changes they are striving to make can only be successfully attempted by a unified front. The Koori music network, reflecting in its processes and conflicts the forces at work in urban Koori society as a whole, lends credence to Bruno Nettl's theory that the socio-musical system is in certain respects a smaller and more easily manageable version of the entire social system (Nettl, 1978: 14). From another perspective, however, the community is not just an enclave, but a symbolic mosaic in Melbourne's intercultural complex. Some of its characteristics can therefore be seen as common to the whole urban environment.

The musical taste of the Koori community has been moulded by the network of Koori musicianship, including Koori radio. The elders still enjoy Country and Western music, but teenagers prefer rock, reggae and rap. Yothu Yindi appeal to young Australians of both Koori[5] and non-Koori descent because the 'in-culture' viewpoint is operative; the peer group finds tracks such as 'Treaty' ideal to dance to. All age groups, however, seem very proud of the achievements of their local musicians. B.B. McGuinness, who has become something of a spokesperson for the network, believes that Koori people need to produce their own music in order to retain part of their heritage, strengthen their own cultural beliefs, provide a more wholesome education for their future generations, and educate and sensitize a vast range of people from varying cultural/social backgrounds who would previously have been ignorant of Aboriginal culture (McGuinness, 1989: 12). Thus Koori musicians hope that positive images of their art will touch people and be transformed into other areas of benefit for Kooris. Strengthening, broadening and deepening the national concept of Aboriginal cultural heritage can be seen to be a firmly ingrained goal in Koori Melbourne.

Koori music and its contexts

The typical Koori band is a microcosm of its immediate expressive culture characterized by strong bonding. Cabarets, parties and community functions provide 'internal' support for musicians and bands, and solo performers are usually easily identifiable for audiences, since the current expressive culture of small-scale community life is, in this case, very dependent on its music and musicians. Ensembles are often characterized by their individuality of style and 'flavour' and their music is usually eclectic, diverse and well-delivered in spite of meagre resources.

The popularity of Melbourne's Koori bands in their own community can be traced back to the activities of earlier groups. One of the first Koori bands to play to non-Koori audiences in Melbourne pubs was the Country Outcasts, led by Harry Williams and Joyce Johnson. The group organized regular Country and Western talent quests and festivals in parks in the early 1970s, which led to the first national Aboriginal Country Music Festival in 1976. In 1975 Country Outcasts Number Two was formed by the next generation of the Williams and Johnson families, together with Henry ('Chooka') Thorpe, and eventually developed into Hard Times, Melbourne's local Koori community band.

In the lead-up to the 1988 Bicentenary of British settlement in Australia, overt nationalism was accompanied by what has been described as 'the commercialization of Aboriginiana' (Crotty, 1992: 6). But the foregrounding of the historical and contemporary treatment of Aborigines through both indigenous and non-indigenous channels (such as the tours, videos and public statements of [white] rock band Midnight Oil) also resulted in a more fundamental change. The inward projection which Koori music manifested in previous decades began to move outwards to the wider community and received appreciation in return. 'Rock Against Racism' fund-raising concerts and the 'Don't Celebrate '88' campaign were followed by 'Bash Against Bicentenary' jams featuring Hard Times at the Burnley Tavern, Richmond. By 26 January 1990, Hard Times were still battling it out at an outdoor Invasion Day, contributing their 'sophisticated urban pop taste in instrumental arrangements, vocal solo style, and high vocal harmonies with triplet rhythms' (Schultz, cited in Breen, 1989: 86).[6]

Grant Hansen, a musician and one of the comperes of 3CR's *Koori Music Show,* has been a key figure and catalyst in encouraging the development of Koori music in Melbourne. Along with colleagues such as Brad and Anthony Brown, he has given morale-boosting promotion to Koori bands. He has also published articles on Koori music in the *Koorier* and, in August 1992, he accompanied Archie Roach and Ruby Hunter on their tour of America, sending live radio reports back to 3CR. Concerned that Koori musicians had been accepting sub-standard equipment and backing for their performances, which kept their reputation amateur, Hansen also initiated the Koori Music Club in mid-1989. Other committee members were Des Smith, Glenda Thorpe, Miki McGuinness, Marion Green and Archie Roach. Although the club only lasted about twelve months, it bore fruit in the following ways. First, the club brought Koori musicians together under one umbrella, giving them the opportunity to sing, play a musical instrument or gain experience in stage management, lighting, sound engineering or roadie work. A regular meeting was held on Fridays at 1 p.m. at Koori Kollij and the club organized Thursday night jam sessions. Lessons were available for both adults and children in drums, bass guitar, rhythm guitar and singing for $2 a session. This type of grounding has equipped Koori musicians to form 'scratch bands', ready for performance at relatively short notice. Secondly, the club edified the wider Koori community. As Des Smith has asserted:

> The Koori Music Club sees a need for channelling talent of all kinds into the community because music is a way to give incentive to Kooris to develop their talents in all the arts. Music gives encouragement, motivation and support. Giving support to everyone and sharing is the Koori way. (1989: 8)

Thirdly, the club was an important incentive on the part of Kooris themselves to bridge the gap between black and white peoples. Non-Koori talent in Koori groups also became 'acceptable' with Grant Hansen's formation of Interaction in June 1989. This cross-cultural group also grew out of a need to provide alternative music for community singing and dancing, and so emphasized 1950s and 1960s rock and roll songs – which suited both young and old – at parties, functions and fund-raisers. The original four-piece band grew to six members and, before disbanding, typical gigs included NAIDOC (the National Aborigines' and Islanders' Day Observance Committee) engagements, a Graduation Night at Deakin University, the AIDS concert at the Myer Music Bowl in January 1990, and the Arts Board Concert at the Arts Centre in March 1990. A further series of music workshops was held at Koori Kollij commencing on 8 May 1990. The workshops, convened by Music Program co-ordinator, Des Smith, were given on songwriting, band organization, management and jam sessions. They were led by respected musicians such as Paul Kelly (who also used the occasion to promote the songwriting talents of Archie Roach).

Apart from clubs and workshops, the recruitment, training and nurturing of Koori musicians in Melbourne operates through households, schools and attachments to specific bands. These have included Koori Youth and Spears (also called Will Shakes Spears) a youth band which performed at the 1991 'Sounds of Survival Festival', and the Next Generation, formed in 1993. Lines of influence are passed on via specialist performer/songwriters, the modern equivalent of tribal songmen. As renowned performers in their own right, these specialists function as mediators between the values of continuity and change. In this sense, the influence of Western music has altered the position and role of the songman in Koori society. Through the example of specialists, younger Kooris are given the incentive to try their hand at music and performance. In 1990 I observed a type of 'apprenticeship' system operating in a Reservoir household. Yal Yal, a teenage boy from Yirrkala (Northern Territory), studied didjeridu and dance with Gnarnayarrahe Waitairie. He busked with his teacher, gave his first stage performance in the *Greenhouse Forum* at the Dallas Brooks Hall, and then made his first television appearance on *The Flying Doctors* shortly afterwards.

The community band Watbilimba provided an excellent example of how training and nurturing occurs in an ensemble situation.[7] Specialists Wayne Thorpe and David Arden led six new Kooris, aged between 20 and 30, in the band's premiere at the Sarah Sands Hotel, making statements about Aboriginal survival via original songs only. In fact, this band wrote twelve original songs together in only one month. Of Thorpe's twenty or more songs, half were written for children, especially his two daughters. Thorpe says:

I believe very strongly that their Aboriginal identity needs to be recognised in their first impressions. Fair enough, they can learn nursery rhymes later on, but I want to make sure that their identity and their Dreaming is instilled in them first, their culture, their heritage, their history – making sure that their belief in themselves is strong. Once you know your identity, your confidence is so much stronger. (Jackomos and Fowell, 1991: 51)

In adopting this proactive approach, Thorpe is looking beyond the fragmentation which has occurred. In his present position as a teacher of Koori students at Northlands Secondary College, Thorpe is seizing the potential for restoration to wholeness, as are other resilient musicians such as Archie Roach and Ruby Hunter. But how does the transience and fragmentation experienced by so many Koori performers affect the historical processes of selection, formation, dissolution, dispersal and reformation of Koori bands?

Early Koori groups were small in size and their members were selected mainly via family ties. Bands have dissolved and dispersed for many reasons, but chiefly through lack of money and equipment. People have also moved geographically, married, died, or joined new groups. It is possible that personal disagreements also caused the dissolution of some bands. Aboriginal groups in Victoria, for all their idealism, have often divided into factions as a result of regional and tribal affiliations to the Riverina, Gippsland or Western District respectively. However, new kinds of Aboriginal bands are developing. These are no longer based on regional and family ties but on a self-chosen style, political position and audience. Schultz has argued that

> This [development] is closely linked with the slowly emerging sense of a single Aboriginal nation where blacks from any region strive to address all other blacks on themes of common concern, and to address the white nation on behalf of all blacks. (Breen, 1989: 111)

There are, of course, a number of other factors which contribute to the breaking up of Koori bands (such as the luring away of outstanding musicians from their home bases, and even seasonal factors, such as waning audiences in bad weather) but the principal threat to the stability of Koori ensembles has been the economic recession and the high cost of modern equipment. For most Koori bands gigging is not a significant remunerative activity, and playing live is usually a supplement to other employment, which is also hard to obtain. Dissolutions, however, are not always permanent, with many bands reforming at later dates when circumstances are more conducive to regular gigging or other forms of support. The re-formation of a Koori band does not always include all – or even most of – the original members. Line-ups are rather designed to suit the context. In 1985, for instance, Hard Times, a group who had operated on an on/off basis for several years, made a video for the Victoria Story Exhibition held at the Melbourne Museum. Screened to the public for three years prior to the Bicentenary celebrations, the video contained three of the band's songs performed to footage of land rights marches, demonstrations, murals and shots of the Melbourne Koori community. As Wayne Thorpe, who rejoined the band to direct the music clip, explained, the band's specific line-up was based on whether past or present members knew the chosen songs (Thorpe, 1985: 20).

Along with Thorpe, Grant Hansen (discussed earlier with regard to the Koori Music Club and Radio 3CR) has also been a key individual in various Koori bands. His original group, Interaction, reunited in mid-1992 as Blackfire, recruiting Selwyn Burns from Coloured Stone. With the 1993

Koori Artist of the Year Award to their credit they soon established a high profile in Melbourne as a hot rock band and toured nationally. Their first album, *A Time to Dream*, was recorded early in 1994. Hansen also started the half Koori/half Latin American band, Mercury Blues, in August 1990. Mercury Blues grew out of the Juke Box Jivers, and mainly performed a 1950s repertoire. Its first female member was Marion Green, who previously sang and played bass guitar for Interaction. Green's career began in 1978, when she performed in the country band Ebon Koorines (Black Daughters) with Debbie Williams and daughters of Joyce Johnson. They played in Melbourne Koori cabarets and toured rural New South Wales before finally disbanding in 1982 due to lack of money and equipment and having families.

At least twenty Koori bands have operated in Melbourne since the early 1970s; nearly three-quarters have been formed since 1988. (The names of some groups speak volumes, wry humour being used as a means of protest.)

My research on Koori bands in Melbourne has shown that each group adheres to one or more of four creative aims, namely to express and reforge Koori identity; to challenge and disturb white Australia; to strengthen, broaden and deepen the national concept of Aboriginal cultural heritage; and to promote harmonious cross-cultural interaction. With some groups only one or two of these aims are evidenced, whereas with some performers all may be present and interrelated. Choice of aims reflects an individual's own personal background as well as a conditioned community response. The fourth aim, forged by the desire of Koori performers to foster dialogue with mainstream Australia, has been manifested chiefly by groups such as Interaction and Mercury Blues, who favoured American rock and roll as a means of building bridges between Koori and non-Koori people; and by Djaambie and Tiddas, who, by including non-Koori performers, managed to ease their way into mainstream engagements. There are clearly a range of musical choices now open to people of Aboriginal descent.

Urban Koori song themes and styles

Urban Koori music has, over the last century, been influenced by styles associated with the dominant (non-Koori) culture, such as early twentieth-century hymns, folk songs, bush ballads and music hall songs; more recently, Country and Western, folk, rock and pop; styles derived from mediated forms of Afro-American and Afro-Caribbean cultures, such as nineteenth-century 'coon songs' and 'plantation ballads'[8]; and, more recently, blues, calypso, reggae and rap. In Schultz's words, Aboriginal musicians 'adopted and adapted them into a folk culture which gave the characteristic mix to early twentieth century non-tribal music traditions' (Breen, 1989: 28). The selection, blending and modification of pre-constituted music styles involves choice and experimentation on the part of musicians and composers. Meyer has argued that composers make choices in the light of the intentions generated by goals that are implicit in the constraints of style and largely set by the ideology of the culture (1989: 36). An increase in external sponsorship since 1988 has been responsible for Koori musicians' growing focus on strategy (as opposed to struggle). As well as involving goal-setting and the art of planning, strategies are also formulated within the constraints of style.

The predominance of Western popular idioms as influences on contemporary Koori music can be interpreted as meaning that Koori music basically uses 'borrowed' apparatus but such a perspective ignores the extent to which musicians always attempt to expand their horizons as new sounds arise. Even before the policy of assimilation had been adopted in Australia, the Koori people had been moved to embrace the dominant culture and build their music into it. With the advent of multiculturalism it gradually became fashionable for Kooris to perform in traditional tribal styles and to combine Western and non-Western elements. If world music can be considered an essentially non-Western form,[9] one notable exception to the more common process of Koori music-making being moulded by Western popular idioms occurred on 14 January 1992 when Joe Geia's Aboriginal chant, *Yil Lull* (or *Yu-la-lei*) featured as an exhilarating finale to Percussion Spectacular, a summer music concert held in the Melbourne Concert Hall. Geia's didjeridu playing was supported by multi-tiered layers of Brazilian, Javanese and West African music, suggesting other possible links and trajectories outside the Western musical mainstream. While in 1995, Geia's CD, *Tribal Journey*, was well received by the Melbourne music press, the problematic issue of its marketing remains – should it be categorized as Aboriginal, ambient or world music?

Table 4.1 attempts to chart the manner in which the various styles within the repertoire of contemporary Koori music in Melbourne correspond with the formulation of their creative aims and, it should be noted, is a preliminary model on which to build further correlations of theme and style. It is based on a study of songs by performers covered in this chapter and identifies four major topics or themes in the songs which are in keeping with the four main creative aims of Koori songwriters stated above. It is of course possible for any musical style to be employed for the portrayal of any theme, but, as can be observed, the constraints of style mentioned by Meyer do seem to prevail. I have therefore attempted to match the four major themes with the dominant styles (and/or genres) in which they are presented.

Both tribal and modern Koori songs provide a strong sense of shared meaning and understanding of the way people understand their lives. As Thorpe has argued:

Regardless whether it's tribal music or contemporary music, we sing about the environment. In tribal times we sang about the different techniques of catching different animals and where's the best spot to hunt that animal. Also about the different journeys that some of the people would take and where they went and what sort of things they left. Today contemporary music is still singing about the environment. It's just that it's changed so dramatically. (1985: 16)

Table 4.1: *Theme/style correlations*

Major themes	Dominant styles/genres
1. Identity	Soul; Country and Western; Folk; Streetwise ballads.
2. Politics	Protest songs; Folk songs; Rock; Calypso; Reggae; Rap.
3. Heritage	Traditional tribal music and dance; Country and Western; Folk.
4. Interaction	1950s and 1960s Rock; Neotraditionalist Rock; Jazz; Koori/non-Koori Fusion; Hymns.

Koori poetry and song emphasize the metaphoric, and link the rhythm and form of music with the metaphorical power of language. Their metaphors reflect direct insights and attempt to communicate them. They express one thing as being another so that a whole experience is communicated as a phrase, picture or a musical expression (Creighton, 1988: 1–2). This can be interpreted in relation to the first creative aim of Koori musicians.

Thorpe aims to express Koori identity, which is sometimes portrayed in contemporary songs through metaphor and is strengthened through the use of tribal names in the text. 'Naming' was an important part of traditional tribal song language, as a name stands for the whole of an object or person (Thorpe, 1985: 9). For example, Thorpe has written songs to help his daughters understand their identity and the songs address the meaning of their tribal names. For his daughter, Pirili Tathra (meaning 'bright star over a beautiful country'), he wrote a song which explains the significance of the star and the land, and for his other daughter, Tallara Murringal (*Tallara*, meaning 'rain which is the spirit of life' and *Murringal*, meaning 'Eucalyptus Wattle'), Thorpe wrote a song entitled 'In Our Dreamtime'. He argues that

These songs help my daughters to understand about their own culture, about their land, about their identity. These things give meaning to life for both my children and help them understand Dreaming. They know their names come from their Father's Dreaming and the names their parents chose are meaningful. They are keeping the Dreamtime alive. (Jackomos and Fowell, 1991: 50–1)

As Koori Larry Walsh has argued, in addition to songs addressing traditional aspects of tribal culture many contemporary songs address the three basic bones of contention for Melbourne's Koori community: land rights; compensation for the mothers of 'stolen' children; and black deaths in custody.[10] Other themes commonly used in songs include urban poverty, alcohol abuse, domestic violence, fear of the police, mental illness, AIDS prevention and Koori leaders' misuse of power. Most Koori radio programmes tend to favour songs with political texts but programmes also feature more light-hearted material whose lyrics link Koori identity with the Dreamtime culture; nostalgia for the country and care of the environment and people; describe historical events; or extol the benefits of positive black/white relationships. Love songs, children's songs and fun songs highlighting the Kooris' sense of humour are also numerous in this contrasting repertoire pool.[11]

Innovation and creativity

The relationship between the Aboriginal traditions which frame Melbourne Koori bands, and the development of styles of music which deviate from those traditions, is complex. Koori musicians do not consciously have to be producing 'Koori Music' in order to do so. It is possible to argue that Koori people share a common 'folk' concept of Aboriginal culture even if they do not consciously articulate or verbalize it. Each individual can be seen to be in the process of developing his/her own expression of Aboriginal culture according to their own background experience, and regardless of whether their creative aims in this regard are conscious or not. Anna Malone (1991) has argued that the use of traditional tribal instrumentation and musical patterns in urban Koori music springs from the desire of performers to use and retain the strengths of contemporary styles of music while giving them a traditional inflection. While the use of instruments such as the didjeridu and sticks to produce a distinctive sound and effect – one aurally iconographic of Aboriginality itself – they are also often peripheral to the central part of more contemporarily-oriented music and may run the risk of being seen as gimmicky and musically dispensable to cultural outsiders (see Smith, 1992: 65). However, as the music of Yothu Yindi has proved, it is possible to integrate rock, dance and traditional Aboriginal music and instrumentation into a coherent and mutually reinforcive sound.[12]

Djaambie is one of the most prominent and accomplished Melbourne Koori bands to have produced an innovative mix of musical approaches. Their music style does not, however, simply derive from musical choices made in isolation. It can rather be seen to reflect their broader cultural project and their concern to promote causes such as ending deaths in custody, establishing land rights and promoting intercultural harmony. In this way, their music can be seen to be inhabiting the same intercultural context as the band itself. A typical Djaambie number begins with a didjeridu introduction over which the band builds up a layered rhythmic infrastructure. The group's 'big band' style is created by the use of trumpet and saxophone and is complemented by the use of (white) female singers performing a responsorial vocal chorus (and live dance movements).

Tiddas, the female trio, use a similarly varied, but more novel instrumental line-up which judiciously combines acoustic guitars, rhythm sticks, cabassa (seed pods from New Caledonia), percussion (or 'chicken shake') eggs and an idiophonic wooden box knocked with a stick. With such subtle instrumentation, the group has to maintain attention to contrast, clear texture and precise expression in their live shows (qualities not always easy to maintain in live sound mixing at rock venues). The band are also notable for the manner in which they have been concerned not simply to adopt styles from the broad 'style-menu' of popular music but rather to interpret and impose their own style of presentation on the music they choose for their repertoire, a process they have described as 'Tiddyfying'. This includes the use of devices such as shift of accent; use of compelling guitar riffs; scatting or the use of monosyllabic backing sequences. An innate sense of musicianship enables the band to avoid gimmickry, and a sense of humour shines through when they put on a drawl in Country and Western songs, use a jazz beat for their version of 'Rock Around the Clock', a change of rhythmic emphasis in 'Summertime', and a barber shop quartet-style vocal arrangement of Bob Marley's 'Freedom'.

Ellis, Brunton and Barwick's research into South Australian Aboriginal music (1988) found that African-American music had a particular significance for Aborigines, and, in the case of Tiddas, Tracey Chapman's music has been a significant influence. They also share a number of characteristics with the American vocal group, Sweet Honey in the Rock (which they supported at Melbourne Concert Hall in August 1992) in that their music is about the grandeur of the human voice and spirit and communicates messages of freedom. A cappella singing, hand-held percussion and clapping are trademarks of both groups. For example, Tiddas accompany their vocals with hand-clapping alone in 'If You Build It, Don't Tear It' and rhythm sticks alone in 'Last Night I Heard the Screaming'. Speech is also an important part of Tiddas's music, being prominent in 'My Brother Has Many Faces' and being superimposed over singing in 'My People's Dreaming'. Tiddas's use of African-American music however, is based on adaptation rather than imitation, and though they use 'blue-notes' and the African-derived call-and-response technique, with its 'filler' variation (short musical responses occurring over stationary spots in the melodies), their music remains proudly and identifiably Koori.

The comparison to African-American music, particularly Soul, has been made with regard to one of Melbourne's most respected Koori performers, Archie Roach, who has been described as Australia's 'first true soul singer'. Roach's musical and songwriting style, like that of his partner and frequent collaborator, Ruby Hunter, is, however, less upbeat than much American Soul and, in the lengthy ballads that typified their early careers, is restricted by dark moods and confined tonal areas. Despite the comparisons to Soul, Roach and Hunter's form of Koori urban balladry possesses the essential markers of unflinching diatonic tunes. This reflects Libby Lester's account of the manner in which, as a 'stolen' child, taken away from his parents and deprived of his tribal heritage, Roach was raised on hymns 'with no history, no language, no dance', a situation in which 'country music filled the void' (1989: 7). Songs such as 'Took The Children Away' represent attempts by Roach to come to terms with his own past and the spiritual violence enacted upon him by white society and its agencies. Hunter's own years on the streets also directly influenced her music and lyrics, and her experiences have been translated into her well-known ballads about Kooris, women and domestic violence. Her song 'Down City Streets' is now the Australian equivalent of Ralph McTell's folk-staple 'Streets of London'. Their songs are also not just addressed to white injustice but also to Koori issues. Roach's 'Walking Into Doors', for example, recorded on his 1993 album *Jamu Dreaming*, appeals to Koori men to avoid violence and to treat their wives and partners with respect.

As two representative musicians who have influenced the course of human development and cultural enrichment for Melbourne's Koori people over the last ten years, Roach and Hunter have earned the esteem, even deference, of both Koori and non-Koori audiences. Their careers represent the manner in which Aboriginal creativity is able to flourish more openly once individuals acknowledge their selves and histories. Although both Hunter and Roach have been victimized by white culture in the past, their songs and music stress messages of hope rather than bitterness. What perhaps makes Koori urban balladry truly distinctive is its profound humanism. Although a minority in their own land, Koori people are neither silent nor passive and their music is a prime medium for them to broadcast their grievances and suggest solutions. In the words of Karl Neuenfeldt, their 'songs give voice to the voiceless, with political overtones of resistance be they overt or covert' (1991: 93). The songlines of traditional Aboriginal culture can be seen to have taken root and new form in urban Koori music. Starting with Joe Geia's recording of 'Yil Lull' in 1988, the urban songlines of Melbourne's Kooris became more audible when Roach recorded songs such as 'Bicentennial Blues' and 'No Celebrations' in 1989 and his albums *Charcoal Lane* (1990) and *Jamu Dreaming* (1993).

Since 1993, Blackfire, Frankland, Geia, Hunter, Roach and Tiddas have all made other recordings. In 1993, Koori music peaked not only with the 'Mabo Mambo' gig but with a whole series of other, well-advertised events. These included the Unity Concert held on St Kilda foreshore on 14 February to celebrate the United Nations Year of the World's Indigenous People; the first annual Brunswick Koori Arts Festival Concert on 14 March; the launch of Seven Sisters Dreaming, Victoria's first Aboriginal theatre restaurant on 4 August; a series of performances by Aboriginal musicians at the Continental Cafe in Prahran; and the foregrounding of Aboriginal performers at the AFL (Australian Football League) Grand Final at the Melbourne Cricket Ground on 25 September and at the Australian Music Day concert on 27 November. By the end of 1996, Hunter, Roach and Tiddas had taken their Koori voices to the world on many occasions. They continue to tour, record and promote their albums. Blackfire, by contrast, continue to make songwriting for the local Koori community of Melbourne their first priority, to the extent that they have largely avoided playing on the mainstream pub circuit. However, in 1996 they performed in all major Australian cities as support act on Carlos Santana's national tour and have plans to perform with Roach and the Naroo Dancers of Northern Queensland on an Asian tour in 1998. Their latest CD, *Big River*, produced by Crowded House musician Paul Hester, features indigenous rock ballads such as 'Stricken Land' and 'Uncle Someone' (about tomorrow's children).

Melbourne's contemporary Koori music scene is diverse and vigorous. New bands such as Bloodlines, Jarrah and the Brolga Boys are featured on the forthcoming *Songlines* compilation album — along with Blackfire and Dead Heart, and soloists Dave Arden, Wayne Thorpe, Carole Fraser (Melbourne's first Koori jazz singer) and the political activist Richard Frankland (who won a 1996 Australian Film Institute Award for his song 'No Way To Forget'). Frankland, and a host of other Aboriginal artists also feature on the Larrikin Records CD *Down Three Waterholes Road* (1997). It is no wonder that Roach views music as the great equalizer. The politics initially enabled Koori music to be promoted but the music now both stands alone and promotes the politics.

Notes

1. This chapter originally appeared in *Perfect Beat*, vol. 2, no. 1 (January 1995).
2. The term 'Koori' or 'Koorie' literally means the local Aborigines of Victoria and New South Wales, most of whom are of mixed racial descent. Some Aboriginal musicians resident in Melbourne were born elsewhere but their contributions to Koori cultural revitalization have been significant and should not be overlooked.
3. The European term 'songlines' is synonymous with the 'dreaming-tracks' of traditional tribal Australian Aborigines, whose music prior to contact was primarily vocal. Long chains of song cycles 'given' to songmen in dreams

were tied to successive geographic sites and often crossed boundaries between tribal groups. To Aborigines they were the 'footprints of the ancestors' or the 'way of the law', intricate sources of personal identity as well as territorial markers forming an oral map of the country: myths related to the beginning of time, when ancestral beings emerged from earth to create the landscape of their particular area. When correctly performed they empowered participants to draw on potent forces believed to have been left at the sites by the ancestors. Bruce Chatwin's novel, *The Songlines* (London: Cape, 1987) popularized the term.

4.   Historical continuity and change in Koori music in Melbourne prior to 1988 is dealt with more fully in the article 'From margin to mainstream: Koori music in Melbourne since 1960', in *Music Since Ca. 1960*, edited by Margaret Kartomi, M. and Purvis, K. (Melbourne: Currency Press, 1997).

5.   'White' and 'Non-Koori' are used more or less interchangeably in this article to refer to the overwhelmingly white Western European derived population who have dominated Australian society and politics since colonization.

6.   The 'sophistication' of Hard Times's music, in which Schultz has detected the influence of calypso (*ibid*.: 86) reflects the training afforded to some members of the band by the Centre for Aboriginal Studies in Music (CASM) at the University of Adelaide. For further discussion of CASM's relation to recent Aboriginal music, see Breen (1989).

7.   According to Wayne Thorpe, *Watbilimba* means literally 'dance and sing you a song' in the *Gunai* dialect (interview, 9 April 1992).

8.   For a discussion of these forms in Australia, see Whiteoak (1993).

9.   See S. Feld, (1988) 'Notes on World Beat', *Public Culture*, vol. 4, no. 1, for discussion of this theme.

10.   Koori Larry Walsh, Orientation Day speech at Melbourne University, 2 February 1992.

11.   Without trying to freeze Koori songs into a system, I can, nevertheless, conclude that the repertoire pools do shed light on actual cultural tendencies. Actual examples of songs representing themes from the two basic repertoire pools are outlined in my thesis, *Koori Sociomusical Practice in Melbourne Since 1988* (Monash University, 1994).

12.   Also see Neuenfeldt (1992), for a consideration of more 'integrated' uses of such instrumentation.

Discography

Blackfire, *A Time to Dream*, CAAMA, 1994.
— *Big River*, CAAMA, 1997.
Richard Frankland, *Down Three Waterholes Road*, Larrikin, 1997.
Joe Geia, *Yil Lull*, Dex (assisted by the Aboriginal Arts Board), 1988 (cassette only).
—*Tribal Journey*, Rosella Music (Larrikin), 1995.
Ruby Hunter, *Thoughts Within*, Aurora, 1996.
Archie Roach, *Koorie*, The Victorian Aboriginal Cultural Heritage Trust and Ruby Hunter, 1989 (cassette only).
—*Charcoal Lane*, Mushroom Records, 1990.

—*Jamu Dreaming*, Aurora, 1993.
—*Looking for Butter Boy*, Aurora, 1997.
Tiddas, *Inside My Kitchen*, ID/ABC Music Deli, 1992.
—*Sing about Life*, Phonogram 1993.
—*Flat Notes and Bad Jokes*, Larrikin, 1996.
Various artists, *Songlines Compilation Album*, Songlines, 1997.

Note: recordings of Djaambie, Mercury Blues, Blackfire and Watbilima are also held at radio station 3CR in Melbourne.

5

Jawaiian Music and Local Cultural Identity in Hawai'i[1]

Andrew N. Weintraub

In the early 1990s Jawaiian, a synthesis of *Ja*maican and Ha*waiian* music, emerged as the most popular musical style in contemporary Hawai'i. At the time of writing (1992), Jawaiian, also called Hawaiian reggae or Island Hawaiian Music,[2] dominates the majority of mass media musical avenues today, including airplay on local music stations, the local recording industry, 'contemporary Hawaiian'[3] music charts (based on record sales), local (as opposed to tourist-dominated) music clubs and major concert venues on O'ahu. This chapter constructs an interpretation of Jawaiian's evolving musical history based on a review of popular media sources, attendance at live concerts and interviews with musicians and audience members. In this chapter I address the question, 'How is Jawaiian perceived as a symbol of local cultural identity in contemporary Hawai'i?' The study aims to understand the perception of Jawaiian's musical meaning within the context of a local cultural identity by examining how this identity is mediated by the sound of the music, the song texts and discourse about the genre by musicians and audience members. A subtheme developed here is the way reggae and its associated images and ideas, when transported to a different social system, take on a different symbolic meaning.[4]

Reggae has been a part of the popular music scene on O'ahu since the late 1970s. The reggae audience consisted of at least three distinct ethnic and social groups, which remained relatively isolated from one another: Jamaicans (many stationed temporarily in Hawai'i for military service), local Hawaiian youth (primarily from the areas of Waianae, Waimanalo and the North Shore on O'ahu) and university students (centred around the University of Hawai'i at Manoa). Bob Marley's live performance in 1980 at the Waikiki Shell was a turning point in exposing reggae to a wider audience in Hawai'i. During the mid-1980s, public parties and dances held throughout the island of O'ahu began consolidating audiences, but reggae was still very much a grass-roots music.[5] Popular musicians, including Brother Noland and Peter Moon, made recordings of reggae-inspired songs which, compared to recent reggae hybrid forms, met with little popular success.

The popularization and commercialization of Jawaiian began in early 1990. The mass media have facilitated the development of reggae from a small, grass-roots music into the most popular music in the state. Over the past two years, Jawaiian has been adapted to modern media, or 'mediaized',[6] via radio and widely distributed recordings.[7] Even the name 'Jawaiian' was originally used as a 'marketing tag for the then-new hybrid of Caribbean reggae and contemporary Hawaiian music'.[8] The role of the media in promoting Jawaiian, from its inception to its current status, is a complex topic that deserves further research.

The reggae musical vocabulary has invigorated the late 1980s and early 1990s contemporary Hawaiian music scene. As reggae musician Butch Helemano states: '5 or 6 years ago record producers wouldn't touch me because they said reggae music isn't gonna go anywhere and now almost every band has a reggae song in their format' (interview in the *Jawaiian Time* video, 1991).

At the time of writing, a large part of the Jawaiian repertoire consists of covers (or 'versions') of reggae tunes. Many of these songs have been localized in order to appeal to a local Hawaiian audience.[9] Jawaiian's popularity may be interpreted as a conjunction of social and musical factors. It unites people through dance at live concerts. As well-known local musician Peter Moon says, 'it is one of the first, if not *the* first, danceable type of local music' (personal communication, 24 May 1991), which explains why local musicians appropriated a fast danceable style of reggae as opposed to, for example, a slow roots reggae sound.[10] Some commonsense explanations attribute the popularity of Jawaiian to:

1. The popularity of reggae throughout the world, as an international style.
2. A desire for local Hawaiian musicians to share a musical style with Jamaicans because of the perceived similarities between the Hawaiian and Jamaican people as historically oppressed populations.
3. The perceived similarities between contemporary Hawaiian and Jamaican 'island' lifestyles, attitudes and climate.

Other explanations suggest that Jawaiian is the latest music/dance trend, the latest example of a synthesis of Hawaiian music with a style popular on the US mainland ten years earlier.[11]

Jawaiian may be the latest music/dance craze, but it has become central to members of a local youth culture in Hawai'i. What defines this youth culture and how are its values expressed in Jawaiian? Jawaiian appeals to a social group popularly referred to as locals, which includes native Hawaiians as well as people from almost every other ethnic group in the state. Here some background information on local culture will be useful as a context for understanding an emergent Jawaiian audience. Jonathan Okamura writes:

> Local has become a symbol of the common identity of people who appreciate the quality and style of life in the islands and who therefore attempt to maintain control over the future of Hawaii and its communities. The shared lifestyle and its associated behaviors, values, and norms is popularly referred to as 'local culture.' (1980: 120)

Historically, 'local culture and society began to emerge when the Hawaiian social system began to incorporate American values, beliefs and modes of activity following the arrival of New England missionaries in 1820' (ibid.). Later, the term ' "local" came into use when ethnic distinctions, maintained on the plantations, were minimized in urban life' (Kirkpatrick, 1989: 305). The presence of 'outsider' groups in Hawai'i was a significant structural factor in the emergence of the term 'local'. The formation of a unified local culture is a way of protecting locals from

> representatives of outside forces of social change, be they tourists, mainland Haoles [Caucasians], immigrants, land developers, or big business in general, [who] are understood as not having this sense of awareness and concern for Hawaii and its communities and therefore cannot be local. (Okamura, 1980: 132)

Local identity is expressed through various character traits or 'values', and in varying degrees. Certain individual values can be emphasized more than others and people can and do assume varying degrees of 'localness' by their adherence to these values. For example, one might say, 'He's so local', or, when I asked the question, 'who listens to Jawaiian?', I got the answer, 'the localest of the local' (personal communication, Marya Takamori, 12 June 1991). Jawaiian song texts, attitudes, and sound reflect the values of the local culture of Hawai'i. I will discuss four of these values here: maintenance of an insider–outsider dichotomy, the aloha spirit, love and defence of the land (aloha'aina) and a symbolic connection to the past.

The Jawaiian music repertoire advocates a sense of group identity as a way of upholding an insider–outsider dichotomy. Example 1 presents the text of a song by Brother Noland which, in no uncertain terms, asks 'Are You Native?', which is also the title of the song.

> Who are these creatures?
> Where do they come from?
> Who are these strangers, with different voodoo?
> Do you feel danger when they are near you?

Chorus
Ask us: Are you native?
Are you native?

They come from outside
And they come inside
Can they make contact and cross your border?
Can they vacate here and drink your water?

Chorus
Can I ask questions?
Will you give answers?
Are we invaders that come to visit?
Or just some neighbors, perhaps we're tourists

'Are You Native?' makes references to the first outsider to visit Hawai'i, Captain Cook, who established 'contact' with Hawai'i in 1778. The new 'invaders', or outsiders, could, as the song suggests, be recently arrived 'neighbours' or 'perhaps tourists'.

Musicians have defined local cultural values in Jawaiian terms. For example, the spirit of *aloha*, one of the guiding principles of Hawaiian social relations, is perceived to parallel the Jamaican term *irie* in meaning.[12] The Ho'aikane cassette cover for the album *Island Irie*, reads: 'The concept of Island Irie is meant to be shared. Similar to 'the aloha spirit', the effect of Island Irie will reach epidemic proportions.' Hoku Tolentino, a member of Ho'aikane, states:

Irie is like aloha ... happy feelings in the islands ... we talked to a lot of Jamaican people about using the word *irie* [because] we don't want to offend them ... It's like someone asking you what does *aloha* mean – good feelings, enjoyable, happy. (Personal communication, Hoku Tolentino, 1 November 1992)

The music of Ho'aikane invokes a symbolic connection to other styles of Hawaiian music by quoting them. The slack-key guitar played in the middle of the song 'Kailua-Kona', and a transition to a Hawaiian song at the end, are both emblematic of traditional Hawaiian music played at local events and parties:

There is a place that is heavenly
A place where life can be so free
Where people work and live easily
That is a place for you and for me

chorus
Kailua-Kona, where the air is clean
Kailua-Kona, where the grass is green
Kailua-Kona, where the fishing's fine
Kailua-Kona, it will blow your mind

Go up the mountains or down to the sea
Enjoy the view or eat sweet opihi
Work and play til the sun goes down
Cruise the beach road to Kona town

chorus
[slack-key guitar solo]
Play reggae music with the Ho'aikane band
Surf at Banyans by the Surf and White Sands
Go north and south as far as you can go
Go Maunakea to see the island snow

chorus
[transition to Hawaiian song]

The area Kailua-Kona on the island of Hawai'i has been rapidly developed as a tourist area in recent years. The song praises this beloved place where the air is still clean and the fishing fine. Implicit in this song is an appeal to protect this area from further development.

Jawaiian's meaning is indeed situated within the *sound*. The band Kapena, like other Hawaiian music groups, has recently added a trap set and a more emphatic bass sound which departs from their former 'cha-lang-a-lang' instrumentation consisting of guitar, ukulele and bass. A cover version of 'Tiny Bubbles' by Bruddah Waltah and Island Afternoon deconstructs the Waikiki nightclub genre's trademark song by taking apart the musical treatment and contextual associations of the original version by veteran tourist entertainer Don Ho. Its politics are mediated via musical parody.

Political messages are explicit and include the interjection of socio-political commentary into song texts. The song 'Hawaiian Lands' concerns the politically sensitive issue of land ownership, and particularly the reclamation of the land by indigenous Hawaiians. Love of the land, or *aloha'aina*, is a characteristic value frequently expressed in Hawaiian music texts (refer also to 'Kailua-Kona'). One of the very few songs containing Hawaiian language lyrics, Ho'aikane's 'Hawaiian Lands' is a call for the people of Hawai'i to maintain control over the future of their land. In addition to the slogan, 'Keep Hawaiian Lands in Hawaiian Hands', another politically charged message expressed in this song is 'We've got to preserve our dying breed', a call for resistance to further dispossession of indigenous groups:

Talk to me my brother
Love one another
It's plain to see
This land is here for you and me
Keep Hawaiian Lands in Hawaiian Hands (yeah) [× 4]

On the road we go
Far from life we stroll
It's an uphill climb (yeah)
Stays with you all the time

Keep Hawaiian Lands in Hawaiian Hands (yeah) [× 4]

Hawaiians say: Ua Mau Ke Ea O Ka Aina I Ka Pono[13]

This is our plea, our destiny flight
We got to be free to claim our rights
Stand up be heard and declare our creed
We got to preserve our dying breed

The literature on reggae posits that the exportation of reggae as sound makes available a set of conventions which can accommodate radical political messages. John Street writes:

> [Reggae's] politics lie as much in its collective character as in its radical lyrics and apocalyptic visions. Even without the words, the sounds are those of a collective resistance, of people making – albeit briefly – a world of their own (1986: 220).

And James Lull writes, 'the hypnotic sound of reggae is unmistakable and universally signals class-based protest' (1987: 168). One must ask whether the sound of reggae has been employed and perceived as a vehicle for expressing 'radical lyrics', 'apocalyptic visions', and 'class-based protest' in Jawaiian.[14] In other words, given the political associations implicit in the *sound* of reggae, why reggae and why now in Hawai'i? This question deserves further investigation into the role of the media, particularly the role of record producers and radio station directors who have been instrumental in creating taste for a local youth market. However, my investigation of some of the strategies and attitudes adopted by participants to invest collective values and a shared consciousness around a musical form addresses these issues as well.

At the time of writing (1992), Jawaiian is not at the centre of a political movement. Jawaiian delivers its message by promoting a reflective, not an advocate position. Jawaiian provides a forum for stating critical issues but does not offer suggestions for solving them. Jawaiian's politics rest in its musicians' and audiences' desire to control or define symbols of their own emergent identity. Music has become so central to the construction of local cultural identity that Jawaiian is now at the centre of a public debate about the negotiation of a Hawaiian identity, defined in terms of certain symbolic activities, explicated through music, and disseminated via the media. A recent public debate about Jawaiian raised the question, 'Is it time to take the 'ja' out of Hawaiian music?' (Chun, 1991: B1). Well-known musicians contest the role of reggae as a symbol of emergent identity because of a perception that the introduction of a foreign music (in this case reggae) may introduce values that obscure, replace, or otherwise endanger the preservation and teaching of Hawaiian values: 'The issue here is not music, but who we are to our ancestors. We have to stop being someone else and create for our own people...' (Chun, 1991: B1, quoting Frank Kawaikapuokalani Hewitt). Hoku Tolentino, band member of the group Ho'aikane, responds by defending the band's use of reggae and notes their commitment to their Hawaiian heritage:

> I'm keeping the Hawaiian *in* instead of keeping it out ... We still have Hawaiian instruments and slack key ... We're not losing it – we're just enhancing it so everyone will like it, young and old (personal communication, 1 November 1992).

Other artists advocate the positive role of reggae for the way in which musicians have interpreted classic Hawaiian tunes as reggae versions, effectively reintroducing them to a younger generation.

One effort to define the genre appeared on the cassette jacket of a 1990 release, *Hawaiian Reggae*, by Bruddah Waltah and Island Afternoon. It reads (italics mine):

> Ja-wai-an (je wi' en', -way'yan), adj. 1: of or pertaining to Jamaican-Hawaiian music *indigenous* to the Hawaiian youth of today. 2: music that makes you feel good.

Bruddah Waltah uses the term 'indigenous' to promote Jawaiian as a music which has roots in Hawaiian culture. Indigenous is a word packed with meaning in contemporary Hawai'i. The indigenous people of Hawai'i are today a small minority of Hawai'i's population, the descendants of the aboriginal people who inhabited the islands prior to the coming of Europeans and Americans in the late eighteenth century. The quote implies that Jawaiian is part of the Hawaiian heritage, a statement supported by long-time radio celebrity Jacqueline Lindsay (aka Honolulu Skylark), who promoted Jawaiian as a way of 'getting people interested again in their culture' (Burlingame, 1991: E3).

These statements are contested by other popular Hawaiian musicians. In contrast to Jawaiian bands, the band Ho'aikane promotes the use of Hawaiian language, maintains the 'cha-lang-a-lang' instrumentation of ukulele, vocal, guitar and bass, and includes hula as an integral part of their performance. At a recent music awards ceremony,[15] a member of the award-winning band remarked:

> We see a yearning for what went with Gabby [Pahinui] and Atta [Isaacs].[16] We're trying to bring that back. And that's really hard, because of the new Jawaiian. We really like the reggae scene, but we feel a commitment to our heritage. (Manuel, 1991: B3).

Ho'aikane represents an extension of the Hawaiian Renaissance movement, an effort begun in the 1970s to revive distinctive elements of
Hawaiian culture, especially music and dance. John Kirkpatrick (1989)
has described the artistic renaissance as a source of identity for residents
of Hawai'i:

> Residents of Hawaii from diverse backgrounds have supported and in many
> cases participated in arts identified as distinctively Hawai'ian. Hula, slack key
> guitar, and other arts are becoming the officially supported culture of the state
> and a source of pride and identity for many who lack Hawai'ian blood or land.
> While many of Hawai'ian blood have come to new understandings of their
> Hawai'ian identity, others draw on similar signs and rhetoric for their own
> self-definition. (1989: 306)

At the time of writing, Jawaiian is not part of the 'officially supported
culture of the state' and is a publicly articulated point of contention
among some musicians who have drawn on distinctive Hawaiian cultural
elements for their construction of a Hawaiian identity. The latter is
founded on distinctly Hawaiian activities that require training in order to
participate. For example, hula should ideally be studied in a *halau*
(school) with its attendant rules, hierarchy and extended length of study.
Skankin', dancing to Jawaiian, is free-form, not bound by conventions,
and it gives local youth the immediate sense of identity they are looking
for.

Jawaiian, now synonymous with 'island-style' and 'local-style', is less
exclusive than other distinctively Hawaiian arts. Its appeal lies in its
ability to 'cross over' geographic, class and racial boundaries. Its domain
extends beyond Honolulu, the locus of an 'officially supported culture of
the state', to areas traditionally under-represented in the centralized state
cultural network. From a local perspective, it is ethnically neutral:
Jawaiian does not belong to any one ethnic group and so cannot be
claimed as any one group's own, but is available to everyone. Its musical
conventions are not tied to the people of Hawai'i, but belong to an
international community of people who identify with the sound and
message of reggae. Reggae music symbolizes a freedom to interpret and
transform contemporary music. As Hoku Tolentino has stated: 'we're
from Hawai'i but we can play different types of music ... To me it's
[reggae] just a different type of music, two different cultures coming as
one and sending a message' (personal communication, 1 November 1992).

Its symbols are not rooted in historical meanings, but are flexible and
open to new interpretations. The red, green and gold colours of the
Ethiopian flag, the lion of Judah, images of Haile Selassie emblazoned on
T-shirts, all kinds of surf paraphernalia and concert posters do not
necessarily symbolize Rastafarian roots, but represent the freedom to
manipulate images that are not culturally bound to Hawai'i.

Jawaiian musical style and dance did not originate *in* Hawai'i, but there is no question that it belongs to the local youth *of* Hawai'i. Composers have consciously maintained local values in song texts, many derived from Hawaiian values (*aloha, aloha 'aina*), and sounds evocative of a 'Hawaiian-style' lifestyle. Composers have defined an identity apart from the 'officially supported culture of the state' but still 'indigenous to the Hawaiian youth of today'.

In this chapter I have tried to interpret some of the ways in which Hawaiian reggae has emerged as a popular musical form. Jawaiian may be the latest musical product of transculturation with a style imported from outside Hawai'i, but it has been transformed in ways that appeal to a specifically local Hawaiian audience. Jawaiian is an example of how reggae and its associated images and ideas, when transported to a different social formation, take on a different symbolic meaning. Like other reggae styles in Jamaica, Europe and the US, Jawaiian has provided a forum for reflecting on political and social issues. It deals uniquely with values shared by members of a local culture in Hawai'i, as these values are expressed in song texts, attitude and sound. As a musical category, Jawaiian may eventually be subsumed by the catch-all term 'contemporary Hawaiian' music. As a case study in cultural construction, Jawaiian has occupied the centre of a local youth culture, illustrating the role of popular music as an arena for reflecting and shaping local cultural identity.

Notes

1. This chapter originally appeared in *Perfect Beat* vol. 1, no, 2, January 1993.
2. Divergent attitudes about what to call the genre reflect the currently contentious nature of the music in Hawai'i. For the purposes of this chapter, I will use the term Jawaiian, the term most preferred by the people with whom I collaborated during my research, 1990–92.
3. 'Contemporary Hawaiian' music is characterized by a synthesis of 'traditional' Hawaiian music with other styles, primarily pop, rock and jazz.
4. This chapter represents the perspective of an outsider, that is, a mainlander who has observed the construction of local cultural identity and music discussed herein. As a graduate student in Ethnomusicology at the University of Hawai'i, 1986–90, I became interested in Jawaiian as a case study of musical transculturation. The research was carried out co-terminously with my work on a larger project pertaining to music and ethnic identity in Hawai'i. I would like to thank Ricardo D. Trimillos, Jay Junker, Sarah Weiss, Terri Teaiwa, Geoffrey White and Eleanor Jaluague for their insightful comments on earlier drafts of the chapter.
5. Personal communication, Jay Junker, 30 October 1992. Junker worked as a DJ for parties and radio shows during the mid-1980s.
6. A term borrowed from Wallis's and Malm's *Big Sounds from Small Peoples* (1984).
7. In 1990 a new Hawaiian music FM radio station began broadcasting

primarily Jawaiian, targeted to a younger crowd than the 'traditional' Hawaiian music AM station. By March 1991, Jawaiian came to dominate the top ten spots (based on record sales) on the 'contemporary Hawaiian' charts. Not since *Honolulu City Lights* by Keola and Kapono Beamer (1978) has an album sold as many units as an album entitled simply *Hawaiian Reggae*, released in 1990 by Bruddah Waltah and Island Afternoon. Concerts at large-capacity venues frequently sell out (venues such as Andrews Amphitheatre and the Waikiki Shell). Beginning in March 1991, a local radio station has sponsored a special series of monthly concerts at the Honolulu Harbor Aloha Tower called Jawaiian Jams, and several local music clubs feature Jawaiian acts on a regular basis. As Peter Moon states: '[Jawaiian] brought people into the stores ... It gave a little bite to the record-buying industry' (personal communication, 5 November 1992).

8. Gary C.W. Chun, quoting Brickwood Galuteria (Chun 31 October 1991: B1). Galuteria, along with others, coined the term 'Jawaiian' to refer to 'jammin' Hawaiians', local musicians who play reggae music (*ibid.*). Musicians do not unanimously accept the label 'Jawaiian', which now encompasses various styles of contemporary Hawaiian music, some with a reggae beat, and some that don't use a reggae beat at all. The music discussed in this chapter has close musical connections to reggae and is identified as such by musicians. A recent World Beat movement has begun in Hawaii, but is not germane to the discussion here.

9. See, for example, the localization of the lyrics of the Bob Marley song 'No Woman, No Cry' (originally recorded in 1975) performed by Bruddah Waltah and Island Afternoon, where localization occurs primarily in the verse.

10. Another characteristic of the repertoire is the predominance of songs played in major keys.

11. This view has been suggested by Ricardo D. Trimillos. A short summary of the history of jazz in Hawai'i, for example, would show how important the 'foreign' element can be. Various styles of jazz, transported from the US mainland, have consistently influenced the popular music of the time in Hawai'i. Around the turn of the century, George Kanahele (1979: xxv) writes, 'Ragtime seeped into Honolulu and engulfed it.' During the 1920s, 'jazzed up' Tin Pan Alley versions of *hapa haole* (half-Hawaiian, half-English) songs were popular, including the jazz-influenced 'Hula Blues', by Johnny Noble, in 1920. The period 1930–60 is sometimes referred to as the golden age of Hawaiian music, characterized by big band music played in Waikiki ballrooms. During the 1960s Kui Lee, who composed songs for Don Ho, used innovative jazz melodies and rhythms. During the 1970s, the Hawaiian Renaissance movement lionized musician Gabby Pahinui, who acknowledged jazz as an influence on his playing style.

12. The spirit of *aloha* emphasizes an easy-going attitude, openness, trust and loyalty to family and friends.

13. Glossed as 'The life of the land is perpetuated in righteousness'.

14. Marcus Breen reports examples of Australian Aboriginal musicians who have used reggae for embedding politically charged lyrics (Breen, 1992: 161).

15. *Na Hoku* awards: the equivalent of the Grammys in Hawaiian music.

16. Musicians heroicized during the 1970s.

Videography

KFVE, *Jawaiian Time* (video), KFVE (Honolulu), 1991.

Discography

Bruddah Waltah and Island Afternoon, *Hawaiian Reggae*, Platinum Pacific Records (Hawaii), 1990.
Ho'aikane, *Island Irie*, Kahale Music (Waianae, Hi), 1990.
Brother Noland, *Native News*, Mountain Apple Company (Honolulu), 1986.
Keola and Kapono Beamer, *Honolulu City Lights*, Paradise (Hawaii), 1978.

6

Hula Hits, Local Music and Local Charts: Some Dynamics of Popular Hawaiian Music

Amy Ku'uleialoha Stillman

Outside Hawai'i, the mention of 'Hawaiian music' still conjures up stereotyped images of lei-bedecked musicians in colourful floral attire serenading at hotel poolsides during the sunset cocktail hour. Nor are the images strictly visual: the sounds invariably include the soft strumming of guitars and ukulele, the languid sighing of the steel guitar and the mellifluous gymnastics of falsetto singers yodelling between vocal registers. Exported since the 1920s and 1930s, these images still shape what ageing tourists expect to see and hear on their arrival in the islands, and there are numerous Hawaiian musicians who continue to earn their livelihood by providing such entertainment for tourists. The Hawaiian music served up for tourism, however, is but one swell among the surging tides of popular musics locally produced and consumed.

The entertainment and recording industries in Hawai'i are heavily weighted toward producing and marketing ethnic Hawaiian music. By this is meant music in specific performance streams that descend from the traditions of the native Hawaiians who are Hawai'i's indigenous inhabitants. However, music production in Hawai'i is complicated by a vibrant coexistence of popular musics alongside ethnic Hawaiian music. Moreover, while Hawaiian musicians perform repertoire which emanates from American popular music, there is also a distinctly local dimension of popular musical production, in which original material addresses and critiques the multicultural pluralism that characterizes contemporary Hawai'i.

'Local' is a category that cross-cuts narrow boundaries between native Hawaiians and Hawai'i residents of other ethnicities. The category 'local' denotes a common culture that is shared among Hawai'i residents (Okamura, 1980, 1994; Sumida, 1991; Yamamoto, 1979). It acknowledges a particular space in which shared experiences of daily living are celebrated, and shared concerns for maintaining this particular lifestyle are articulated. It involves an appreciation of the land and environment as well as an easy-going style of interaction that guides social relationships. It also involves expressed opposition to threats of social, economic and political changes, especially when perceived to originate outside Hawai'i (Okamura, 1980: 132). Local music, then, refers to a repertoire that specifically explores local perspectives on issues of shared concern, as well as common sentiments and aspirations that unify Hawai'i's ethnically diverse population.[1]

Performed using an eclectic variety of musical styles, local music cross-cuts ethnic Hawaiian music in interesting and even surprising ways. The purpose of this chapter is to survey some of the dynamics through which ethnic Hawaiian and local Hawaiian musics intersect. My discussion is framed within the perspective of repertoire, for 'hits' on local charts emerge out of a complex matrix of trends that are variously artist-driven, performance-driven and sentiment-driven. I shall explore relationships among 'hula hits' – songs that rise and ebb in popularity within the contemporary hula scene, the production of commercial recordings and the world of local music, taking into consideration local charts that track popularity.

The Hawaiian music performance scene that flourishes currently owes its robustness to the phenomenal resurgence of Hawaiian cultural practices, popularly referred to as the 'Hawaiian Renaissance', that began in the early 1970s and continues in the present. Young adult musicians, previously attracted to American rock and roll music in the 1960s, turned back to Hawaiian music in a quest to affirm a Hawaiian cultural identity. The efflorescence of Hawaiian music is evident in dramatic increases in commercial record production, which reached a peak in 1978 with the release of an average of ten recordings each month (Buck, 1984: 148).

Much of the Hawaiian music that circulated during and since the 1970s consists of revivals of songs composed since the late 1800s. These songs are categorized as 'modern' Hawaiian songs, for they use Western melodies and harmonies, and instrumental accompaniment is provided by Western stringed instruments including guitar, bass and piano, as well as ukulele and steel guitar, which are held to be Hawaiian inventions. At least three named genres of modern Hawaiian songs are distinguished. *Hula ku'i* are Hawaiian-language songs intended for performance as hula. The poetic texts are organized into stanzas, each stanza consisting of two lines or one couplet of text. In performance, one melody is repeated for all stanzas, and stanzas are separated by a brief instrumental interlude, popularly called the 'vamp', during which dancers perform a conventional movement sequence whose function is to separate stanzas. *Mele Hawai'i* are Hawaiian-language songs modelled on the alternating verse–chorus format used widely in Hawaiian-language Christian hymns called *himeni* (the only distinction between the two categories is the subject matter of poetic texts; Christian in the latter, secular in the former). *Hapa haole* songs are English-language songs whose lyrics are about Hawai'i or some aspect of Hawaiian culture. A vast majority of *hapa haole* songs conform to the 32-bar popular song format that has prevailed in American popular music.[2]

With the renewed popularity of Hawaiian music in the early 1970s, quests for material led recording artists to pursue two strategies. One was the recovery of previously performed repertoire. While hundreds of songs had been published in folio song books since the late 1800s, much repertoire remained in private family collections or in archival collections. This repertoire was renewed through original arrangements by musicians who drew on their familiarity with performance styles from American popular music as well as conventions of performing Hawaiian music.

In addition to revived repertoire, recording artists also presented songs newly composed in English and Hawaiian languages alike. Moreover, newly composed songs often commented on concerns relevant to life in Hawai'i in and since the 1970s. These concerns extended beyond the culture of native Hawaiian people and addressed a broader heritage and lifestyle shared by Hawai'i residents of all ethnicities.

While some of the newly composed repertoire adhered to the formats of *hula ku'i*, *mele Hawai'i* and *hapa haole* songs, many do not. For the moment, I propose the label 'contemporary Hawaiian songs' as a catch-all for newly composed repertoire whose variance from conventions of pre-existing song formats precludes their inclusion in those categories; I also propose that the label apply to songs whose format does allow classification as *hula ku'i*, *mele Hawai'i* or *hapa haole* songs, but whose subject matter is relevant to contemporary social and cultural concerns.

Hula hits

I use the term 'hula hits' to refer to songs in the modern Hawaiian music performance stream that rise to popularity in the hula world. The dynamics involved are unique to Hawai'i, for the commercial recording enterprise is brought into a close relationship with the thriving hula performance tradition as practised within the Hawaiian community, where it is, for the most part, not commercial. Dancers are overwhelmingly students of culture who do not aspire to professional careers in performance, and whose principal employment lies outside the fields of entertainment and tourism. The hula community contributes to sustaining the performance of ethnic Hawaiian music, for live music is an important component of hula performance, and continuous turnover in repertoire is necessary to maintain the interest of audiences and participants alike.

Hula aficionados are also a substantial group of consumers whose purchases of commercial recordings support the continued production of ethnic Hawaiian music. The largely amateur hula world expands upon the production/consumption dyad, because requirements for live music and continuous streams of repertoire ascribe a functional dimension to music performance that transcends mere consumption. The power of the hula world to elevate individual songs to hits is not measured solely by sales of commercial recordings, but by use in performance as well.

Hula performance, like Hawaiian music, owes its vigour to the resurgence of cultural practices in and since the Hawaiian Renaissance of the 1970s. Renewed interest in native Hawaiian performance traditions motivated youth and adults alike to seek instruction from knowledgeable teachers, thereby swelling enrolments at public recreation classes and privately-run hula schools. A new generation of teachers emerged by the mid-1970s, contributing to the proliferation of private hula schools. Increased participation in hula was further stimulated by the establishment, since 1973, of formal competitions among the hula schools (see Stillman, 1996). Among the competitive events, the Merrie Monarch Hula Competition held each April in Hilo, and the King Kamehameha Chant and Hula Competition held each June in Honolulu, are the most prestigious.

Within the hula world there are several ways in which songs become hits. Hula performers are always searching for original material, and will often look for songs that have been out of circulation. What follows is a provisional survey of various trajectories that hula hits may follow, on their way to becoming hits, as well as after their fortunes begin to rise. These trajectories cross-cut the output of commercial recordings in ways that demonstrate intimate links between recording artists and the hula world. Hula hits may be revived 'oldies' or new compositions; choreographers' interest in specific songs may be stimulated by the subject matter of the song itself, a particular performed rendition or an original choreography. Recording artists who subsequently issue songs that can be considered hula hits are capitalizing on renewed interest in the song within the hula world as a selling point for their recording.

1. Revivals of old compositions can be initiated either by hula performers or recording artists. A new recording of an old song can stimulate interest in the hula world, but not necessarily among other recording artists. An example of this trajectory is the song 'Honolulu Harbor' by Mary Robins, first recorded by Johnny Noble's Hawaiians in 1928, then published in 1929 in Noble's *Royal Collection of Hawaiian Songs* . The song enjoyed a continuous presence over the decades in a steady stream of recordings by (in roughly chronological order) Sol Hoopii and His Novelty Trio (*c.* late 1920s or early 1930s), Julia Nui's Kamaainas (*c.* late 1940s or early 1950s), Kawai Cockett and the Lei Kukui Serenaders (*c.* 1960s), Leinaala Haili (*c.* late 1960s or early 1970s) and Sonny Chillingworth (1977). The 1986

recording of this song by the Makaha Sons of Ni'ihau on their album *Ho'ola* is what stimulated renewed interest in the song within the hula world, for the group enjoyed enormous popularity among hula troupes. The song was subsequently presented in hula competitions by five different groups: in the Merrie Monarch Hula Competition in 1987 by Puka'ikapuaokalani, and by Hula Halau o Kamuela in 1992 (a performance that earned them first place); and in the King Kamehameha Chant and Hula Competition in 1992 by Hula Hui o Kapunahala, Kealakapawa and Halau Hula o Hokulani. The song 'Honolulu Harbor' does not appear to have been recorded commercially by other artists since 1986.

Another example of this trajectory, and one that demonstrates how the worlds of commercial recording and hula are closely entwined, is the song 'Kuhio Bay' by Keliana Bishaw. This song was first published in 1929 in Johnny Noble's *Royal Collection of Hawaiian Songs*. Recordings that predate the era of hula competitions (i.e. prior to the late 1970s) are mostly arrangements that are not particularly suitable for use in hula; they include choral performances by Kamehameha Schools Glee Clubs (*c.* late 1950s) and the Prince David Kawananakoa Hawaiian Civic Club Chorus (*c.* 1970s), an instrumental slack-key version on Waikiki Records, and vocal versions by Wainani Kanealii and Nina Keali'iwahamana. Gary Haleamau's recording in 1987 in hula tempo was followed by the song's appearance on hula competition stages. In 1988 the troupe Keolalaulani Halau 'Olapa o Laka performed the song as their choice number at the Merrie Monarch competition; they were accompanied by the group Ho'okena, who included the song on their debut CD, *Thirst Quencher*, issued in 1990. The song was performed in 1990 by Halau Hula Ka Noeau in the King Kamehameha competition, and in 1991 by Hula Halau o Kamuela in the Merrie Monarch competition. It was recorded by Israel 'Iz' Kamakawiwo'ole on his 1993 CD, *Facing Future*.

2. In some instances, a revival of an old song on the hula stage precedes, or virtually coincides with its renewed appearance on commercial recordings. The song 'Alekoki', which dates from the late 1800s, has been issued prior to the era of hula competitions on recordings too numerous to list here. Its initial appearance in competition was apparently in 1979, when Halau o Na Maoli Pua presented it at the Merrie Monarch competition. Its next appearance was in 1993: it was performed as a solo by Maelia Loebenstein who won the 'Miss Aloha Hula' title that year. She represented Ka Pa Hula O Kauanoe O Waahila, a troupe directed by her grandmother, Mae Loebenstein, who was (presumably not coincidentally) co-director of Halau o Na Maoli Pua in the late 1970s and early 1980s. In 1994 the song 'Alekoki' was released on a CD by falsetto singer Tony Conjugacion. The song was also presented in 1994 by the troupe Na Pualei o Liko Lehua in the King Kamehameha competition;

they were accompanied by the group Ho'okena, who subsequently issued the song on their 1996 CD. Most recently, the singer Darlene Ahuna, also closely associated with hula troupes who enter the Merrie Monarch competition, included the song on her second release, *Ku'u Lei Poina 'Ole* (1996).

3. Newly composed songs can enter the hula repertoire after their introduction on a commercial recording; the song becomes popular among hula performers and continues to be recorded by other artists. An example of this trajectory is the song 'Pua Hone', composed by Rev Dennis Kamakahi. A member of the group Sons of Hawaii, he recorded the song on the Sons' 1977 album. Prominent hula exponent Leinaala Kalama Heine created a choreographic routine for her show with the Brothers Cazimero, and also taught the choreography to her halau (privately-run hula school), Na Pualei o Liko Lehua. The Brothers Cazimero included the song on their 1978 album *Ho'ala*; the song was also included on their live album in 1982, and the original recording was anthologized on their *Best of* CD issued in 1987. Although it has been performed only once in the 1989 King Kamehameha competition by the troupe Halau Mehana o ka La from Tokyo, the song has been extremely popular among hula troupes. It has continued to be popular among recording artists, too, for subsequent recordings were issued by Ned Ka'apana (1980), Gary Haleamau (1988), Sugar Sugar (1989), Hawaiians Unlimited (1991) and Scott Williams (1993, 1994).

4. Original songs may be specially composed for specific kumu hula, and presented in performance. The song is recorded later, after which it becomes available to other halau. Two examples of this trajectory are offered here. First, the song 'Ke Alaula' was debuted in the Queen Lili'uokalani Keiki (Children's) Hula Competition in 1993, by Jawna Lono, a dancer representing the troupe Na Mamoali'i o Ka'uiki. The lyrics were composed by William Panui, husband of the troupe's director Namahana Kalama-Panui; the music was composed by Louis 'Moon' Kauakahi, lead singer of the Makaha Sons, the group who provided the musical accompaniment. The Makaha Sons released the song on their 1994 CD. Another hula troupe, Halau o Kawaili'ula, presented their own choreography of the song as their choice number in the 1995 Merrie Monarch competition, accompanied by the Makaha Sons. Second, the song 'Hopoe', composed by Frank Kawaikapuokalani Hewitt, was performed by Pi'ilani Smith, a dancer from Halau o Na Maoli Pua, at the World Invitational Hula Competition in 1992. Smith was accompanied by her aunt, Loyal Garner, who issued the song on a 1993 recording. In 1995, the troupe Keolalaulani Halau 'Olapa o Laka performed the song in the Merrie Monarch competition and the World International Hula Festival, with musical accompaniment by associates of

the halau, including director Aloha Dalire. The Makaha Sons included the song on their CD issued at the end of 1996.

5. A new CD becomes a hit, the artist is propelled to popularity because of it, and songs from the CD are choreographed and taught in hula troupes. The example that comes immediately to mind is the artist Keali'i Reichel. His 1994 debut CD *Kawaipunahele* enjoyed enormous success. After garnering awards in five categories in the Hawai'i recording industry's Na Hoku Hanohano Awards in Spring 1995, it spent nearly two months on *Billboard* magazine's World Music chart later that Autumn. His much anticipated second CD, *Lei Hali'a*, appeared in late Autumn 1995.

The popularity of songs from Reichel's debut CD extended far beyond Hawai'i, as is evident by their presentation in competitive hula events. Although only one Hawai'i group, Kealakapawa, chose one song from the first CD, 'Hanohano Ka Lei Pikake', for performance in the Merrie Monarch competition in 1996, at least five other contestants entered three other songs in at least two other events. At 'E Hula Mau', the first annual hula competition in Southern California in 1995, the song 'Kauanoeanu-hea' was performed by soloist Alapa'i Kanamu of Hula Halau O Kamuela II (who repeated her performance in the World Invitational Hula Festival) and by the troupe Kaulana Ka Hale Kula O Na Pua O Ka Aina. The song 'E Ho'i I Ka Pili' was also performed by soloist Kehaulani Kelly of Halau Hula O Keoniana. At the World Invitational Hula Festival held in Honolulu in November 1995, the song 'E Ho'i I Ka Pili' was performed by soloist Dagmar La'ela'e Sundberg from Germany, and the song 'Kawaipunahele' was performed by soloist Mikaela Joy Maka'ala Willis from Chicago. At the 1996 Merrie Monarch competition, 'Toad Song' from the second CD was performed by Halau Hula o Kawaili'ula.

Keali'i Reichel was the headline act at the concert that concluded the first E Hula Mau competition weekend in southern California in 1995. As he sang songs from his first CD, dancers from participating troupes rose to their feet and danced the songs that they knew. The result was a feast of multiple choreographies performed simultaneously, illustrating dramatically how repertoire from Reichel's CD had spread so thoroughly throughout the hula world – as displayed in California, no less.

Local music

While Hawai'i's recording industry is ostensibly weighted toward the production and marketing of ethnic Hawaiian music, and this production is closely intertwined with the hula world, there is also a segment of music production and consumption that appeals to broader audiences. Within this segment, there is some imitation of continental American popular music trends. However, it is particularly striking that a number of groups have established followings on the basis of songs and song packages that address specifically local interests and concerns in ways that transcend ethnic boundaries among Hawai'i's multiethnic and multicultural population. Among performers and groups that engage in broadly local (rather than ethnic Hawaiian) music, three strategies of focus on repertoire can be identified. These strategies demonstrate how local groups do, or do not, intersect with ethnic Hawaiian music.

First, many local groups include at least one, and sometimes two or more Hawaiian-language tracks on most, if not all, of their recordings. For example, the artist Willie K. (Willie Kahaiali'i) has one Hawaiian-language song on each of his three recordings: 'Ho'onanea' on *Kahaiali'i* (1992), 'Waiulu' on *Here's My Heart* (1992) and 'Makee Ailana' on *Uncle Willie K.* (1995). The female duo Leahi has also included at least one Hawaiian-language song on each of their recordings: 'Nani Ka'ala' on *Island Girls* (1989), 'Kanaka Waiwai' on *Hawaiian Holiday Island Style* (1990), and 'Ahulili' and 'He 'Ono' on *Live from Tahiti* (1990). The group Kapena, whose members are native Hawaiian and Samoan, have consistently included Hawaiian language songs on most of their recordings. By their fourth release, *Stylin'* (also 1990), the group had begun adding Samoan and Tahitian-language songs; their latest 1996 release, *I'll Build You A Rainbow*, includes two Samoan-language songs only, and no Hawaiian songs. The Ka'au Crater Boys also included three Hawaiian-language songs on each of their first two recordings: 'No Ke Ano Ahiahi, Kawika', and 'Sweet Lei Ka Lehua' on *Tropical Hawaiian Day* (1991); and 'Noho Paipai, Palolo' and 'Ka Uluwehi O Ke Kai' on *Valley Style* (1993). The group Hawaiian Style Band included two Hawaiian-language songs, 'No Ke Ano Ahiahi' and 'Kaimana Hila' on their first CD, *Vanishing Treasures* (1992), and one Hawaiian-language song, 'Wahine 'Ilikea', on their second CD, *Rhythm of the Ocean* (1994). The lead singer, Robi Kahakalau, continued the inclusion of Hawaiian-language tracks on her solo CD, *Sistah Robi* (1995). As an aside, the vast majority of Hawaiian-language songs cited above are *hula ku'i* songs.

Second, there are at least four groups whose early recordings demonstrate their members' initial affiliation with ethnic Hawaiian music, but whose subsequent recordings show a gradual move toward exclusively English-language material. These groups include Ho'aikane, Mana'o Company and 3 Scoops of Aloha. Ho'aikane debuted with two recordings in 1986: on *Pu'uanahulu*, eight of ten selections were in the Hawaiian language; *Kiho'alu ... On The Back Porch* consisted of instrumental selections in the Hawaiian-guitar style known as slack key. By 1990, with the release of Ho'aikane's fifth recording *Island Irie*, the group had moved away from Hawaiian material and had established a presence in Hawai'i's reggae scene (see pp. 81–5 and below). Mana'o Company had four Hawaiian-language tracks on their 1990 recording *Just*

Beyond the Ridge; their 1993 recording *True Inspiration* is entirely in English, and their 'greatest hits' anthology, issued in 1994, *Ke Hoomanao Nei*, contained only one Hawaiian-language song. The group 3 Scoops of Aloha issued two recordings in the late 1980s, *Kinohi Loa* (The Very Beginning) and the self-titled *3 Scoops of Aloha*, that had a balanced mix of Hawaiian and English language material; their 1990 release, *That Was Then, This Is Now*, contained only one Hawaiian-language song, and their 1992 release, *Live, Laugh and Love*, is entirely in English.

Third, there are performers who eschew Hawaiian-language material entirely. Those performers who are allied with the performance of reggae (at one time dubbed 'Jawaiian'; see Chapter 5 of this anthology), including Bruddah Waltah and Island Afternoon, Butch Helemano and the Players of Instruments, Ho'aikane, Simplisity, Sistah Sistah, and Sundance, form a sub-group distinct from those whose material is in a more mainstream popular style, including Brother Noland and Pagan Babies. Interest in reggae exploded in the late 1980s, leading up to the release of three recordings in 1989: *Hawaiian Reggae* by Bruddah Waltah and Island Afternoon, *Reggae Fevah* by Butch Helemano and the Players of Instruments, and *Pure Jawaiian* by Simplisity.

What unites reggae with other more mainstream styles is the use of the medium to express concerns for, and commentary on, everyday life in the islands. Songs such as 'Hawaiian Lands', 'Hawaiian Roots', 'Island Reggae', 'Jawaiian Wave' and 'Sweet Lady of Waiahole' are clearly about subject matter unique to Hawai'i, dispelling any notions that Hawaiian reggae may be nothing more than imitations of Jamaican exemplars. In this vein, local groups have also incorporated use of rap to convey commentary on local living. The selection 'Island Stylin'' by Kapena, recorded on *Wild Heart* in 1992, celebrates local music by claiming uniqueness ('Island music's got a different style'), then continuing on to laud specific performers:

> The Mana'o boys, they've got the groove
> Hoaikane's got the jockey move yeah
> Uncle Willie K., he'll make your day
> Kapena's here to make everybody party
> Cause eveybody is Island Stylin'

The track culminates in a rap that is self-promotional:

> Now the people of Hawaii find it natural to move
> And the boys of Kapena find it natural to groove
> So when you put these things together then you get a funky jam
> And then you'll know it's true Kapena Island Stylin'
> 'Cause many bands them rock it in a different style
> But Kapena's got the sound that drives the whole world wild

The female trio Na Leo Pilimehana occupies a special niche in the annals of local music. The title track of their debut recording 'Local Boys', released in 1985, sparked a storm of controversy that culminated in charges of racism. The song was an innocuous celebration of Hawai'i's unique multiethnic profile, yet its statement of preferences was read as exclusionary:

> Blue eyes and blond hair don't thrill me
> Cause I'm in love with the local boys
> Don't try to convince me
> Because the local boys are *no ka oi* [the best]

Local music plays a major role in defining local culture in Hawai'i, because it creates a multicultural space that is shared by all Hawai'i residents who identify themselves as local. In this light, the seemingly exclusionary 'local boys' can be construed as inclusionary, for no one ethnicity is specified over others. The song 'Living in a Sovereign Land' (recorded by Hawaiian Style Band in 1992, and again by co-composer Israel Kamakawiwo'ole in 1996) marks the gathering of native Hawaiians on the 1993 centennial of the overthrow of the sovereign Hawaiian monarchy. The second verse addresses all people, irrespective of ethnic descent:

> Island people come together as one
> For future generations under the sun
> Singing songs of freedom
> Singing songs of love
> Living in a sovereign land.

Among performers of local music it is striking to note what can be called 'crossovers' – performers not noted for performing ethnic Hawaiian music issuing at least one recording devoted primarily to material in the Hawaiian language or with Hawaiian cultural subject matter. Two in particular stand out: *Satisfaction Guaranteed* by Kapena (1990) which contains only three songs not in the Hawaiian language, and *Puu Nui* by Butch Helemano (1993), which contains only one song not in the Hawaiian language. This leads to the observation that among artists who focus on non-Hawaiian material are musicians who are skilled in performance styles of ethnic Hawaiian music. Three singers in particular are especially talented in male falsetto singing: Willie Kahaiali'i, Kapena's Kelly De Lima and Russell Mauga, a founding member of Ho'aikane who left the group by 1990 and released a solo CD, *He Kakahiaka Nani E*, in 1996.

Table 6.1: KCCN *Top Ten lists for July 1996*

Hawaiian Top Ten (heard on 1420 AM)	Island Top Ten (heard on FM100)
1. 'Kuikawa' – Makaha Sons	1. 'Kuikawa' – Makaha Sons
2. 'Lei Hali'a' – Keali'i Reichel	2. 'Lei Hali'a' - Keali'i Reichel
3. 'Flying With Angels' – Na Leo Pilimehana	3. 'Flying With Angels' – Na Leo Pilimehana
4. 'Acoustic Soul' – John Cruz	4. 'Acoustic Soul' - John Cruz
5. 'Broken Hearts' – Darren Benitez	5. 'Score' – Fugees Refugee Camp
6. 'Kawaipunahele' – Keali'i Reichel	6. 'Broken Hearts' – Darren Benitez
7. 'Pua'ena' – Reverend Dennis Kamakahi	7. 'Resistance' – Big Mountain
8. 'Sistah Robi' – Robi Kahakalau	8. 'Kawaipunahele' – Keali'i Reichel
9. 'O Ka Wa I Hala' – Tony Conjugacion	9. 'Sistah Robi' – Robi Kahakalau
10. 'Island Radio Hits' – Various Artists	10. 'Island Radio Hits' – Various Artists

Local charts

Local and ethnic Hawaiian musics come together in the context of Hawai'i's recording industry. Points of overlap and non-overlap between the two domains call attention to the fact that relationships are constantly shifting. This is clearly illustrated in two tracking mechanisms: a 'Top Ten' album list compiled by local radio station KCCN, and the record industry's annual awards structure, called 'Na Hoku Hanohano' (Stars of Distinction).

The Top Ten lists compiled by KCCN radio are derived from two sources: listeners' requests and in-store sales at Tower Records. The distinction between ethnic Hawaiian music and non-ethnically specific local music is reflected in two different categories: Hawaiian Top Ten, and Island Top Ten. The Hawaiian Top Ten list factors in listener preferences on the AM station which has a programming focus on Hawaiian material. The Island Top Ten list factors in listener preferences on the FM affiliate which purportedly covers a broader range of local music than the narrower ethnic focus of the AM station; the FM station is noted for playing more reggae and other contemporary styles.

The Top Ten lists for July 1996 are reproduced in Table 6.1. The overlap is striking: the first four spots on both lists are occupied by the same recordings; four other recordings share the remaining six spots. The recordings at numbers seven and nine are specific to the Hawaiian Top Ten, while those at numbers five and seven are specific to the Island Top Ten. Given this amount of overlap, one can generalize that audiences and their preferences overlap, for even on the FM station which purportedly programmes more local music, listeners are requesting many of the same recordings as on the AM station. It is possible, of course, that from any given recording, different tracks were being requested on the two different stations. A fan on the Internet reports the following on Keali'i Reichel's recording *Kawaipunahele*:

> Some radio stations here hardly ever played 'Kawaipunahele', 'Hanohano Ka Lei Pikake', 'Kauanoeanuhea', or any of his Hawaiian tunes from the first album, but they played 'Wanting Memories' every two hours, and 'If We Hold On ...' at least twice a day.
> (Donaghy, posting on NahenaheNet, < http://www.nahenahe.net >, 14 March 1997)

Diversity of musical styles in Hawai'i's local recording industry is clearly evident in the structure of categories for annual awards established in 1978. These awards, named 'Na Hoku Hanohano' (Stars of Distinction), are co-ordinated by the Hawai'i Academy of Recording Arts, whose voting members are industry professionals. The coveted awards recognize achievement in a variety of categories, including best artists (male, female and group), best new song and technical production. For the purpose at hand, I shall focus on the categories that pertain to albums. Ethnic Hawaiian and non-ethnic recordings are considered separately; among ethnic Hawaiian recordings, a further distinction is drawn between 'traditional' and 'contemporary', ostensibly referring to performance style. The three categories have been defined on the ballot and in the awards ceremony programme as follows:

1. Traditional Hawaiian Album of the Year – best performance of traditional Hawaiian music;
2. Contemporary Hawaiian Album of the Year – best performance of the music of Hawai'i in contemporary style;
3. Contemporary Album of the Year – best performance of contemporary music by a local resident artist;
4. Album of the Year – best LP or cassette release of the year.

In 1995, the category names underwent two cosmetic modifications. First, 'Traditional Hawaiian' became 'Popular Hawaiian'. Second, 'Contemporary Hawaiian' became 'Island Contemporary'. The separation of categories acknowledges two fundamental realities in the local recording industry, namely that not all musicians engage in ethnic Hawaiian music, and that within ethnic Hawaiian music, there are separate approaches to performance. The division between 'traditional' and 'contemporary' allows for creativity to be weighed separately from performances that adhere to conventional approaches in performing ethnic Hawaiian music.

What emerges from this arrangement is a portrait of valuation by members of the recording industry, who comprise the voting members of the Hawai'i Academy of Recording Arts. The historical reality is that ethnic Hawaiian recordings have predominated in the Na Hoku Hanohano awards over the years. Yet among them, contemporary Hawaiian recordings have predominated in the Album of the Year category. A compilation of the finalist nominees for Album of the Year by categories illustrates this clearly. Contemporary recordings have garnered the Album of the Year Award in only two years – 1989 and 1992; over other years, Contemporary Hawaiian recordings have outnumbered Traditional Hawaiian recordings.

Table 6.2: *Finalist nominees for Album of the Year*

| | Number of nominees | | Winner |
Year	Traditional Hawaiian	Contemporary Hawaiian	Contemporary	
1978	?	?	?	Traditional Hawaiian
1979		2	1	Contemporary Hawaiian
1980	1	4		Contemporary Hawaiian
1981		3	2	Contemporary Hawaiian
1982		3	2	Contemporary Hawaiian
1983	1	2	2	Contemporary Hawaiian
1984		3	3	Contemporary Hawaiian
1985	1	4		Contemporary Hawaiian
1986	4	1		Traditional Hawaiian
1987	4	1		Traditional Hawaiian
1988				Contemporary Hawaiian
1989	1	2	1	Contemporary
1991	2	1	2	Traditional Hawaiian
1992				Contemporary
1993	2	2	1	Traditional Hawaiian
1994	2	3		Contemporary Hawaiian
1995	4	1		Traditional Hawaiian
1996	2	2	1	

Conclusions

Hawai'i's recording industry consists of multiple domains that are simultaneously separate yet overlapping. The coexistence of ethnic Hawaiian music with local (i.e. non-ethnically specific) musics constitutes a rich mix whose intersections are vividly mapped out in the production and valuation of commercial recordings. Moreover, the dominance of ethnic Hawaiian music in local charts such as KCCN's Top Ten lists and the Na Hoku Hanohano awards points to the integration of ethnic

Hawaiian music in the commercial entertainment industry to a level not readily seen in other locales, such as New Zealand, where indigenous music production is largely marginalized outside of the major popular music production apparatus (see Chapter 2 and Mitchell, 1997: 84–6). In Hawai'i, ethnic Hawaiian and local musics are fairly integrated, even if differentially weighed at awards time.

The presence of Hawai'i's flourishing hula scene adds a distinctive dimension, in that commercial recording is directly related to and, to some extent, even driven by trends and demands outside of record production itself. Intersections among ethnic Hawaiian and local musics demonstrate that artists as well as consumers acknowledge not only the traditions of Hawai'i's indigenous inhabitants, but also realities of everyday life for Hawai'i residents of all ethnicities who identify with local culture.

Notes

1. For purposes of this chapter, notions of unity within local culture take precedence over closer attention to the racial tensions that can and do erupt on occasion. For an analysis of 'fissures and cracks' in the local fabric that are apparent in various configurations of nationalism proposed in locally produced literature, see Fujikane (1994).
2. This format is also called 'AABA', where A represents one melody sung for verses, and B represents a contrasting melody sung for the section of text often called 'chorus' or 'bridge'.

Discography

Brothers Cazimero, *Ho'ala*, Mountain Apple, 1978.
— *Captured Magic*, Mountain Apple, 1982.
— *Best of the Brothers Cazimero, Vol. 1*, Mountain Apple, 1987.
Bruddah Waltah and Island Afternoon, *Hawaiian Reggae,* Platinum Pacific, 1989.
Sonny Chillingworth, *Sonny*, Poki, 1977.
Kawai Cockett and the Lei Kukui Serenaders, *Beautiful Kauai*, Hula, (n.d.).
Tony Conjugacion, *Ku²*, Creative Native, 1994.
Loyal Garner, *Sounds of Progress*, Piilani, 1993.
Leinaala Haili, *Hanohano Olinda*, Lehua (n.d.).
Gary Haleamau, *Big Island Style*, Liko, 1987.
— *Ke Aloha o Ka Makualani*, Liko, 1988.
Hawaiian Civic Club Choruses, *Mele Ho'olaule'a*, Hula (n.d.).
Hawaiian Style Band, *Vanishing Treasures*, Top Flight, 1992.
— *Rhythm of the Ocean*, Top Flight, 1994.
Hawaiians Unlimited, *For the First Time*, Bluewater, 1991.
Butch Helemano, *Puu Nui*, Aha Hui, 1993.
Butch Helemano and the Players of Instruments, *Reggae Fevah*, Dread Lion, 1989.
Ho'aikane, *Kiho'alu ... On The Back Porch*, Kahanu, 1986.

— *Pu'uanahulu*, Kahanu, 1986.
— *Island Irie*, Kahale, 1990.
Ho'okena, *Thirst Quencher!*, Hoomau, 1990.
— *Ho'okamaha'o*, HICD, 1996.
Sol Hoopii and His Novelty Trio, *Honolulu Harbor*, Columbia (n.d.).
Willie K. (Kahaiali'i), *Kahaiali'i*, KDE, 1992.
— *Here's My Heart*, KDE, 1992.
— *Uncle Willie K.*, Round Island Records, 1995.
Ned Ka'apana, *Niihau-Hawaii*, Pumehana, 1980.
Ka'au Crater Boys, *Tropical Hawaiian Day*, Roy Sakuma, 1991.
— *Valley Style*, Roy Sakuma, RSCD, 1993.
Robi Kahakalau, *Sistah Robi*, Kanai'a, 1995.
Israel Kamakawiwo'ole, *Facing Future*, Big Boy, 1993.
— *In Dis Life*, Big Boy, 1996.
Kamehameha Schools Choruses, *Folk Songs of Hawaii*, Scholastic (n.d.).
Wainani Kanealii, *Songs of the Pacific*, Lehua (n.d.).
Kapena, *Satisfaction Guaranteed*, KDE, 1990.
— *Stylin'*, KDE, 1990.
— *Wild Heart*, KDE, 1992.
— *I'll Build You a Rainbow*, KDE, 1996.
Nina Kealiiwahamana, *Songs from the Island of Hawaii*, Music of Polynesia (n.d.).
Le'ahi, *Island Girls*, Hana Hou, 1989.
— *Live From Tahiti*, Hana Hou, 1990.
— *Hawaiian Holiday Island Style*, Hana Hou, 1990.
Makaha Sons, *Ke Alaula*, Poki, 1994.
— *Kuikawa*, Poki, 1996.
Makaha Sons of Ni'ihau, *Ho'ola*, Poki, 1986.
Mana'o Company, *Just Beyond the Ridge*, Kenford/Kaniu, 1990.
— *True Inspiration*, Kaniu, 1993.
— *Ke Hoomanao Nei*, Kaniu, 1994.
Russell Mauga, *He Kakahiaka Nanie*, Shell, 1996.
Na Leo Pilimehana, *Local Boys*, MDL, 1985.
Johnny Noble's Hawaiians, *Honolulu Harbor*, Brunswick, 1929.
Julia Nui's Kamaainas, *Honolulu Harbor*, 49th State 71 (n.d.).
Keali'i Reichel, *Kawaipunahele*, Punahele, 1994.
— *Lei Hali'a*, Punahele, 1995.
Simplisity, *Pure Jawaiian*, Hana Hou, 1989.
Sons of Hawaii, *Eddie Kamae presents the Sons of Hawaii*, Hawaii Sons, 1977.
Sugar Sugar, *Forever*, Kahale, 1989.
3 Scoops of Aloha, *Kinohi Loa (The Very Beginning)*, Kahanu, 1985.
— *3 Scoops of Aloha*, ACK (n.d.).
— *That Was Then, This Is Now*, Hana Hou, 1990.
— *Live, Laugh and Love*, Hana Hou, 1992.
Various, *Hawaiian Slack Key Guitar*, Waikiki (n.d.).
Scott Williams, *The Adventures of Scott Williams*, Altitude, 1993.
— *Scott Williams*, Mountain Apple, 1994.

PART II

Music, Commerce and the Media Industries

7

Developments in Papua New Guinea's Popular Music Industry[1]

Malcolm Philpott

Introduction

Papua New Guinean (PNG) popular music has come a long way since independence in 1975. This chapter takes the view that a handful of music entrepreneurs, broadcasters and sound recording engineers have been largely responsible for encouraging and facilitating local musicians in the creation of a local music scene. What has happened has to be seen in context. The nation is very much a product of its geography. The most populous nation in the Southwest Pacific – close to four million people – one country, yet fragmented by mountainous terrain and by vast expanses of ocean, PNG presents a rich tapestry with over 800 different languages and dialects and a corresponding number of markedly contrasting cultures. The elimination of the cultural cringe – the veneration of imported products and cultures over the local – and the renaissance of local music, which began in the early 1980s, have not come about through any one plan or programme. Yet what has happened has been a minor triumph against many odds, and has confounded the fears of many media analysts with their predictions of cultural collapse in the face of the superior forces of alien technology and the superior marketing strengths which propel the global culture.

PNG is, by world standards, a small market. The disposable income of all but a few of the urban elite is very limited. The country, like other Pacific Island nations, has experienced the full force of acculturation in recent decades, yet the potentially negative impact of new communication technologies has failed, so far at least, to completely obliterate a variety of distinctively Melanesian cultural expressions. Indeed, a growing number of Papua New Guineans are beginning to explore their past, as well as their present, by using modern multi-track sound recording and video production – as well as traditional dance-drama and music performance –

in their quest for self-expression and self-esteem. Those associated with the music industry are convinced that PNG is poised to make a bid for attention in the international market place; and this chapter privileges their voices, experience and opinions in its analysis of its topic.

A brief history of PNG popular music

Webb and Niles (1987) have provided an indispensable introductory overview of the nation's music history. They have divided the historical record into three periods: up to the 1870s, which they term the 'true traditional'; the period between the 1870s and 1945, which they term the 'early external influence'; and the period since 1945, which they call the 'recent external influence'. It is with this third period, and particularly with industry developments since independence in 1975, that this chapter is concerned. Webb and Niles's detailed chronology of significant dates and events ends in 1986. This is unfortunate for researchers in that evidence points to the emergence, since then, of a growing sense of self-confidence and professionalism in performance and recording, and of excitement concerning the pace of change. In fact a number of local observers are beginning to talk about the need to identify a fourth period, but as yet there is no consensus as to the date this fourth period might have begun.

Webb and Niles determine the end of period two and the beginning of period three as the end of World War Two. They argue that with the increasing accessibility of guitars and ukuleles after 1945, a completely new Papua New Guinean music form germinated.[2] The acoustic stringed instruments Allied servicemen had used in the war found their way to the villages where amateur musicians developed a wide variety of approaches to melodic and rhythmic playing.[3] Acoustic instruments were favoured because of their relative inexpensiveness but, with the lifting of a legal ban on nationals drinking alcohol in taverns in 1962, the need for more sound to fill the entertainment areas in urban hostelries prompted the introduction of so-called 'power bands' using amplified equipment.

On 24 November 1994 readers of one of PNG's two English dailies (*The National*) were reminded – in a full-page, full-colour obituary of Terea Iro, killed in an ambush – of a seminal event in the history of string band music.[4] Iro, guitarist, composer, songwriter, bandleader and singer, created PNG music history when he founded the Paramana Strangers in early 1967. At first the group was a trio with brothers Kiki and Verao Geno. Two years later Sam Pepena, Vagi Geno, Rupa Kala and Wari Iamo (now director of the National Research Institute) joined, and in 1972 Alu Gerega teamed up, making it one of the most formidable and entertaining bands to come out of the Central Province to date. Terea and his Aroma Coast colleagues set the standards by which the string band music era in PNG is judged. Iro went on to make history in other ways too. He set up the first locally owned recording studio – Paradise – in 1978. The Paramana Strangers were the first ever national group to tour overseas. Performing on acoustic guitars, they visited Fiji, the Cook Islands, Western Samoa and Tonga before their professional career ended in 1983.

Nineteen seventy-four is another date of significance to the chronology. In that year both the Institute of Papua New Guinea Studies (now the Cultural Studies Division of the National Research Institute) and the Creative Arts Centre (later to become the National Arts School and now the Faculty of Creative Arts at the University of Papua New Guinea) were established. Among the first graduates of the NAS were students who became foundation members of the music group Sanguma, an offshoot of the School's creative music course, in 1977. These young musicians used traditional instruments such as kundu and garamut (hand-held and slit-log drums respectively), kuakumba (Highland side-blown flutes) and Jew's harp in addition to amplified instruments. Although Sanguma were not commercially popular they made a great impression on their contemporaries and foreign audiences, completing a number of successful overseas tours. Sanguma made extensive use of traditional music, which they rearranged, sometimes employing a blend of Afro-American styles. The use of traditional instruments was to be taken up by other groups some years later – for example the group Tumbuna '84, and, more recently, Tambaran Culture. Mention should also be made at this point of the Black Brothers, a pop-rock group resident in PNG after being exiled from Irian Jaya. They had a large following before being deported in 1979, and as Webb and Niles have noted, 'the reggae sound which they incorporated into their own music influenced the direction of some PNG bands' (1987: 59).

The 1970s were also a significant time for PNG broadcasting with the National Broadcasting Commission (NBC) inheriting the role of the Australian Broadcasting Commission (ABC) at the time of independence. In 1977 they began to encourage local music by recording and releasing cassettes of locally produced pop. Their lead was followed by commercial companies, with the establishment of Paradise (now defunct) in 1978; Chin H. Meen Studios (CHM), currently the largest PNG label, in 1980; Soundstream (which closed down in 1982); and, in 1983, Pacific Gold, which remains CHM's main commercial competitor (see pp. 114–16, 'The Entrepreneurs', for further discussion). NBC has been through difficult times since 1975 (see Philpott, 1992), but their ongoing responsibility to promote local cultures, in addition to informing, educating and entertaining, has been recognized by PNG National Information and Communication Policy (see National Information and Communication Policy Committee, 1993; Philpott, 1993).

The NBC reaches its nationwide audience through its AM Karai service. Its main function is information and education, but it broadcasts imported and local music in a ratio of about three to one. NBC's FM Kalang service (which promotes itself as 'The Entertainer') was launched in 1982 and broadcasts a largely musical format, in roughly the same ratio (with news bulletins, in brief, on the hour). Its principal shortcoming during the 1980s was that it implemented a pay-for-play policy, charging PNG companies for playing their records. This was an imposition on the local music industry because the same policy could not be applied to the predominantly overseas material being broadcast. This impediment to air play of local music was not finally resolved until 1989 when the station dropped the policy. Nau-FM, a clone from the Suva-based parent company, Communications Fiji Ltd (and 25 per cent owned by them), began broadcasting 24 hours a day from 14 November 1994. The arrival of television and the emergent video industry have also had an impact on the cultural profile of the local music industry and the popularity of artists who have been able to successfully exploit the video format.[5]

Mediating the music

Krister Malm (1993) has convincingly demonstrated that the dissemination of music by the mass media can be traced back to the beginning of the twentieth century. Such technological developments came to PNG somewhat later but when they did arrive they only served to accelerate trends in cultural exchange which date back to first contact with traders and missionaries. Local music in PNG has been picking up elements from transcultural music since the arrival of Christian missionaries in the late nineteenth century; and the introduction of schooling, and the arrival of foreign workers (such as gold-mining personnel) and the portable gramophone early in the twentieth. But it was really only after World War Two that radio, one of the most potent means of both preserving and effecting change in musical traditions (Malm, 1993: 351) arrived upon the local scene.

On 1 July 1946 the ABC acquired the Army Amenities station 9AA (in Port Moresby), restored the call sign to 9PA and commenced its Papua New Guinea Service.[6] Until independence in 1975, the ABC provided the national information, education and entertainment service, whilst the Administration Broadcasting Service, which was established progressively from October 1961, concentrated on regional and local matters. This latter service was destined to become the Kundu service when the present-day national broadcaster – the NBC – took over both the ABC and the government stations. The ABC broadcast mainly imported music because the local music industry, spearheaded by the string band phenomenon, was still in its infancy. The Administration network played a great deal of traditional music, most of it recorded by local broadcast officers, but this was supplemented, with the advent of the LP, with imported music. Country and Western was, perhaps not unexpectedly, also popular.

When the NBC took over from the ABC it inherited both its good and bad points. People associated with the changeover, both expatriates and nationals, insist that the NBC acquired good studio equipment (unfortunately, a lot of it is still around!) and the professionalism associated with its parent. It also inherited a bureaucracy whose appropriateness is questionable. A fascinating study of the PNG urban music scene, carried out by students of the National Arts School (NAS) and authored by staff member Sandra Krempl-Pereira (1984), reveals, for instance, that of the five NBC staff members selected at random to be interviewed, none had musical training and yet all were responsible for scripting an assortment of programmes including music entertainment and music information programmes. The study also suggests that the fault was not that of NBC alone and argues that the government education department had to seriously consider music education as part of the school curriculum, since, without this, it was going to be difficult for the NBC and other music-related organizations to improve their output and develop towards an internationally accepted standard. The study noted that, to that time, the NBC had never employed music graduates (although several had applied) and went on to comment that overseas comparisons suggested that upwards of 30 per cent of staff ought to be trained in music.

The NAS study also contained comments on the (then) infant local recording industry which have relevance to what follows:

The National Broadcasting Corporations [sic] policy towards the playing of cassettes produced by other companies[7] on air is simply that it will not unless the company buys air time. This has caused much conflict between [local] recording companies and the NBC. (Krempl-Pereira, 1984: 8).

In April 1983 a top twenty programme was introduced on the Kalang service, sponsored by the clothing company Haus Bilas. There were problems with the show however, since although CHM paid for airtime, other sponsor support declined and the show collapsed in early 1984 when Haus Bilas pulled out and no further sponsor could be found. In 1983 CHM went one step further and bought air time to run a series entitled *Chin H. Meen Supersound*, featuring their own recordings of local bands and material from other Pacific recording companies for which they held the PNG agency.

Broadcasters' perspectives

The NBC's 'pay-for-play' policy during the 1970s and 1980s was, in large part, due to pressure applied by the Public Accounts Committee for the national broadcaster to charge for its services. This policy was however at variance with Section 9 of the Broadcasting Commission Act, which requires that the national broadcaster 'give adequate expression to the culture and the needs of the people of the various parts of Papua New Guinea'. Reflecting this, the *Times of Papua New Guinea* called for a fair go for local music in its 21–27 September 1989 issue.

Despite dropping the pay-for-play policy in 1989, Kalang's managing director, John Malisa, has declared himself unrepentant about the station's approach during the 1980s, arguing that

> We had to think about our own releases … you've got to realise that we were strapped for both funds and equipment. Before Kalang came along the NBC studios could hardly cope with the broadcast demands made on them, let alone be used for commercial ventures.

Notwithstanding the difficulties most government instrumentalities experience when they attempt to operate commercially, Malisa has emphasized that 'before the commercial studios got started we [i.e. NBC] were the ones who were promoting local music'. As Malisa stresses, NBC's role in the early development of PNG recording was significant. Although the Institute of PNG Studies released music cassettes as early as 1975, the NBC released some of the first recordings of the then popular 'six-to-six' groups, village string bands, school bands, bamboo bands as well as, perhaps somewhat surprisingly, local performances of the pop operas *Ipi Tombi* and *Jesus Christ Superstar*. Taking everything into consideration – poor management, poor equipment maintenance and underfunding – the national broadcaster has played its part, making a valuable contribution to the national cultural scene, a role which it now shares with television and, more recently, with the new music radio station Nau-FM.

One of the most significant individuals behind Kalang's promotion of local music has been Justin Kili, one of PNG radio's most popular music presenters and current programme manager of Kalang. Kili, usually referred to as 'JK', comes from Buka Island in North Solomons Province and began his career in radio with his local station in 1971. After a year he was sent to Port Moresby for two years to train as a journalist, returning to Bougainville for a further year before secondment for a time with the ABC in Port Moresby. In an interview with the author, conducted in November 1994, he recalled that his initial desire to develop contemporary PNG music through radio came about as a result of his *dislike* of string band music, seeing it as inferior to imported western music in terms 'of both performance and sound recording quality', emphasizing that:

I preferred traditional music to string band music. What really turned me off at the start was the fact that there were far too many cover versions. PNG bands at that time were just not creating their own music. They were copying western music and making a terrible job of it. When Raymond [Chin, managing director of CHM] asked me if I wanted to be a part of a push to promote PNG music I said, 'I hate the stuff I'm hearing now, so why not?'

Despite the competition between the NBC and the principal commercial companies CHM and Pacific Gold Studios, JK is unequivocal in his recognition of the contribution made by CHM and Pacific Gold to contemporary PNG music culture, stressing that

the NBC had a purpose when it made recordings. That purpose, later endorsed by the Kalo Report,[8] was to preserve PNG cultures and traditions through music ... to catalogue our many cultures, and it did that. It would not, could not, have done much to develop PNG music because its primary role was the preservation of what was there already. I think that without Greg [Seeto, Pacific Gold's managing director] and Raymond [Chin] PNG music wouldn't be where it is today. They might not get on [i.e. personally], but both work full bore to promote PNG music ... They took risks which the NBC didn't have the resources to do. And they continue to do so.

One of the prime radio sites which showcases the continuing contribution of PNG record companies to the development of PNG music is Kalang's 'PNG Top Twenty' on its *PNG Music Requests* show, which JK presents. Given that PNG is effectively a long-form (i.e. album), cassette-only market (with CDs just beginning to be phased in), with no neutral retail monitoring service to provide weekly sales figures for audio product, the *PNG Top Twenty* is drawn up as an interpretation of listeners' requests. JK explains its operation as follows:

since the introduction of that programme, letters asking for local music have been streets ahead of requests for the overseas stuff. The ratio? I'd suggest three to one in favour of the local music ... the selection of the songs is a matter for the Music Department. But I do have some influence on how long they stay there [in the Top Twenty]. I don't think it's a good thing to have songs coming in one week and going off the next, purely at the whim of our postal service. So I try to stop the 'yo-yo' effect and cushion the decline. There's probably no stopping a winner from getting to the top quickly. But it doesn't look right to see that same song pop in one week and drop out the next.

Although keen to emphasize that *PNG Popular Requests* is not the sole arbiter of public taste in music in PNG, citing EM-TV's popular music shows, *Mekim Musik* and *Fizz*, as significant agencies, JK argues that the desire to get tracks in the PNG Top Twenty has encouraged a professional approach to music production. This perception of an increasing professionalism and quality in local music also leads him to believe that one day there'll be a PNG sound. There have been a lot of hangovers from the past. And the radio playing too much overseas music hasn't helped [but] I truly believe that there will be a PNG sound, and I say that because Papua New Guinean audiences are listening to more PNG recorded music and more PNG created lyrics than ever before. They're much more critical than they used to be.

The entrepreneurs: against the odds

One of the principal problems facing commercial record companies in PNG is the relatively small market for their product. PNG may well be the largest nation in the South Pacific, but 85 per cent of its people are rural and many live in isolated villages. And the remaining fifteen per cent who live in the towns and cities have, unfortunately, only limited purchasing power. For this reason alone Pacific Gold owner Greg Seeto and CHM head Raymond Chin recall the 1980s, and the survival and expansion of their companies since, with a mixture of pride and satisfaction. As the record company mottos which prefaced this article suggest, both men see themselves as involved in an important cultural – as opposed to merely commercial – activity. Seeto, for instance has stressed the role of the PNG music industry in developing local music. He regards his studios as something more than just a recording venue, arguing:

> they're that, of course. But they have a second – an educational function. The studio's the place [the musicians] learn about music and the discipline required in playing together. Above all the studio is a happy working environment. We all enjoy what we're doing.

Reflecting the different characters of the two entrepreneurs, Raymond Chin prefers to talk about the risks involved in producing music in PNG. He is of the opinion that there is insufficient recognition of the money that has been invested in promoting local music, arguing that

> what you've got to realise is that it's we who took the risks. We paid to put local music on air and on television until commercial companies sponsored the shows. We paid to prove PNG music could make it. Of course we had the motivation ... and we had the sound engineers too.

Although both entrepreneurs speak enthusiastically about live concert promotions and overseas tours, there are considerable logistical problems with both. Live concerts outside Port Moresby, as Krempl-Pereira (1984) has pointed out, are hampered by the fact that travel and freight costs are high, given that there is no road connection between the Central Province and the population centres along the Highlands Highway and the North Coast. To visit them, and potential island province venues, it is necessary to resort to air transport, with Chin estimating that CHM usually has to air freight around 700 kilos of sound equipment alone to offshore locations, a factor which contributes greatly to the costs involved. Major sponsorship is necessary in order for record companies to recoup their outlays and, in this regard, the Benson and Hedges-sponsored 'Golden Tones' music tour of PNG in 1996 was a significant venture. Featuring the Reks Band, Sagothorns, Rabbie Gamenu, Tarikana, Wali Hits and the Tumbuna Superband, Sanguma II and Australian-American guitarist Diesel, the tour played in Lae, Goroka and Port Moresby.

Despite similar difficulties with organizing overseas tours, Chin has aggressively pursued a market expansion into Melanesia through ventures such as the April 1994 'Superband' tour of the Solomon Islands and Vanuatu. This tour featured top PNG artists Charles Kivovon, Henry Kuskus, Lista Laka, George Telek, George Luff, Basil Greg, Hitsy Golou and Steve Lahui, alongside the Australian singer Nadya (Golski) and Irian Jayan act Trio Wespa (both of whom released debut cassettes on CHM in 1994). Pacific Gold has also mounted successful overseas tours, such as Barike's visit to Vanuatu in November 1993, and Sanguma II's trip with John Wong to Noumea in 1996, to play at a festival raising funds for the establishment of the Jean-Marie Tjibaou Cultural Centre. PGS also organized the December 1993 visit of Australian country music vocalist-guitarist James Blundell. Blundell headlined a day-long, outdoor concert at Port Moresby's Sir John Guise Stadium, sponsored by the tobacco company, Benson and Hedges, which was billed in the media (and on promotional T-shirts) as 'The Event of the Year'. Supporting artists included the Clansmen Band (from the University of PNG's Faculty of Creative Arts), the Banditz, Tarbar, the Riot Squad Band and Barike.

The annual Port Moresby Show also provides an opportunity for public music performance. In June 1994, the show was extended from the traditional three days to four, and provided thousands of patrons with the opportunity to see and hear bands and solo artists from all over PNG in a successful collaborative venture between CHM, Tumbuna Traks and Kalang Radio. CHM was represented by some of its star performers – including Telek, Henry Kuskus, Leonard Kania, Chako Chako, Saugas, Lista Laka and Ronnie Galama. A wide range of other acts appeared, such as provincial artists The Old Dog and the Offbeats, Lemeki and Yondik and other popular acts such as Dabsy Yapuc, Higher Vision, Lamaika and Helgas.

The devastation of Rabaul in the volcanic eruptions of September 1994 also prompted Pacific Gold Studios to mount two major Volcano Relief concerts, featuring Pacific Gold artists, in Port Moresby. The first, in late September and only a few days after Tavurvur and Vulcan erupted, featured a number of Tolai artists who had been performing at the Goroka Show as part of the Independence weekend celebrations the week before, but who found themselves stranded and unable to return home.

Acts appearing included Barike, Painim Wok, John Wong, Jade, Julie Toliman, Riot Squad and the re-formed Sanguma. Following this first, hurriedly-arranged concert, which was somewhat sparsely attended, Seeto and his staff at Pacific Gold directed some of their energies into creating a benefit album entitled *Rabaul Volcano Town*, which contained numbers written in 1983 when Rabaul had last been threatened, together with new versions of songs such as 'Rabaul Town', 'Dust Over Rabaul', 'Volcano Song', and 'Wan Kantri'. A second concert was held in the Sir John Guise Stadium on 11 December to launch the album. This featured Sanguma II, John Wong and visiting overseas artists Island Queens, Sharon Bowman and Colin Atkins, and was, like the first, compered by Kalang's JK and William Mairi.

There has been a growing tendency for overseas acts to both tour, and, more recently, record in PNG in the 1990s. Such projects follow on from the well-documented collaboration between the Australian group Not Drowning, Waving; Telek; and other musicians from Rabaul; facilitated by Pacific Gold Studios; who recorded together in 1988, released the album *Tabaran* (entitled *Not Drowning, Waving* in its PNG version) in 1990 and performed live gigs together in Australia and PNG in 1991 and again in 1996.[9] In addition to James Blundell's performance there have been visits from other Australian bands such as Yothu Yindi and Sunrize Band, and from the Fijian act Seru Serevi. The Australian acts, Nadya (Golski) and Kalabash, toured, recorded and released cassettes on CHM (entitled, respectively, *Haiwe Driva* and *Kalabash*) in 1994. Pacific Gold also released the Island Queens album *Waikiki Tamoure* in December 1994 as a joint venture with the Australian label Assault Studios and an eponymous album by Bowman and Atkins (which features a guest appearance by John Wong). Both Chin and Seeto see such collaborations with overseas artists as confirmation of the improved standing of the local industry as well as being a valuable learning experience for local musicians and the sound engineers.

The sound engineers

The sustained improvement in musicianship and performance in PNG music over the last decade is attributable in no small measure to the efforts of the major recording studios and their technical staff. The role which the studio sound engineers have played in training PNG musicians can best be illustrated by reference to the experience of two well-known exemplars of the art – one a Papua New Guinean, the other an expatriate Australian.

Thomas Lulungan is a Tolai from the Gazelle Peninsula in East New Britain. Lulungan was chief sound engineer with CHM until 1995, when he left the company and returned to start his own recording studios in

New Britain. Whilst he lays no claim to inheritance of the talents of the traditional Tolai musicians – the *Buai na pepe* (School of Composers) – Lulungan leaves one in no doubt as to the significance of music in his and every Tolai's life.[10] Starting his working life as a schoolteacher and music educator he developed an interest in sound recording. Lulungan was awarded a teaching fellowship at the National Arts School in 1984. There he encountered the musicians who formed Sanguma. He recalls the tremendous impression Tony Subam, Sebastian Miyoni and Tom Komboi made on him and the other students, since

> The music they were making was so very different from the prevailing Central Province string band sound. For a start they made great use of traditional instruments, and they arranged a lot of traditional music too.

Although Sanguma were not widely influential on the PNG pop scene at the time, the prevalent string band sound was gradually replaced in the mid-1980s by another musical wave, local rock. Lulungan joined CHM in 1986 and recalls that early developments in PNG rock involved a reworking of traditional forms:

> I think it all began with the Rabaul-based bands, especially Painim Wok, and later the style was picked up by groups like the Junior Unbelievers, Barike and Narox ... Most of the songs that [the Rabaul-based] bands did at the time were actually string band music rewritten to fit contemporary pop arrangements ... you had a four-piece band coming in with acoustic drums, electric bass, lead guitar and rhythm guitar, and perhaps the occasional keyboard.

Lulungan's career as a recording engineer – a term used in PNG in preference to the more common 'record producer' – has involved him working with both traditional music and local forms of pop, rock and reggae. The recording engineer performs a pivotal function in PNG popular music, acting as producer, engineer, arranger and studio musician. Lulungan identifies the ability to read a score as crucial and adds that 'to be able to participate in ensemble playing is a bonus'. Lulungan, like his fellow engineers Dika Dai, Basil Greg, George Luff and Lista Laka, was formerly a member of the CHM Superband. An able musician in his own right, he regularly provides studio backings for solo artists, such as Leonard Kania, and has performed live before large audiences both at home and overseas. Following Telek's move to CHM from Pacific Gold in 1993, Lulungan worked on a series of his albums, citing his fellow Tolai as a 'genuine *buai na pepe*'[11] and attributing his success with all age groups to his ability to compose songs which comfortably combine 'roots with imported music', noting that 'he's managed it as few others have done so far'. Although recording engineers and session players play an important role in CHM recordings, Lulungan stresses that he adopts different approaches for different performers. Comparing two of CHM's most prominent artists for instance, Lulungan observes that

> [Telek] is slower with some arrangements than Leonard [Kania] and he relies much more on the work we're doing in the studio. Leonard on the other hand comes better prepared. He's been around for five or six years now, and I like the way he works. He [Leonard] can't play a single guitar chord, but he can really write top lyrics ... and straight from his head. When we go into the studio to lay a new track Leonard's first take is always the best.

While Lulungan's influence on PNG music reflects his cultural background as both an indigenous Papua New Guinean and a Tolai, the other most influential PNG engineer has a markedly different cultural background. Mike Wild, Pacific Gold's chief engineer until 1995, first came to Papua New Guinea in 1984. Unlike Lulungan, his ear had been tuned almost exclusively to Western music before his first visit. He recalls that he was immediately impressed by the Tolai bands and – like many westerners in PNG – was also fascinated by the use of traditional instruments, as well as by the way PNG musicians worked. He sees his role as primarily that of a facilitator for the artists he has worked with. Wild observes that there have been 'tremendous developments' in PNG popular music, 'even in the time I've been up here', and cites inventive use of new technologies as a key factor, commenting that

> groups like Barike, using MIDI technology and sequencing, as well as incorporating all the traditional techniques of playing we used to associate with the string bands, have now developed a more subtle sound ... a more professional technique.

Another area he identifies as significant is local musicians' modification of imported music styles, arguing, with regard to the local form of reggae, known as Island ('Ailan') reggae, that

> Not content with Jamaica's one and three [rhythm], island reggae is taken faster than the original, and to the tune of four beats to the bar, with the emphasis on the last beat. The fans love it, even if it baffles visiting West Indians.

Of all the bands he has worked with, he singles out Tambaran Culture, with whom he worked in 1992–3, producing their cassette album *Tambaran Culture of PNG*, as the most impressive. He argues that

> They even take Sanguma a stage further because of their virtuoso musicianship. Listen to them and you hear some amazing time fields ... rhythmic structures and percussive structures. As a western musician I find what Papua New Guineans are doing absolutely fascinating. You'd be amazed at the

rhythmic and percussive structures a group like Tambaran Culture are building into their tracks. I think it all has to do with their roots. One thing any newcomer notices right away is the melody line. They don't just sit there and set a beat, then do a melody line over the top. They set about it in reverse. They set the melody and then work out the beat underneath. Most musicians I've ever worked with played a drum beat, then they went for a chord structure over that, and finally sang a melody line over the top of that. Up here it's a bit like building a house starting with the roof first, and finishing up with the basement and the foundations. Whatever, it sounds great.

Towards the millennium

In the years leading up to independence, and for perhaps the ensuing decade and a half, indigenous popular music in PNG, as happened in other Third World countries, was affected by a predominantly one-way flow of cultural products and the threat of a cultural 'grey-out'. As a consequence, PNG local popular music lost some of its authenticity and social relevance in the move to accommodate and mimic alien musical forces and forms. However, with the benefit of hindsight it is now possible to view the post-Independence years as a new beginning, forged through the combined efforts of the mediators – broadcast music presenters, especially JK, William Mairi and Patrick Patu; EM-TV's *Fizz* programme; and the major recording studios and sound engineers, especially Seeto and Wild at Pacific Gold, and Lulungan, Dika Dai, Basil Greg and Lista Laka at Chin H. Meen.

Whilst those involved with the local music industry have become increasingly confident that PNG popular music is gaining ground both at home and overseas, all the individuals interviewed for this article agreed that it was premature to speak of it having achieved an international profile and status. Although overseas tours to the Solomons and Vanuatu have done a great deal to promote PNG music in the rest of Melanesia, both leading PNG music video makers Titus Tilly, and Thomas Lulungan believe that songs which made it to the top of Radio Kalang's PNG Top Twenty would be unlikely to appeal to any but specialist audiences in North America, Europe and even neighbouring Australia. Tilly, like Lulungan, notes an improvement in local musicianship and sound recording technique over the past decade, and concedes that the efforts of the local entrepreneurs to use the studios as a learning experience have borne fruit, but concludes that 'We are not quite ready to compete on that stage ... perhaps in five or ten years time, but I don't think we're there just yet.'

One event which cast a very real cloud over the undoubted successes of the local music industry over the past two decades, was the 1994 Rabaul volcanic eruption. Throughout the 1980s at least, Rabaul was perhaps *the* most significant geographical centre for PNG popular music. Despite their mutual antipathy – an antipathy which many have seen as a key driving force in PNG popular music – both Seeto and Chin are of PNG Chinese origin and grew up in Rabaul, attending the same school. Pacific Gold first set up a studio in Rabaul in the early 1980s, and were followed, soon after, by CHM. The Rabaul studios developed and popularized the Tolai sound (described on pp. 116–19) which became the dominant force in PNG music throughout the decade. However, the Rabaul connection was abruptly severed by the cataclysmic eruption of Tavurvur and Vulcan on 19 September 1994. Rabaul Town was devastated for the second time this century. Both Pacific Gold and CHM studios were destroyed by the collapse of buildings, the result of tonnes of ash falling upon their roofs. The majority of studio equipment was either destroyed, sent off for repair and/or subsequently relocated to Port Moresby. Most of the personnel and recording artists have transferred to Port Moresby. Both Chin and Seeto have expressed the intention to resume their recording operations in New Britain, either in Rabaul or nearby Kopoko. As yet, these intentions have not been realized and Lulungan's studio has yet to open.

The last word is perhaps best left to a Papua New Guinean. Asked for his predictions about where PNG music might be headed in the next five years, Lulungan offered the following prognosis:

> I've done some research into Tolai music and into other traditional music around PNG, and as much as I hate that music being transformed and taken out of their traditional settings I think it's inevitable if we're going to see any development of PNG-oriented music here. Certainly I foresee there's a risk of a little bit of damage to our cultural heritage. It's luring young people away from knowing about the traditional ways, the way I did when I was a young man. And that's sad. But again we've got to accept change. We can't stand still. So I'm encouraging people to include traditional instruments in their arrangements.
>
> In five years time I think there'll be a very big change. Not so much moving away from the style we have now, but technically speaking. There's new equipment coming in all the time. And of course sound engineers like myself will want to use the new machines to their fullest ... the sound quality will be so much better that nobody will even realize it's PNG music any more ... unless that is we include traditional arrangements and traditional instruments. It's all going to be drastically changed ... by the studios and because of the technology.

Notes

1. NB. All quotations from PNG music industry personnel cited in this chapter, are, unless otherwise attributed, taken from interviews with the author conducted in Port Moresby in 1993 and 1994.

   Thanks to Raymond Chin, Ian Fry, Philip Hayward, James Kila, Justin Kili, Thomas Lulungan, John Malisa, Wilma Marakan, Neil Nicholls, Don Niles, Father Vince Ohlinger, Mark Rogers, Austin Sapias, Greg Seeto, John Taylor, Titus Tilly, Louie Warupi and Mike Wild who willingly offered both their time and, more importantly, their thoughts.

   This chapter originally appeared in *Perfect Beat*, vol. 2, no. 3 (July 1995).

2. Other forms introduced during the second period also continued to be used in both the schools and churches and the continuing late twentieth century popularity of Gospel music can be traced to the hymnody so firmly planted by the early missionaries.

3. See Webb and Niles (1987: 54) for further discussion.

4. The obituary, written by Mohammed Bashir, is headed 'Terea's music will live on' and is memorable for the statement by Sam Pepena, chairman of the PNG Oil refinery, that he would get 'the boys' together and re-record the entire fifteen albums produced by Iro's band in order to raise money for his bereaved family.

5. Analysis of this topic is however beyond the scope of this article. Various aspects of PNG music TV and music video are, however, discussed in Chapter 10 of this anthology.

6. Amalgamated Wireless opened the country's first broadcasting station, 9PM Port Moresby, in October 1935.

7. The NBC began releasing its own cassettes in 1977.

8. The Kalo Committee, which reported to the Government in 1987, dealt with a range of broadcasting issues. Of major concern at the time, given that television had just arrived and videos were becoming freely available throughout the country, was the potentially adverse impact of alien images, violence and pornography. However, the committee also concerned itself with the run-down state of the NBC and called upon the broadcast media to encourage local cultural production.

9. See Hayward (1998); Webb (1993).

10. For details of the significant role music plays in Tolai society see Lulungan (1983).

11. Telek, having undergone a rigorous initiation ceremony, is well-versed in traditional *malira* (love magic) and *warbat* (magic love songs).

Discographic note

Full details of all PNG music releases can be found in the publication *Commercial Recordings of Papua New Guinea Music*, and a series of supplements, compiled by Don Niles and published by the National Research Institute (GPO Box 1432, Boroko, NCD, PNG). Chin H. Meen (CHM) has issued two full-colour Supersound catalogues with reproductions of the cover of every cassette released. Requests for more information should be addressed to

CHM Head Office, PO Box 1106, Boroko, PNG. Pacific Gold Studios have only issued a leaflet, but more information on releases of PNG and international recording artists may be obtained by addressing their head office, PO Box 4470, Boroko, PNG. Details of cassette releases on the Kalang label can be obtained from the Sales and Marketing Manager, Kalang Advertising Pty Ltd, PO Box 1534, Port Moresby, PNG.

8

Questions of Music Copyright in Papua New Guinea[1]

Don Niles

While some type of copyright over traditional music and dance at a village or regional level is a common feature throughout Papua New Guinea (see Niles 1992), the development of the commercial recording industry in the country has not seen Papua New Guinea become a signatory to any international copyright legislation. Alongside locally produced recordings of PNG pop are sold pirated overseas cassettes, also mostly locally produced. This is no black market enterprise, but standard business practice nationwide. A valuable overview of the legal question of copyright is provided by Nonggorr (1990). The brief comments below benefit from that article, but focus on music, particularly in relation to two important aspects of the whole discussion concerning music copyright in PNG. Tauwala (1984) also speaks personally on the same issue.

Although the PNG parliament passed the Copyright Act of 1978, which stated PNG's acceptance of the Universal Copyright Convention, the act stipulated that 'a work shall not be eligible for copyright unless deposit has been made in terms of the Statutory Deposit Act 1978'. As the latter Act was never passed, PNG's sole copyright legislation has been unenforceable. Yet the issue of the right to copy PNG popular music has been of considerable importance amongst fans as well as musicians.

An important argument in favour of copyright legislation has been that it would encourage local composition. This would come about for at least two reasons:

1. The increased costs of imported materials would mean fewer people would spend their money on them, opting instead for cassettes of local bands.

2. Royalties generated by the increased sales of cassettes by local bands would encourage more local creativity (and this creativity would be in original compositions, rather than the imitation of other bands).

Obviously, imitation is a very important element in gaining musical competence, but the PNG public has often been sensitive to simple imitation being an end in itself, rather than a step towards developing a band's own musical style. Certainly the first electrified bands in PNG relied heavily on cover versions of overseas songs. One very popular 1960s band was simply called the Copycats. In the mid- to late 1980s, when the PNG music industry was becoming more competitive and releases more numerous, many written comments on these developments were sent to the local newspapers. These comments were often highly critical of local bands that copied overseas songs, even if the language was changed from English to Tok Pisin. Typical comments included: 'What fools would be proud of such copycats denying themselves their own ethnic musical identity?...[bands] must try to produce something that Papua New Guineans will be proud of' (Toturi, 1985: 4); and, 'If you're interested in music, then write and produce your own (or otherwise forget it). You are out of the tune and style of another person's record' (Kange, 1985: 4).

Concern has also been raised if local bands from one region copy a style from another region. For example, in certain parts of the country lengths of bamboo are struck with rubber thongs to provide a bass part to string bands. Many writers complained that the use of these bamboo bands by musicians from a province not usually associated with such instruments was an embarrassment to the province as a whole:

> Whenever I hear some string bands from West Sepik playing bamboos, the bamboos just don't sound good. The guitar strings sound weird and the voice of the man singing is really strange. Such mistakes really spoil their songs ... Don't copycat. We'll just try it out and it won't be good. The stringband will be totally spoiled. We must use our own style.   (Ruina, 1986: 15)

> Can't you Vanimo people find your own style? Work hard to find the sound of West Sepik itself.   (Kombi, 1984: 4).

Beyond just copying of styles, however, the theft of local songs between bands has also been reported. Letter writers frequently told bands simply to get their own songs: 'I would like to tell stringbands to record their own songs and not to copy other people's compositions' (BB Kings Fan, 1984: 4) or question who gave permission for a certain song to be included (e.g., 'Novorab Kid', 1984: 4). Yet things take on a new dimension when overseas bands are responsible for the theft. The most well-known example of a theft of a PNG song by an overseas band was reported in 1983. Sanguma, a band originally formed of students from the National Arts School, gained a widespread reputation within Papua New Guinea and abroad for their experimentation in incorporating traditional music and instruments into their music.[2] In 1977 they released their first (eponymously titled) cassette, which contained the song 'Yalikoe', a hunting song from East Sepik province, arranged by band member Aron Murray.

The Black Brothers, a band from the Irian Jaya province of Indonesia, were based in Papua New Guinea in 1979–80 and gave a number of performances before being evicted from the country – eventually resettling in The Netherlands. In 1982 they recorded their own version of 'Yalikoe' which became a popular dance track in the Western European club circuit,[3] and was for some time available in Papua New Guinea on an Indonesian cassette entitled *Disco Festival 83*, which also included songs by Madonna and a number of other less well-known bands. On the cassette, 'Jalikoe' (*sic*) is identified as being performed by 'Papua' (the name Black Brothers used while resident in The Netherlands) and, in contrast to the other songs on the cassette, its text is not included in the accompanying sheet of lyrics. The members of Sanguma reacted, with one member stating:

> We haven't been referred to at all by the Black Brothers about the song. They should have at least asked us to use it instead of sneaking it out like that. (Joku, 1983: 3)

Note that simply 'asking' was all that was requested – the usual way of handling such things in PNG, yet applied here even though the context was no longer local.

Along with arguments that the introduction of copyright would increase local creativity is a strong statement against its introduction – namely that copyright would result in a great increase in the cost of music cassettes for local buyers. In the past, PNG has seen many pirate cassettes of overseas popular music (mostly of UK and US bands), primarily manufactured in Singapore and Indonesia. Today, however, the vast majority of such pirate cassettes are locally made, reflecting recent international Top Twenty hits of the past few months and popular albums. Chin H. Meen, the most prolific producer of cassettes of PNG bands, is also the main producer of pirated cassettes of overseas music. Consequently, locally made pirated cassettes of foreign music are less expensive (*c*. 3.50 kina, approx. Aus $3.50) than locally made cassettes of PNG bands (*c*. 6.50 kina, approx. Aus $6.50). Lack of copyright keeps the cost of pirated cassettes low, but cassettes of PNG bands remain expensive because studios absorb production costs. (Although a couple CDs of PNG popular music have been released locally, they are presently of no importance to the majority of buyers of PNG music recordings. CDs of both local and overseas material sell for 16 to 20 kina.)

Pat Siwi, a well-known musician from the former Wahgi Hellcats and presently part-owner of Kumul Studios in Goroka argued that, as well as for other reasons, copyright should be introduced to increase the low price of pirated cassettes (Siwi, 1990: 6). Yet, another writer considers the low cost of pirated cassettes to be a great blessing and one that politicians should think twice about before introducing anything which will affect such prices, lest they might not be elected again (Henry, 1983: 4). This view is also predictably echoed (minus the threat) by Chin H. Meen itself (Avei, 1989: 3).

Many of these comments have been heard frequently over the past two decades of independence, especially whenever parliament is said to be considering yet another bill concerning copyright. But the calls for copyright seem to be getting louder, particularly with the general rise in the interest concerning the 'world music' market. Bands would love to gain international fame for themselves, as well as their country. But they are also concerned about theft of what is theirs and, more generally, what is Papua New Guinean. How would PNG bands be promoted? Who would really benefit? PNG music must not become known through disembodied samples featured on Western releases such as the Future Sounds of London's *Papua New Guinea* CD (1992).[4]

At the end of January 1995, PNG officials held meetings with a specialist in copyright from the UNESCO office in Paris. Opinion is still divided as to whether internal copyright should be taken as a first step or whether PNG should immediately go with one of the international models. Furthermore, a National Library and Archives Act 1993 has now been passed, making deposit at the National Library a legal requirement. All of these steps promote the right environment for copyright legislation. But unless there is a powerful lobby for its introduction, it is doubtful that parliament will move in this direction with any speed.

Notes

1. This chapter originally appeared in *Perfect Beat* vol. 2, no. 4, January 1996. I very much appreciate the assistance of Neil Nichols and the comments of the *Perfect Beat* editorial board, especially Philip Hayward, in the preparation of this chapter.
2. See Webb (1993: 61–6) for further discussion.
3. Joku states that 'Jalikoe' reached third place on the European disco charts (Joku, 1983). Precisely which chart she is referring to remains unclear, however, as there was no commonly accepted European disco chart during the 1980s.
4. Released with no attribution of the Papua New Guinean sample on the sleeve credits.

Discography

The Future Sound of London, *Papua New Guinea*, Jumpin' & Pumpin', 1992.
Sanguma, *Sanguma*, National Art School, 1978.
Various, *Disco Festival 83*, Kings Record, 1983.

9

Te Wa Whakapaoho i te Reo Irirangi: Some Directions in Maori Radio[1]

Helen Wilson

The bicultural policies of much of the public sector in Aotearoa/New Zealand are based on the Treaty of Waitangi. The settlement of Treaty claims involves a recognition of colonial injustice and an attempt at redress, though the results are always a compromise and far less is offered to Maori than was taken from them in the past. The backlog of cases before the Waitangi Tribunal is enormous and its resources far from adequate. Indeed the Tribunal has been described as 'a panacea which helped stabilize, and later actively legitimize, the Pakeha state' (Kelsey, 1991: 108). But the present development of Maori radio is an outcome of some crucial Waitangi Tribunal decisions.

Broadcasting is taken by many Maori to be an important means of empowerment, especially with regard to cultural revival and language maintenance. In the field of broadcasting there have been three major cases before the Waitangi Tribunal. The Te Reo Maori Report (Spoonley *et al.*, 1986) identified the Maori language as a valued possession which the Crown ought to have protected. The BCNZ (Broadcasting Corporation of New Zealand) Assets case, on which a decision of the Court of Appeal was made in 1992, addressed, among other things, the obligation of a state-owned television broadcaster to provide Maori programmes in prime time (Wilson, 1993). In introducing its new spectrum management regime in 1990, the Crown had pledged AM frequencies for specific Maori use, but in its Spectrum Report, the Waitangi Tribunal called on the Crown to make extra frequencies available (FM frequencies in the major metropolitan centres of Auckland and Wellington) to cater for Maori youth. For this reason and for reasons of cost, FM became the preferred medium for Maori radio. This paper deals with some aspects of the use of these frequencies for *iwi* (tribe) based radio stations, aimed primarily at a Maori audience for the promotion of Maori language and Maori culture.

Some of these developments since 1989 have dramatically changed the nature of radio in the country at a time when the number of outlets continues to increase due to the government's tendering of frequencies. Maori radio is now a dynamic presence in all major markets, particularly in the North Island, extending the range of radio sounds and services and in some cases challenging the established stations. There is much change and upheaval in the stations and many issues present themselves to Maori programme makers, broadcasters and funding bodies.

The stations were in the first instance primarily funded by the body which collects the public broadcasting fee from television households, NZ On Air, and from 1995 by the new Maori broadcasting funding body, Te Mangai Paho. Partly guided by ministerial directives, NZ On Air took its responsibilities in this area seriously. It spent 10 per cent of its funds ($7.3 million) on Maori radio in 1991 (Annual Report no. 2), opting to support the model of autonomous *iwi*-based local stations linked for programme exchange purposes by Telecom lines. This was in keeping with government policy at the time, which involved devolving the management of Maori assets to *iwi* authorities (Fleras, 1991). Licence holders have to be a recognized *tangata whenua iwi* body, who can then assign the running of the station to a broadcaster who will respect and fulfil the language and culture *kaupapa* (philosophy).

NZ On Air set limits on the funding it would provide for new stations. They had to serve a population of at least 10,000 Maori, and $200,000 was the maximum operating funds per year, with a one-off establishment grant of $100,000 also available. NZ On Air funded 22 of the 24 stations on air by 1993, when there were also many other aspirant groups, and most continued to be funded on the same basis by Te Mangai Paho. The funding of $200,000 per year was enough to employ perhaps five full-time staff. Though volunteer labour was instrumental in establishing the stations, many later dispensed with it, seeing regular and reliable workers as essential. Most stations have a manager and programme director, an administrator and some announcing and writing staff. There is a severe shortage of experienced Maori broadcasters and station staff, and salary levels are likely to attract young Maori only into programming positions. The gap of experience is being filled in a few cases by Pakeha as station managers, but they, and indeed Maori with experience in mainstream broadcasting, may bring with them certain professional values and commercial orientation as well as management skill.

NB. All quotations attributed to radio sector employees in the following section are, unless otherwise indicated, taken from interviews conducted by the author in 1993–4. All comments attributed to Graham Pryor are taken from an interview conducted by Karen Neill in October 1996. All Maori words used in the text are translated in the Glossary at the end of this chapter.

Music and youth

Music may take anywhere from 40 to 90 per cent of *iwi* stations' output, and one hears a lot of familiar music on tuning in randomly. The question of whether music brings the appropriate audience for the policy of promoting Maori language and culture, or indeed can bring people to the language, desperately needs addressing, as some of the current music practices of the stations are not obviously defensible in terms of the stations' stated purpose. Appropriate music policies which take account of the role of singing *waiata* in *marae* protocol, the issues of *reo*-preservation, contemporary Maori artists and postmodern, hybrid musics have arguably yet to evolve.

The music policies of the stations are far more varied than any other sector (except perhaps community access stations) and are largely driven by listener requests and dedications, as the day is divided into bands of different assumed audiences. Typical during the day is easy listening or Country music, often broken up with traditional Maori music. The national Maori network, Radio Aotearoa, appealed to potential advertisers in 1993 by describing its policy as

> A music mix that ranges from classic hits to the latest releases. Music with a distinct urban flavour (soul, blues, funk, etc). Our classic hits are Motown rather than Liverpool. Kiwi music. A commitment wherever possible to the local. Definitely no rap.

Aotearoa is closer to a Classic Hits format than any of the iwi stations. Most of the stations have a *rangatahi* slot in the late afternoons, in which they play contemporary music, much of it black American urban dance and rap, but with very little, if any, Maori language, and Maori music does not tend to get requested in this slot. This causes dismay among the activists who fought for Maori radio as part of the project of rescuing the language, for it was Maori youth who were considered to be the particular problem (Waitangi Tribunal, 1986).

One station, Mai FM ('Auckland's Hottest Music!'), has directed its entire programming to this audience, using an experienced team of varied backgrounds to develop a fully commercial but unique format – global youth culture, predominantly black, with a Maori accent. Mai's ratings success (number one music station in Auckland in summer 1996) is providing a major challenge to other *iwi* and mainstream broadcasters. Its audience is the largest for any *iwi* station, with a weekly cumulative audience of over 100,000. The plan for a youth-oriented station was developed by station manager, musician Taura Eruera, in conjunction with the Runanga (council) of Ngati Whatua, and it went on air in July 1992. Mai's *kaupapa* is, in Eruera's words, to promote Maori language and culture 'through the discipline of commercial radio'. Of the station's

45 staff in 1996, 18 were claimed to be fluent Maori speakers by new manager Graham Pryor. Many of them work in sales. Its deals with Coca-Cola, Reebok and other major advertisers are a contrast with the low-key advertising on other *iwi* stations, and raise issues about the compatibility of mainstream commercial styles and values with the promotion of Maori interests. Mai has also chosen, however, to promote causes such as a secondary schools cultural festival, a gay festival and various *marae* projects and *hui*.

Since the large Maori population of South Auckland is basically English-speaking, Eruera explained that the station's target audience is no different in linguistic ability from the Pakeha population, though its commitment to the language is greater. Sales Manager Vivien Bridgewater is quoted as saying that about 83 per cent of Maori people in Auckland are under 35: 'If we want them to listen, we have to play the music they like. We are making Maori into something that's hot, contemporary, positive and empowering' (*NZ Herald* 22 July 1992).[2] If Auckland radio is the *marae*, then Radio Aotearoa, the national network, is the meeting house and Mai is the cookhouse. Maori children hang around the cookhouse but will wander into the meeting house, according to Eruera.

With the demise of the contemporary hit radio format in New Zealand, as most stations target the 25-plus demographic, the outlets for contemporary music, especially New Zealand music, have declined, leaving the field to the margins of student and *iwi* radio. Mai's format is almost entirely urban dance music, including a small amount of New Zealand music, particularly by Maori artists. One columnist noted that its 'funk, hip hop, rap, dance and sweet beat' made it one of two stations not playing 'museum music' in Auckland in early 1993 (*The Listener* 8 May 1993).[3] The closure of the contemporary RNZ station 89X in early 1993, followed by 91FM's change of format to 'The Breeze' (album-oriented rock), was a gift to Mai. The sales charts in June showed that Mai was the only Auckland station playing seven of the top ten singles, and it is said that the singles sales charts are directly influenced by Mai.

In contrast to many other *iwi* stations, Mai FM is not fussy about the language of the song, but is very particular about its musical qualities. Speaking on the *Mana Hour* on 17 June 1994, Eruera called on the record industry to provide more 'hot tracks' by Maori artists. He said that existing Maori recorded music was not suitable for radio, and cited his teenage relatives' love of live Maori music but their utter rejection of it as radio material. There is an appropriate local music industry, with record companies such as Deep Grooves and Tangata Records producing contemporary music by Maori artists, both in Maori and English,[4] but its product has not had significant airplay on mainstream stations. Mainstream record companies cannot handle *iwi* stations' 'lack of format'. Most Maori stations will play any new music by Maori artists that comes their way, but how much exposure new records by small companies, such as Tangata, get is uncertain without the feedback of playlists. They, in turn, feel inhibited about recording music in Maori for fear that it will not get commercial airplay.

NZ On Air has set up a programme to assist New Zealand music on radio. This has involved the funding of more than 100 music videos over the last two years (including clips by Moana and the Moahunters, Jools Issa, Annie Crummer, Upper Hutt Posse and other Maori and Polynesian artists),[5] which have helped them make the crossover to commercial as well as Maori radio airplay. NZ On Air also funds feature programmes about New Zealand music for commercial and student radio stations, runs an innovative funding scheme which rewards record companies for 'significant' commercial radio airplay and produces a monthly CD which is a compilation of new releases chosen by NZ On Air in consultation with the programme directors at a number of contemporary format radio stations. Thus *Kiwi Hit Disc* was first released in June 1993, and was greeted enthusiastically by the record producers, who have trouble financing their products on CD and thus ensuring airplay, and by radio, because the disc provides ready access to New Zealand music. Many of the tracks on the first two discs were from such small companies, and many of them fit Mai's format. In an interview with the author in 1994, NZ On Air's Brendan Smyth saw Mai as 'a significant new force' in the promotion of New Zealand music, and it remains one of the stations advising on the selection of tracks for the *Kiwi Hit Disc*. A welcome development in 1996 was the first *Iwi Hit Disc*.

Elsewhere in NZ On Air, Mai was more of a challenge for its lack of commitment to talk radio, let alone *te reo Maori*. Its format is entirely music, with very short news bulletins initially from the private commercial network. Eruera explained that their 'yaya audience' hates 'audio traffic cops'. There was only one high-profile announcer, Robbie Rakete, formerly the presenter of television's *RTR Countdown*. In press profiles he acknowledged his lack of knowledge of the language, but his willingness to learn in his new job (*Mana*, no. 2, 1993: 65). The language level on Mai is extremely low, and basic, such as a brief conversation about the meaning of Pukekohe, a town near Auckland (*puke* means hill, *kohekohe* a kind of tree). But it is accessible, and the style of address, along with the slogan, 'it's cool to korero' may be doing more to promote respect for the Maori language among Auckland's urban Maori youth and multicultural youth generally, than the less inviting styles of other stations.

Though it is highly regarded in the radio industry, Mai has had to fight on every conceivable front except with their own *iwi*. It has been denounced by private radio operators, who may have paid up to $750,000 for their frequency, for taking government money to run a commercial music station. As a result Mai has joined the Independent Broadcasters Association as well as the *iwi* association, Te Whakaruruhau. It thus finds itself in two camps, supporting dedicated Maori services, and in a lobby group that pushes for minimal government interference. Following complaints from this sector to the Minister of Broadcasting, Maurice Williamson, Mai invited the minister to visit and open the station. He took his guitar and, jointly with the station staff, played 'Pretty Woman' to an appreciative crowd, subsequently directing NZ On Air to provide two years funding upfront, in order to help the station meet its goal of being self-sufficient by 1995. Mai may have won the minister over, but policy-makers in the Ministry of Commerce and NZ On Air remained dubious about whether it was sufficiently promoting Maori language and culture.

From June 1994 the station stopped receiving public funds and by 1996 had declared a profit of almost $200,000 (*National Business Review*, 4 October 1996: 58). Though now operating as a straight commercial station in a very open market, manager Pryor maintained Mai FM's continuing commitment to the original kaupapa and on-air sound. The station had set up its own sales agency for Maori stations, Mai Media, and was involved in a joint venture with Christchurch station Tahu FM to bring the urban dance format to the South Island. In 1996 it also won Te Mangai Paho FM's tender to provide a trial programme service, the National Maori Radio Service.

The postcolonial phenomenon of Mai FM was the subject of much policy and public debate in the 1990s, and is a salutary example of the innovations possible in a rigid policy framework, where the major broadcasting institutions are under severe pressure. It is an inspiration to many other *iwi* stations, and a measure of the choices available for Maori radio. Many Maori, however, decry the tendency of the stations to target youth in order to justify low levels of language content. Despite the clear successes of *iwi* radio in bringing Maori speakers and musicians to the medium, it could be argued that without Mai's profile and ratings success, *iwi* radio would be much more marginal and contained, perhaps the way governments intended it to be.

Localism and networking

There is some tension between the aspirations of individual stations to serve local communities and the capacity of dedicated, state-of-the-art networking technology to create a national Maori audience for the output of any station or any combination of stations. Funded by Te Mangai Paho, the NZ On Air-funded Star network (Starlink or Starnet) is described by one experienced station manager, Kevin Loughlin, as 'one of the most innovative and effective structures for broadcasting' in any organization he has worked in. It was set up as a transmission system operated from Radio New Zealand in Wellington, providing random access, two-way traffic over seventeen lines.

Most *iwi* stations use this facility to take a proportion of their content from the programme suppliers Mana Maori Media and Mai FM's Ruia Mai, as well as from other stations, but there was concern in NZ On Air that it was not being used to maximum advantage by stations committed to running an autonomous operation. Te Upoko o te Ika's morning current affairs and talkback programme was taken by some stations, as were Radio Aotearoa and Radio Tainui's midnight-to-dawn-shifts. Some take longer segments from other stations, but these remain by and large local in orientation, and hearing them has the quality of visiting another place rather than being part of a larger audience community.

The Star network quickly became overloaded as new stations came on air. NZ On Air considered possibilities for re-configuring the network so that, for example, some stations became hubs and others would operate more as relays. For lack of reliable information about programmes distributed through Starlink actually being broadcast, NZ On Air also had reason to doubt the cost-effectiveness of its $892,000 investment. Mai inherited this problem of a lack of ready use of the network when it began its programme service Ruia Mai, providing free programme provision for iwi stations. This was designated as a 100 per cent Maori language service, consisting of three hours of current affairs in the morning and a youth/sport/music programme in the evenings, plus news bulletins. The entire output was broadcast in Auckland on an AM frequency, but it appeared to be getting a mixed reception from other *iwi* stations, with only about six stations known to be regular users, and public criticism of its quality.

New private commercial stations were set up in the same period as the *iwi* stations, but many are programmed according to shared formats. This means that the *iwi* station in many markets may have the edge on truly local content. Announcers are normally locals and *panui* or local announcements are a common feature. Kev Loughlin, manager of Te Reo Irirangi o Whanganui, reported that despite the new stations in Wanganui in 1993, his was the only one in the market to provide local talkback.

With the possibilities for localism and the complex networking facility of Starlink, there are unlimited opportunities for sharing and collaboration, but this requires imagination and technological sophistication. One innovative use of the network was a link between Wanganui and Christchurch early in 1993, when a woman in the Wanganui studio spoke and sang songs with her daughters in Christchurch. Papa Ruru on Aotearoa's midnight-to-dawn shift sings with many of his callers and accompanies them on various instruments. Interviews and discussions can be conducted from different stations and the technology can also be used to record music programming, thus building up station collections.

One useful form of information sharing is the *iwi* stations' Top Ten, compiled each week by a different station and broadcast in the Mana

Hour on Thursday nights, where music is the theme. Te Reo Iriraki ki Otautahi (Christchurch) only includes songs by Maori artists in its hit chart, and its programme director sees the service as a good way to learn about new music and artists around the country. Other stations are more eclectic.

Advertising on individual stations may be a problem for networking. Before it began its national service, Mai was supplying programming via the Star network to other *iwi* stations, especially in the evenings, but this became more difficult as Mai charged for its programming (including advertising, which the competitors to the *iwi* stations depend on). The Maori Broadcasting Association, Te Whakaruruhau, began to develop national sales of advertising to be placed in networked programmes. The most likely users of such slots are government departments, for whom national Maori radio sales are a cost-effective way of getting messages across. There were also moves to standardize many station operations, such as accounting systems, programming software and studio equipment, so that there are maximum efficiencies between stations.

News and sport

Mana Maori Media is a Maori news agency, also initially funded by NZ On Air, which compiles five national bulletins per day, in both Maori and English, and a nightly Mana Hour of interviews on the themes of arts, current affairs, education, health, music and sport. In 1993 it had 30 staff, 12 of whom were young Maori journalists. There were separate editors for the Maori and English bulletins, so stories might be chosen and packaged differently in the different languages. By 1996 the organization's radio operations were substantially reduced, though it was running a successful glossy magazine. *Mana News* was also broadcast on National Radio, New Zealand's most authoritative talk network, run by Radio New Zealand, formerly part of the public service broadcaster. Thus news from a Maori perspective also reached a wider audience, although in competition with the major news programmes on television, and not on any commercial radio station. Items from the programme sometimes made their way into the flagship *Morning Report*. *Mana News* was strikingly different from mainstream news in the length and presentation of its items, and the historical perspective which was put on contemporary issues.

Until September 1993, when a cut in RNZ funding shortened the programme to twelve minutes, *Mana News* normally had between five and eight items in 22 minutes, all of which concerned Maori and sometimes other indigenous peoples. The programme covered national politics, regional politics, environmental issues, sport, culture and media. Familiarity with Maori issues and terms was assumed. The sound bites of spoken voices were characteristically unhurried (though doubtless less so in a shorter programme) and these might range from politicians defending policies affecting Maori, to Maori people with *mana*, but not necessarily authority, in the Pakeha world. The Maori commentary was appreciated by the liberal middle-class among National Radio's listeners, but how many young Maori listened was unknown. There were several issues for RNZ in Mana Maori Media's success. Mana provides a model for the free market lobby in broadcasting, which would like to see National Radio entirely run on the basis of contracting in this way for programme provision. Not only was RNZ a major determinant of Mana Maori Media's viability, it was also a competitor. Comparisons were often drawn with its own Maori programmes, which had less impact and credibility.

Some *iwi* stations find *Mana News* too narrow and too extended for an audience used to two-minute bulletins on the hour on commercial radio, and have subscribed to mainstream services as well as or instead of *Mana News*. Negotiations were going on in mid-1993 between some stations and Mana Maori Media over the provision of shorter and more comprehensive bulletins, and hourly bulletins were also being developed. The issue remained unresolved, as RNZ was undermining the effort by selling its news service at a cheaper rate to an increasing number of *iwi* stations, and Mana's funding was cut.

News provision is one of the central programming issues facing *iwi* radio, and is indicative of the strategies being adopted in the face of funding uncertainty. While some stations take a mainstream news service in order to keep their audience from crossing to a competitor, others decry the tendency to copy mainstream radio rather than following the particular kaupapa of Maori radio. But most of the Maori audience has been raised on Pakeha media and it is an open question how much of this they want to or should give up.

Radio Aotearoa began as a BCNZ (the public service broadcaster at the time) plan 'for a Maori radio network based in Auckland and repeated from the Bay of Plenty, Wellington and Christchurch' (Whaanga, 1990: 67). It was intended to serve urban Maori of all tribes with AM frequencies, and began in Auckland only with NZ On Air funding in 1989. It became a middle-of-the-road station, not altogether successful at generating advertising income, with some bilingual content. Aotearoa developed a network operation, but outside Auckland this was taken as unwelcome competition for the new *iwi* stations. It has never had the grassroots support of the *iwi* stations, and its generous funding, largely due to ministerial directives, has been anomalous. With new management, however, Aotearoa was in the 1990s beginning to establish better relations with other Maori broadcasters.

In 1996 Radio Aotearoa established its own youth-oriented station, Soul FM, a direct competitor to Mai. Radio Aotearoa did not take Mana

Maori Media's services until 1993, but the new co-operation between the national bodies promised better programme supply to *iwi* stations. Mana produced Willie Jackson's sports talkback programme on Sunday mornings on Aotearoa, for example, for national distribution. Sport is a programming priority for Maori radio, though sports sponsorship may be a problem for those Maori averse to commercial directions. A welcome development in 1993 was a Maori language simulcast of the coverage of the New Zealand *vs*. Great Britain rugby test series. TVNZ funded the simulcast, which was broadcast via Starnet.

Current issues

Some of the issues currently being addressed by the stations, the government and Te Mangai Paho are to do with training, funding, how to get more stations started and linked together, and relations between broadcasters and *iwi*.

Training

Training staff for *iwi* radio falls outside the current policy framework and is a major omission. Because of the colonial heritage of educational institutions, few Maori have received high-level broadcasting training. Specific programmes oriented to the needs of the new sector are required, or the stations will be forced to continue to train on the job and/or recruit staff trained in mainstream radio.

Funding policy

NZ On Air claimed in 1993 that 70 per cent of Maori received a primary signal from at least one Maori station, but indicated that the present level of funding could not be assumed indefinitely, so there was an expectation that the stations must generate some income themselves. NZ On Air was aware that its present allocation was preventing new stations from starting and was freezing precious assets in a way which may not have been giving Maori as a whole the best value. Its planning was also hampered by regular ministerial intervention.

NZ On Air operates in New Zealand's economic rationalist orthodoxy, rigorously accounting for money spent, so it had an issue with the effectiveness of its funding allocation to Maori radio, and had trouble designing appropriate performance measures. The brief 'to promote Maori language and culture' would seem to indicate that a station's success should be measured in terms of the amount and quality of broadcasting in the language on Maori matters. But there were problems, for a quota of Maori language might seem an obvious measure, but this was unacceptable to the government, who were ideologically opposed to quotas as a form of content regulation. Te Mangai Paho has more leeway in this area. A survey of the audience for each station would require enormous resources, so NZ On Air opted in mid-1993 for a national survey of Maori radio listeners, in which 1500 Maori were asked about their listening and judgement of their local station. This had gratifying results, with high levels of principled commitment shown to Maori radio.

Devolution of funding

The Broadcasting Amendment Act was passed in July 1993, and set up a Maori funding agency, later to become Te Mangai Paho. It has seven appointed members who have, from January 1995, allocated the money formerly in NZ On Air's brief for Maori broadcasting, plus an additional initial $3 million, followed by $5 million in the second and third years. Though granting control of Maori resources to Maori was clearly overdue, a debate on the *Marae* programme on TVNZ in May 1993 between Derek Fox of Mana Maori Media and Minister Williamson emphasized how little the Crown was providing in contrast to the magnitude of the wrongs against Maori specified in the various Treaty of Waitangi claims. There is a sense in which the problems of settling the Treaty claim for ownership of radio frequencies have been too difficult for the government, so it was convenient to be able to hand them all over in a magnanimous gesture to Maori. Whereas NZ On Air was set up to execute government policy, Te Mangai Paho is much more autonomous, and faces an unenviable job. It has, for example, addressed the recalcitrant issue of Maori demands for prime time television programming, and in 1996 allocated temporary funding to Aotearoa TV to run a channel in Auckland with 50 per cent Maori language content. But many Maori were critical of its lack of action in other areas.

Iwi–*broadcaster relations*

Iwi differ in what they give their radio stations, which may be located in supportive environments such as on marae or in educational institutions. The new form of power a radio station brings can variously articulate with the complexities of *iwi* politics, and there may be disputes between the licence holder and the broadcaster. The case of Tuwharetoa in Turangi resulted in the establishment of two Maori stations in the town, one supported by the *iwi* authority and NZ On Air and the other effectively a pirate station using disputed equipment. When more than half a tribe may live outside its tribal area, there is also a need to serve pan-tribal communities, especially in the cities, but there are no guidelines on how to do this.

The requirement of *iwi* authorities as licence holders has meant changes for the pioneering station Te Upoko o te Ika, founded by activists aware of the power of radio to bring people to the declining language. It has always had a political commitment to high levels of language use and Maori-oriented talk, and a greater level of programme makers and talk broadcasters than other stations. But its funding was reduced in 1993 because one Wellington *iwi*, Te Atiawa, proposed their own station, and this was in keeping with NZ On Air's guidelines, for Te Upoko o te Ika's licence was not held by an *iwi* body.

Coverage

The main issue is the South Island, with a low Maori population generally, and only one *iwi* station in Christchurch with a wide coverage area over flat terrain. A second commercial station, Tahu FM, from 1996 programmed by Mai, was set up in 1994. Another station, Wairau FM in Blenheim, has been refused funds because Blenheim's Maori population is less than 2000, and there are larger concentrations in Dunedin and Invercargill.

Conclusion

The political struggles by Maori for control of radio frequencies have been based on the fate of the language, whose decline has been parallel to the growth of electronic media in New Zealand (Waitangi Tribunal 1986). But there is an issue about whether the success of Maori radio should be measured in terms of the revival of the language, as implied by the Broadcasting Act and the funding regime it sets up. The rapid development of dedicated stations testifies to the commitment of Maori to their own radio sector, but the different trajectories of the stations, even in these early days, point to different notions of Maori radio. Some focus on Maori control and the Maori audience, while others concentrate on Maori content. As in all areas of Treaty settlements, the question of Maori control of resources is central, but it is not clear in the case of broadcasting that ownership alone ensures a cultural and linguistic outcome.

Mai FM's success in achieving its stated aim of promoting Maori language and culture 'through the discipline of commercial radio' is contentious, with prominent Maori such as musician Moana Maniopoto Jackson publicly criticizing it. Yet its financial health and ratings success, on the one hand, and its new existence as a Maori language programme supplier, indicate an extraordinary ability to survive in a difficult environment. Mai's strategy of first ensuring an audience underlines the extent to which the radio market is an integrated whole in which an audience can only be gained by providing a service for which a gap exists, and doing it by knowing the medium well. The difficulty of programming Maori content for youth on most *iwi* stations means that Mai is bound to have imitators, and as other models for youth-oriented radio fade, Mai's urban contemporary sound may become a dominant youth format, for Maori and Pakeha alike.

The policy issues about whether youth-oriented radio deserves public subsidy will continue in Aotearoa, as elsewhere. Graham Pryor comments:

> Youth cultures are worldwide. I think culture is becoming more worldwide than related to a specific geographic area, but we still have strong cultural ties to where we come from, and Maori are no different to any other indigenous culture around the world. They still hold on to their indigenous cultures very strongly, but they may listen to a lot of other cultures as well, due to the communication technology that makes it possible to listen to other cultures very easily now.

While *iwi* radio has shown a capacity to fill the youth market niche, it also has the potential to develop as the most local medium in some areas, as private stations use imported formats and news services. If the Starnet facility remains the exclusive property of the *iwi* stations, innovative networking arrangements could become a feature of the sector, avoiding the dominant tendency of network structures to centralize output and control (Mulgan, 1991). And if all this is done while acknowledging and celebrating New Zealand's biculturalism, many interests are met.

There are, however, some who would protest at the way Maori radio has developed, particularly the activists who fought the original claims. They see the development as too fast, without proper attention to planning and training so that the stations can be sustainable. Piripi Whaanga was one of the founding broadcasters of Te Upoko o te Ika, later working as a trainer and consultant to NZ On Air. He thinks there is an infatuation with Pakeha broadcasting methods and styles, seeing no justification for *iwi* stations being stretched around the clock, for example. He regrets the lack of political purpose in many of the stations, and what he judges to be a lack of appreciation of how best to use the medium. This vision of Maori radio as considered and strategic cannot happen without a secure institutional environment, but it is not clear that this could develop within the existing structures.

The framework of Whaanga and others is one of biculturalism in broadcasting, in which 'the Maori world is respected, is resourced, and is in a true state of equity' (Ritchie, 1992: 11). While this project is pursued to the benefit of Maori generally, questions remain about the variety of media needed to satisfy particular groups, and the way Maori stations fit into the larger radio context. Both Mai and Aotearoa see their role as urban broadcasters to be largely set by the larger radio environment. While Mai has fallen outside the official policy net, Radio Aotearoa remains within it. Mai perhaps fits more readily into the historical category of postcolonialism than the official one of biculturalism. Postcolonialism draws attention to hybrid characteristics of ethnically complex societies following histories of colonialism and migration. While this might describe Mai, it is very likely that Mai could not have happened without a policy of biculturalism. It is hard, for example, to imagine an Aboriginal equivalent while indigenous broadcasting policies in Australia are so patronizing and haphazard (Molnar, 1994). Clear bicultural policies to guide the settlement of grievances are therefore arguably necessary to create the space for the unpredictable cultural mixes of postcolonialism.

Glossary

wa   time
hui   meeting
iwi   tribe
kaupapa   philosophy
korero   speak
mai   towards the speaker
mana   prestige, power
te mangai paho   the mouthpiece of broadcasting ('this is what people say')
marae   formal meeting place
pakeha   white New Zealander
panui   notice, announcement
rangatahi   youth
ruia   sow
runanga   council
tangata whenua   people of the land, indigenous people
te reo irirangi (*iriraki* in South Island)   broadcasting, radio
te reo   the language
waiata   song
whakapaoho   turn
whakapuaki   announce
whakaruruhau   association

Notes

1. This chapter originally appeared in P. Hayward *et al.* (eds), *North Meets South: Popular Music in Aotearoa/New Zealand* (Umina, NSW: *Perfect Beat* Publications, 1994).

A version of this chapter was given at the Postcolonial Formations Conference at Griffith University, 7–10 July 1993. The research for it was funded by a grant from Christchurch Polytechnic as part of a larger study on Radio in New Zealand. I am grateful to staff of the New Zealand Broadcasting School and NZ On Air for comments on an earlier draft, and to staff of Te Matauranga Maori for help with Maori language. Special thanks to Karen Neill for conducting the interview with Graham Pryor in October 1996, and to Wendy Hewson and Annie Murray for a general update.
2. No page details – supplied through collation service to staff at Christchurch Polytechnic.
3. *ibid*.
4. See Chapters 2 and 11 of this anthology for detailed discussion.
5. See Sheridan and Hayward (1994) for further discussion.

10

A New Tradition: Titus Tilly and the Development of Music Video in Papua New Guinea[1]

Philip Hayward

In the mid-1980s there was considerable debate in Papua New Guinea about the introduction of commercial television broadcasting.[2] One of the major concerns was the likely impact of foreign programmes (and the broader 'culture' of commercial television) upon the indigenous culture(s) of the country. A second, associated theme was whether Western (and specifically in this case, Australian-owned) television companies could be trusted to produce material which reflected PNG culture. With regard to the latter anxiety, the fears of many appear to have been justified. PNG's national broadcaster EM-TV has developed as a highly commercial service with close similarities to its Australian parent company, Channel Nine. Although it has produced a series of impressive station 'idents' (short non-narrative sequences ending with the EM-TV station logo), showing scenes of PNG culture and landscapes, it otherwise produces and shows little local material and has not supported the production of local TV drama.

The impact of such programming upon PNG society is more difficult to gauge. Although Western culture, social values and economics are rapidly changing the perceptions and lifestyles of all but the most remote tribal communities in PNG, this does not necessarily imply incipient cultural collapse. Similarly, there is, as yet, little evidence to demonstrate that there has been a simple and unequivocal westernization of PNG culture. Indeed, it is possible to argue that PNG culture continues to show signs of diversity, development and accomplishment both in the face of and, more significantly, *through* the agencies of its 'modernization'. As Malcolm Philpott outlines in Chapter 7 in this anthology, this is nowhere so obvious as in the case of popular music, which has thrived over the last decade. Local music has also been culturally significant in another sense too, as it has come to constitute a powerful presence amidst the (foreign-dominated) schedules of EM-TV. Somewhat paradoxically, this enclave of local culture has established itself within the heart of Coca- (and Pepsi-) Cola culture itself – the TV music video show. This paradox illustrates the complexities and contradictions of the internationalization of the Western music industry, commercial television and popular culture itself.

Since its development as a marketing tool in Britain and the USA in the late 1970s and early 1980s, music video has developed into an international form.[3] Western, and primarily Anglo-American videos, are now widely broadcast in European, North American and Australasian markets and in parts of Latin America, Asia and Africa. Many of the countries in these regions have also begun to produce their own music videos, usually intended to promote locally produced music tracks in local or regional (as opposed to global) markets. Since the introduction of television broadcasting in 1987, PNG has followed this model by becoming both a consumer of Western music videos and, more recently, a producer of its own.

This chapter addresses the development of music video in PNG with particular regard to the role of video director Titus Tilly; the nature of the styles of video he has produced; the cultural motivation and project of his work; and the pivotal role of Tilly's company, Pacific View Productions, in providing the (post-) production base for the video production sector in PNG. It does not, however, simply represent an attempt to identify and elevate Tilly as *the* auteur of an emergent field of media practice (although the analyses advanced in this study could be seen to support such a characterization).[4] It rather attempts to analyse how Tilly's initiation and development of music video production in PNG reflects a conscious perception of the medium as a strategic site for the development of contemporary forms of PNG culture. The chapter thereby also analyses how Tilly and, to a lesser extent, other PNG video makers have interpreted and inflected the standard styles and approaches to music video popularized by Western producers. In this way, the concerns of this chapter parallel those of Nancy Sullivan's discussion of the emergence of film and television production in PNG – looking at the way production has been used as a tool for local cultural development and 'for casting the local in terms of the national and even the international ... "indigenizing" television as they "naturalize" its mode of production' (Sullivan, 1993: 533); and examining the extent to which local production has 'been subject to innovation along local patterns of social organization and local empowerment' (*ibid.*).

NB. *All quotations attributed to Titus Tilly and Ronnie Galama in this chapter are, unless otherwise specified, taken from interviews conducted by the author in Port Moresby in 1994.*

Context

As Malcolm Philpott outlines in Chapter 7, the PNG music industry began to take off in 1977, when NBC (the National Broadcasting Corporation) began to release cassettes of locally produced pop music. In 1980 the first two commercial labels were set up – Chin H. Meen (CHM), now the largest PNG label, and Soundstream (which folded two years later). In 1983 the Pacific Gold label also entered the market and is now CHM's main commercial competitor. Television broadcasting followed in January 1987, with the launch of the short-lived NTN (Niugini Television Network),[5] and became more firmly established in July 1987 when EM-TV began transmitting. In the period 1989–90, the only regular TV pop music show broadcast in PNG was the Australian-franchised *MTV* programme. This mixed Australian and Anglo-American material with MTV USA 'stings' and packaging, was produced in Sydney and compered by expatriate New Zealander Richard Wilkins.[6] The first locally produced music show, *Mekim Musik*, closely modelled on the *MTV* format, was introduced in October 1989. Packaged by EM-TV at Boroko (a suburb of the capital, Port Moresby) and sponsored by Coca-Cola, the show is compered by a local VJ in the standard MTV style. For its first two years of operation it broadcast a selection of Australian and Anglo-American videos and later added locally produced clips (when they began to come on stream) and a selection of South African videos.

Music video production in PNG was initiated in 1989 by local independent video maker, Titus Tilly and encouraged by the readiness of EM-TV and its director, John Taylor, to broadcast early clips.[7] The increasing availability of PNG clips in 1991–92, financed by the two major PNG recording companies, led EM-TV to introduce a second music video programme in February 1993, showing entirely local material. The prime mover behind this programme was CHM managing director Raymond Chin.[8] Prior to the introduction of this second programme – entitled *Fizz* in allusion to its sponsor, Pepsi-Cola – CHM had paid EM-TV for airtime to run music videos (as extended adverts for CHM music cassettes). *Fizz* both gave CHM (and its competitors) access to broadcast airtime and a regular and identifiable TV slot for PNG music.[9]

One element which differentiates PNG music video from its Euro-American antecedents is the conscious national-cultural project which has informed it from its early days. In a similar manner to that of the PNG music industry – which was initially set up as an initiative to preserve and promote PNG music – music video production was also conceived of as a way of boosting local music and breaking the dominance of foreign product on the screens of EM-TV. In the hands of Tilly, at least, it was also conceived as a means of preserving and re-presenting traditional music(s) and local customs in the era and arena of broadcast television. Tilly's key role in this narrative reflects his generation and the significance of that generation in the establishment of cultural identity and the culture industries following PNG's independence. Tilly was born in 1958, in Pum on the island of Yela (formerly known as Rossel Island) in the far east of the Louisiade archipelago in Milne Bay province. Tilly was educated in mission schools before going on to join the first generation of students to undertake higher education courses at the National Art School in Port Moresby (NAS) after independence. His diploma in visual arts course included work with drawing, painting and photography. The new NAS diploma courses taught at this time in subjects such as music and visual arts had a strong orientation to traditional PNG culture and emphasized the virtues of preserving that culture, rather than simply attempting to reproduce displaced Western models and aesthetics. Art students were, for instance, required to go on field trips to examine and work with ideas from local cultures and music students were encouraged to learn traditional instruments and become familiar with the diversity of PNG's musics.[10]

The emergence of PNG music video

During the 1980s, when the PNG music industry began to take off, Tilly worked on government-sponsored radio projects and as a press photographer before moving into video production with the short-lived NTN in 1987. After working for EM-TV, Tilly left the organization in late 1989 to join the independent company Pacific View Productions, set up by former NTN production manager Craig Marshall. During his time at EM-TV, Tilly became convinced that PNG should produce music videos to counter the monopoly that Anglo-American-Australian products had via their presence on the *MTV* show. In order to convince PNG record companies and audiences of the potential of local 'indigenous' music video production, Tilly produced a demonstration piece which became PNG's first music video.

The music for the video was produced by former NAS students and members of the band Tambaran Culture, Pius Wasi and Jeff Chalson. Their only brief was that it should be 'traditional ... in a new style'. The track, entitled 'Kame', opens with a gentle flute and keyboard passage which fades to a keyboard and bass interlude before moving into the song's main form – a choppy, syncopated, mid-tempo instrumental groove over which the two vocalists sing unison melody lines. To this soundtrack Tilly shot both traditional and modern images, illustrating the 'two worlds' of PNG music and culture. After an opening sequence showing a landscape of lakes and hills – complementing the delicate flute introduction – the video mixes sequences of Wasi and Chalson on location in the forest (wearing traditional garb), with sequences of the musicians working in the studios and miming the vocals, wearing 'sharp', city-style clothes. The video also makes extensive use of Fairlight effects, creating gentle patterns in the traditional scenes and dynamic background graphics for the mimed studio sequences. Unconsciously adopting an approach reminiscent of what is commonly regarded as the first Western music video, David Mallet's 1976 clip for Queen's 'Bohemian Rhapsody', and a whole series of subsequent videos (discussed in detail in Hayward, 1991), Tilly used the Fairlight effects to 'excite the audience ... excite them with some magical images that they wouldn't be used to'.

Tilly completed the clip in July 1990 and showed it to EM-TV boss Taylor, who, he remembers, was 'very excited and very pleased' by it. Rather than show the video as an isolated item, Taylor agreed to Tilly's suggestion that the video should be dropped (unannounced) into *Mekim Musik* (which, until then, comprised entirely foreign produced material). According to Tilly, 'viewers were so excited that they called the station immediately asking about the clip and asking to see it again ... it stayed very popular and was shown many times over the next year' (despite the fact that the music was not released on audio cassette to 'support' the video). The publicity and public 'buzz' over the video, which far exceeded Tilly's expectations, were sufficient to convince CHM and Pacific Gold to begin to produce videos for their own artists' releases and, as might be expected, Tilly was an immediate beneficiary of their commissions. Since this first production Tilly has worked exclusively for CHM (shooting, directing and editing in excess of 130 videos),[11] with Pacific Gold shooting most of their footage in-house and editing it at Pacific View Productions.[12] Average budgets for video production are currently around 500 kina (approximately US $400) – a tiny sum by international standards but one which must be considered against the markedly smaller size of the PNG music market.

Following Tilly's initiative, filmmaker Albert Toro – who co-directed and starred in the first feature film to be directed by a Papua New Guinean, *Tukana: Husat i Asua?* (1982)[13] – began to produce music videos through his company Tukana Media.[14] Reflecting Toro's interest in drama, his video clips usually feature (skeletal) enactments of the song's emotional themes and/or mini-scenarios, performed by the singer and other band members or 'extras', in a mode similar to, if not derived from, mainstream Anglo-American music videos. This tendency is also evident in the small body of videos produced from the National Art School's video unit (as a commercial sideline) and several videos produced by Vanessa Daure for Pacific Gold prior to her death in 1992. Although a number of Tilly's videos also use this approach, his conviction that

> We in PNG do not yet have the skills in our actors and singers to do these types of dramas, this 'song acting', in a convincing way – we might in the future but I don't think it works very well for the kind of productions we can do now ... on our budgets and our limited shooting times

has led him to explore other approaches to music video production. Several of his videos eschew pseudo-realist set pieces and instead demonstrate an attempt to develop synchronic, 'poetic' uses of images to illustrate and complement the lyrical themes of songs. This is perhaps most marked in the traditionally-orientated Ronnie Galama trilogy, with its emphases on traditional dance (see pp. 148–52) but is also explored in videos for more contemporary songs such as Lamaika's 'Baba' (1993).

Dismissing arguments that music video is a form over-determined by its Western origins, styles and applications, Tilly explains his work in the music video medium as strategic and functional, arguing that

> You've got to capture and have some kind of archival history of your culture – and TV and music video are one medium for doing this, for capturing movement, sound, image and colours ... music videos are one means of recording history.

While such claims for the importance of music video as a form may appear unusual and over-stated to those familiar with Western media, they have to be understood in the context of PNG and its media environment. Given the almost complete dearth of indigenous drama (filmic or televisual), music video (together with television advertising and station idents) has become the prime televisual site for the representation of PNG culture. The textual practices of music video, however prescribed by their promotional function, can be understood as 'enabled' audio-visual spaces and thus strategic sites for expression.

Productions

Kerema

Following the popularity of 'Kame' with audiences, which, as previously discussed, Tilly attributes to the mix of traditional style music and the technological 'magic' of the video, he attempted to develop this style further in his 1991 clip for Hollie Maea's song 'Kerema'. The song was already one of the most popular on the band's 1990 cassette album, and had been played widely on radio for 4–5 months before CHM decided to re-promote the song and cassette with a video. Unlike 'Kame', 'Kerema' was an assertive, up-tempo, funky, pop-orientated song, sung in pidgin, with prominent lead guitar lines. The song's principal theme is the government's neglect of the Kerema region (in the Gulf of Papua). Aspects of the song's lyrics are directly visualized in the video, most notably when the names of other cities such as Rabaul, Madang and Goroka appear as graphic backdrops at appropriate points in the verses. Reflecting the considerable amount of post-production time his ideas for the clip required, Tilly secured a budget of 750 kina for the video. Unlike many of his later location videos, Tilly decided to shoot Hollie Maea performing the song in a high-tech, chroma-keyed visual environment, whose 'development' was thereby far more marked than the Kerema region itself. After shooting the lead singer Robert, his back-up singers and dancers in the studio, against a blue screen, Tilly produced the rest of the images using the Fairlight. The final video featured vibrant, swirling effects behind the male members of the band lip-synching the lyrics, intercut with four female dancers, either shot in group formation or solo.

Like 'Kame', the video was a major success with audiences – who responded to the technological 'wow' factor – and re-promoted the Hollie Maea cassette so successfully that it sold out in Port Moresby after the video's first broadcasts, requiring a new batch to be manufactured. The success of the video prompted a number of bands to request similar videos from Tilly, a move he resisted on the grounds that

> Particular songs need different treatments, ones appropriate to their music, their song themes and their atmosphere. The chromakey and Fairlight suit some songs not others ... I had to educate the [musical] artists and try and get them to think creatively about it.

While this statement is obviously one based on the director's own taste rather than any objective criteria, it reflects Tilly's attempts to interpret music tracks creatively rather than simply packaging them in the most obvious or demanded styles.

The Ronnie Galama trilogy (1991–93)

In a similar fashion to some Western video makers, Tilly differentiates his video productions into standard commissions and those he regards as special creative projects, 'artistic videos which I make as an artist'. Although Tilly is at pains to point out that he takes all his video production seriously and perceives it as an 'important view on PNG's cultures for its audiences', he sees projects such as the trilogy of clips he produced for Ronnie Galama in 1991–93 as his 'most important work'. Galama, like Tilly and Subam a former NAS student, has recorded three cassette albums for CHM to date – Ronnie Galama Volume One: Saidi (1991), Volume Two: Saidi – Very Best (1992) and Volume Three: The Legend of Naviu Marona (1993). These feature traditional songs from Maopa in Central Province, arranged in various styles,[15] alongside more syncretic PNG pop. In a manner similar to that of Australian band Yothu Yindi's use of traditional Gumatj material, Galama's use of traditional Maopa songs and dances has been sanctioned and encouraged by clan elders. As Galama explains, the elders see his music as one way of ensuring that the traditions can 'stay alive' and appeal to young people who otherwise 'only listen to contemporary PNG pop or overseas music'.

As house director for CHM, Tilly was commissioned to make a video of one of the tracks from Ronnie Galama's first cassette album. Upon listening to the album, Tilly was struck by a traditional-style track called 'Rinunu', a vocal chant sung over a slow, emphatic, bass guitar riff (with continuing, faster-paced percussion 'filling in' the rhythm spaces), and chose this to work with in preference to several more pop-orientated pieces on the album. Although Galama was not seen by CHM as a potential major selling artist in PNG, due to the traditional orientation of much of his music, Tilly was encouraged to submit an imaginative treatment for the song and, on acceptance of the treatment, was awarded an unusually high production budget for the video. CHM director Raymond Chin describes the budget of 1500 kina as a 'gamble' on his part;[16] one which was based on both Tilly's ambitious proposal for the video and CHM's interest in developing Galama as an artist who might have international appeal (with the video therefore also intended to function as a potential promo for international record companies).

Completed in October 1991, the 'Rinunu' video blends the singer's lip-synch miming with dance sequences (featuring Galama and a group of female dancers) and brief narrative vignettes. The song's narrative tells the story of a proud young man who is driven out of his village, speared by his uncle, then flees to the sea where he meets three beautiful mysterious women. He marries them and eventually returns to his village as a 'big man'. The story of the lyrics is interpreted by Tilly in a series of brief visual motifs – sequences which do not lend themselves to easy linear interpretation. This was a conscious move on the director's part since, as he has explained:

> I try not to just tell a story from A–Z by following the vocals on the soundtrack. I like to mix the story up, select and juggle it around. The story lines are there but they are in themes, images ... It's my artistic interpretation and the audience is able to interpret the images in the way they want ... maybe differently. In this way I try through my videos to add levels to the song.

The video opens with the image of a face and chest rising up out of the sand and then cuts to a spearing and shots of a young man running away and falling exhausted on a beach. Three women come and turn him over and the vocals begin, lip-synched by Galama and the female dancers. Galama features as vocal performer and/or actor in the narrative and shots of the spearing and the rise from the sand recur throughout the video as the video's narrative develops elliptically (and does not reach the [lyrical] conclusion of the hero's return to his community). Alongside these sequences are images of the women's slow group dance, sequences where they are shown as if planting crops, and images of their faces and bodies. Three of the women appear both as dancers/ members of the vocal chorus and as the women in the narrative who restore the hero to health. Overall the video works thematically and atmospherically rather as conventional narrative.

The role and prominence of the dance and dancers in the 'Rinunu' video is particularly significant in the light of Galama and Tilly's conscious cultural project. In traditional PNG cultures, songs, music, costume, dance and ritual are not separate, semi-autonomous practices but part of an 'organic' social practice. As Anne Gee has emphasized, 'traditional music in Papua New Guinea, with very few exceptions ... always involves singing, dancing and musical accompaniment' (Gee, 1991: 38). The dances associated with songs have ritual and/or symbolic meanings and, if separated from the songs and dispensed with in 'modernized' musical versions, diminish the re-representation of the traditional form. The inclusion and prominence of the dance in the 'Rinunu' (and other) videos thereby retains at least a trace of the basic symbolism and significance of the live dance accompanying traditional performances of the songs. In this manner, the sequences of the dance in the 'Rinunu' clip serve to reinforce (one of) the 'messages' of the song (which Galama summarizes as 'not hating each other while we are alive because we can't say sorry when we are dead') with the linked arms and unison movement of the dancers symbolizing clan bonding and friendship.

Despite the obvious contrasts between music video (and the broadcast context of EM-TV) and forms of traditional Maopa culture, Galama's community were keen to participate in the production of the 'Rinunu', 'Goruna' and 'Uana' videos. As Galama has recalled:

> My people were happy to appear in the videos before they passed away – they wanted to keep their image alive so that they would be there after, in the future, for their children and those that come after.

This enthusiasm also extended to their subsequent broadcast:

> My people liked the videos a lot when they saw them on TV. They made their memories come, made them sad as the songs and dancers made them remember their ancestors who passed away.

Along with Tilly's video for the Helgas's 'Pore Vavine', shot on location in the Central Province in September 1991, 'Rinunu' was the first PNG clip to feature vocalists and dancers in traditional costumes and the first to feature images of female performers appearing in traditional bare-breasted style. Illustrating the differences in notions of 'decency' in public media between PNG, with its dual cultures, and Western countries, the video attracted no comment or censorship from the censor's office. This is in direct contrast to the heavy restrictions on more explicit Western-style representations of sexuality which were introduced by the censor's office shortly after 'Rinunu' was first broadcast. Following controversy over the screening of explicit material featuring Madonna on EM-TV in early 1993, the office introduced new guidelines requiring all foreign music videos to be submitted for assessment in advance of intended broadcast[17] (with an estimated 33–50 per cent of these now being deemed unsuitable for screening on PNG television).[18] Local videos which are perceived to adopt similar approaches are also subject to censorship. Tilly's video for Nokondi Nama's 'Olei Olei' (1992) for instance, a song with lyrics concerning the deployment of the female posterior in dance, was banned by the PNG censor's office, after several screenings on *Mekim Musik*, on account of its focus on the (clothed) rumps of female dancers.

The stylistic approach developed by Tilly for 'Rinunu' was continued in his video for 'Goruna' (first screened in February 1993), a song from Galama's *Volume Two* cassette. Although credited to Galama alone, 'Goruna' principally comprises a female vocal chorus singing over a mid-tempo kundu drum pattern. Made on a similar budget to its predecessor, the song is performed on screen by Galama and the dancers who appeared in 'Rinunu' (and two other male percussionists). Like the 'Rinunu' clip, the video's scenario is based on the song's lyrics. These tell the story of a chief's sister who breaks her brother's magic wooden charm. He tries to punish her by spearing her but misses and turns her into an eagle instead. This story is visualized through a fleeting and fragmentary introductory sequence and subsequently through an exchange of looks between Galama (as the chief) and a dancer (as his sister), images of a spear and images of an eagle's face and claws. Much of the video's effect comes from the slow, repetitive (collective) motions of three groups of dancers on the beach; movements that create an intense, trance-like visualization of the vocal performance. This atmosphere is further heightened by shots of a mysterious, processed, ghostly image of a male face.

The video for 'Uana', a track from *Volume Three*, made in October 1993, differs from the 'Rinunu' and 'Goruna' videos in its choreography (with dancers ranked in several parallel lines); its more literal visual depiction of a specific event; and its high, 3000 kina budget.[19] The video mixes two strands: the performance of a traditional Maopa song, sung by Galama and the Vali Pakuna Clan girls, and images of fire and destruction. The latter sequences illustrate the song, whose lyrics mourn and commemorate the accidental burning down of a village in the 1920s, bringing them to life through re-enacted scenes staged for the clip. These re-enactments involved the construction of a replica set close to the site of the original village, which was then set on fire, with Tilly shooting footage of village members running through the smoke and burning wood. In this manner, the aural-linguistic and melodic record of a traumatic community event became re-enacted, reinscribed and perpetuated by another non-literary medium: video.

In complete contrast to videos such as 'Kame' and 'Kerema' (and much Anglo-American production) 'Rinunu', 'Goruna' and 'Uana' have a slow stately, sparingly edited, visual 'ambience' which makes them resemble particular styles of video art rather than standard industry rock clips.[20] Video art, understood as a Western art practice with its own histories, genres and contexts, is, of course, alien to PNG, which is currently at a point of emergence into the video-filmic era. In this manner, the Galama videos can perhaps be better understood as examples of a nascent indigenous 'music-video-art' which circulates, paradoxically, within a highly commercial TV system primarily reliant on western programming.

Lei Polo

Despite Tilly's emphasis on the Ronnie Galama trilogy as a conscious attempt to represent traditional PNG culture in a modern medium – and thus attempt to preserve and renew it – much of what he regards as his 'standard' video production has also provided valuable, accomplished and effective cultural records of the context of the music tracks. Indeed, it is possible to argue that some of these have a composed documentary relevance and immediacy that is equally important as a cultural record as the more complex and traditionally referential work of the Galama trilogy. Tilly's video for PS II's 'Lei Polo', made in March 1993, is a case in point. PS II (Paramana Strangers II) are an offshoot of the successful Paramana Strangers band, formed by younger brothers and cousins of the original members. The 'Paramana' in the band's name refers to their village, in the Cental Province, and the song is sung by PS II's lead singer Navo. The track is an up-tempo song based around a jaunty keyboard riff and prominent bass guitar line.

The 'Lei Polo' video was shot on Paramana beach and features three main performative levels:

1. The singer's lip-synched mime to the vocal track, alongside the female dancers' rehearsed 'hula' style dance routine.

2. The performance of locals, who are incorporated into the video as either spectators, passively observing the shoot, or as (impromptu) participants, improvising dance moves which are cut rhythmically into the video.

3. The non-participatory performance of those fishermen who arrived on the beach and disembarked with their catches only to find themselves – and their customers – (unexpectedly) in the middle of a video shot. Their 'performances' have a documentary aspect and take place *despite*

the shoot – occasionally intruding, as when two figures casually carry baskets across the rear of the screen during a lip-synch vocal sequence.

Level 1 comprises specifically rehearsed routines. The singer's lip-synch performance draws on conventions of live music performance and music video mime and expresses these within a range of physical gestures which are also drawn from both local performance traditions and broader PNG pop conventions. The dancers' routines and costumes are more strongly derived from traditional dances from the region, but are presented in the video as a performance-for-camera (rather than performance for live audience), with the dancers orientated to a central visual point (i.e. the camera). Level 2 represents an incorporation of members of the band's community into the video, where they are not simply featured as 'spectators' in the Western model (i.e. as fans, audiences or puzzled locals stumbling across a shoot) but rather as social participants attending what becomes a social occasion. Level 3 involves the fishermen as participants in the video who perform both the function of 'real people' (as opposed to participant performers), shot in documentary style; and as 'authentic' visual signs which illustrate the song's theme of fishing. The three levels are also linked in sequences such as the scene where a female member of the crowd humorously improvises during the singers' mime by presenting him with a fish, which he then flourishes as he dances. The referent of the song – a real fish – becomes inserted into the visualization of a song about fishing, shot in the precise location the song is addressed to.

The mere combination of levels 1–3 is not of course necessarily profound, complex or significant. Indeed, 2 and 3 in particular might well be seen as accidental intrusions in another video. Yet the 'Lei Polo' video can be seen to operate with considerable subtlety and complexity if read with attention to the song's lyrical address and the 'embeddedness' of the song, performer and band with their community and the location in which the video is shot. These aspects provide more complex levels of textual operation than clips such as Tilly's video for Steve Lahui's 'Tura Lalokau' (1993), which also feature similar lip-synch and dance routines on a beach. Due to its contextualizing elements, 'Lei Polo' becomes a video which not only represents the song's representation of the community but also represents it within what it seeks to represent – inscribing the artifice of the cultural product within the 'organic' of the social and its specific geographical point of origin. In this way, the 'Lei Polo' video fulfils the archival function Tilly envisages for his work but goes further by situating its representation within the scene of what it represents.

Local and international contexts and exposure

For all its accomplishment, some aspects of Tilly's work are somewhat problematic within its originating cultural context. One of the problems faced by producers emerging in a new medium such as PNG music video (let alone more self-consciously artistic versions of this) concerns issues of audiences and critical responses. Tilly can be seen to have been both a key agent in the establishment of music video as a form in PNG and a producer who has attempted to produce more complex, traditionally-orientated versions of that form. There is a sense in which the direction of his trajectory has been premised on a cultural project that is both outside the standard operation of music video (both in PNG and internationally) and the nature of EM-TV's standard (commercial, import-dominated) programming. Although Tilly – and, significantly EM-TV boss John Taylor[21] – have emphasized the Galama trilogy as notable and culturally innovative work, Tilly has himself pointed out that some of his most *popular* videos with audiences were the early 'technology heavy' ones such as 'Kame' and 'Kerema' – videos made in a style which Tilly was reluctant to repeat. In this manner, the Galama videos are exceptional in address and orientation (as well as accomplishment), being made, in many ways, without an audience in mind. Viewed as a kind of indigenous music-video-art, as discussed earlier, they could be seen to be out of context when broadcast on the *Fizz* show with its repeated and heavily-emphasized adverts, its plugs for Pepsi-Cola and its upbeat style of VJ presentation. As Galama himself has commented:

> Old people and people who like the traditional ways like the videos [i.e. the Galama trilogy] best – the young people don't like them so much, they are not all 'fast', they are not the kind of stuff they like today.

As outlined in this chapter, videos such as the Galama trilogy require more reflective readings than either the broadcast context or the target audience for TV music shows conventionally provide. This is not, however, an attempt to simply characterize PNG viewers, PNG youth or the international audience for music videos as innately deficient or superficial in their viewing; but rather to point to the manner in which broadcast material is a form watched *contextually* by all but its most academic audiences. The industrial logic which invariably relegates unusually subtle, complex or experimental TV programming to ghetto slots is not simply over-caution on the part of broadcasters but rather acknowledges audience expectations of schedular context and flow.

As big budget videos produced for an artist who sells significantly less than major PNG acts such as George Telek or Henry Kuskus, the Galama trilogy is also exceptional. The explanation for the nature of this investment is, in part, that CHM saw Galama as a possible international act – a local entry into the potentially lucrative world music market.[22] In this manner, the difference between the Galama trilogy and other PNG music videos (whether produced by Tilly or other video makers) is in their attempts to begin to commodify Galama in terms of his traditional ethnicity and cultural identity. Such approaches are far from standard in the PNG music industry but *are* part of the standard (Western) packaging and promotion of world music. In this sense, Galama can be understood to have been groomed for an international market in advance of CHM's gaining access to that market. The videos thereby represent a kind of speculative R&D (research and development) project which, in the curious logic of World Music, involves a move towards traditional local cultures in its attempt to reach the inter-national.

Despite CHM's investment, Galama did not succeed in gaining access to the World Music market. Indeed, after the production of the 'Uana' video Galama declined to record a fourth album for CHM, preferring to seek a recording deal which offered greater remuneration and artistic autonomy (a deal which has not yet materialized). Tilly's collaboration with CHM also ceased shortly after, in 1995, with CHM (informally) boycotting PVP due to Chin's perception of their inflated production costs. Tilly's own involvement with PVP ended in 1996, after a company takeover, and he has not produced a music video since. *Fizz* and *Mekim Musik* continue to be broadcast on EM-TV. Tilly's involvement with music video making and, more pointedly, the creative autonomy he secured in 1991–94, can be seen as a piece of cultural opportunism, a strategy which succeeded in a niche or, perhaps more appropriately, 'cramped space' within EM-TV's scheduling and the public culture of contemporary PNG. However temporary this space, Tilly's work in the music video medium provided a remarkable example of the manner in which indigenous societies can re-produce and reinscribe their cultural traditions and practices using new media genres and technologies.

Notes

1. An extended version of this chapter originally appeared in *Perfect Beat* vol. 2, no. 2, January 1995. Thanks to Steven Feld, Ronnie Galama, Craig Marshall, Sarah Miller, Don Niles, Malcolm Philpott, John Taylor and Titus Tilly for their various assistances with this chapter.
2. See J. Horsfield *et al.* (1988) for further discussion.
3. Music video, or 'film clips' as they were more usually known, were also produced in other countries – such as Australia and New Zealand – at this time but the international form can be seen to have developed more specifically out of the UK and USA.
4. In this regard it should be noted that Tilly himself has acknowledged and emphasised the influence of Australian director Craig Marshall, who he began working with at NTN, and video editor Tahirih Homerang, who edited several of his early clips, on the development of his style. (Personal correspondence with the author, August 1994.)
5. NTN shut down in March 1988, due to financial difficulties experienced by

its Australian owner Kevin Parry. Shortly before going off-air, production manager Craig Marshall had gained approval for NTN to begin production of a weekly PNG music magazine show – a format which EM-TV did not develop until *Fizz* in 1993 (interview with Craig Marshall, Boroko, September 1994).

6. *MTV* ceased being produced in 1993 when its Australian franchise expired.
7. EM-TV's enthusiasm for PNG video material derives from both *Fizz*'s ability to deliver cheap local programming (on a network dominated by Australian and US product) and the interest of Australian-born director John Taylor in local music and culture.
8. CHM's association with EM-TV began in 1989 when they began providing EM-TV with background music for EM-TV's test pattern broadcasts.
9. CHM also continues to buy airtime for video screenings of new releases in a five-minute prime time evening slot, broadcast on EM-TV on Monday–Tuesday and Thursday–Saturday, entitled *Chin H. Meen Supersound New Release*
10. Tilly's fellow students at the NAS at this time included Tony Subam, who subsequently founded the pan-traditional rock band Sanguma. (See Webb, 1993, for further discussion.)
11. And also working on other documentary projects for PVP, including shooting items for ABC TV Australia's *Foreign Correspondent* programme.
12. For further discussion of Pacific Gold's music video production see Wild (1993).
13. The first feature film usually credited as a local production was Oliver Howes's *Wokabut Bilong Tonten* (1973).
14. See Sullivan (1993: 537–9) for further discussion of Toro's film work.
15. Galama has characterized Maopa music as 'songs of our place, we don't have harsh sounds, singing ... rhythms. Our songs are soft like the soft southerly wind that blows on our place ... With the songs they have a tune, a flow – people are not so excited by song melodies but the lyrics ... what they mean, the poems we sing ... what the songs give you a feeling of' (Interview with the author in Boroko, PNG, September 1994).
16. Unpublished interview with Malcolm Philpott, Boroko, June 1994.
17. See Hayward (1993a: 80–1) for further discussion.
18. Tilly's rough estimate, precise figures on this are unavailable.
19. Chin identifies the extra costs on 'Uana' compared to its two predecessors as being due to factors such as vehicle and driver hire to travel to the location; (unspecified) payments to the village community to ensure their collaboration and participation in making the video; and the cost of constructing the structures built for (and burnt down in) the video. (Unpublished interview with Malcolm Philpott, Boroko, June 1994.)
20. And it was in this context, as a 'video artist', that Tilly was introduced to an overseas audience for the first time at the 1994 Adelaide festival when he spoke in a forum on 'Video as Open Form' organized as part of the Festival's Artists' Week.
21. Taylor, in phone conversation with the author, November 1993.
22. In this manner, CHM can be seen to have approached Galama as another possible Sanguma, since Sanguma's international reputation was not matched by their local sales.

Videography

A wide selection of Tilly's works (though not 'Kame') can be found on CHM's 'PNG Supersound Video Clip' compilation series (begun in 1992, and currently continuing). There are, at present, no dedicated compilations of Tilly's video work available.

Discographic note

All Tilly's videos (with the exception of 'Kame') have been made to promote material released (in cassette only form) on CHM Records. Details of the release dates of relevant cassettes are included in the main body of the text.

11

The *Proud* Project and the 'Otara Sound': Maori and Polynesian Pop in the Mid-1990s[1]

Tony Mitchell

In 1994, Crowded House, New Zealand's most successful band, released their fourth album, *Together Alone*. The album featured the Te Whaka Huia Maori Cultural Group Choir on backing vocals on three songs, including the title track, which also features a brass band and a group of Cook Islander log drummers. These elements were included in a conscious reflection of indigenous Maori and Polynesian music which gives the album a distinctive sense of place. As part of the promotion of the album, Crowded House played a free concert in Manukau City Square, in the predominantly Maori and Polynesian-populated area of South Auckland, in February 1994. The group used the occasion to promote Maori and Pacific Island musicians in the area by putting three local support acts on the bill, including the rappers Radio Backstabber, DJ Playback and Purest Form. Lead singer Neil Finn also invited two Polynesian men from the audience on stage to play on a version of Bob Marley's song 'Exodus', in acknowledgment of what he described as 'a great resource ... that's not recognised by the rest of New Zealand' (Moore, 1994: 19).

The Crowded House concert in Manukau was also held in support of the *Proud* Music Project, a local Polynesian musical initiative set up by the Manukau City Council, and promoted by Enterprise Otara, a committee of local business people, police, representatives of all the Polynesian communities in the area and the local polytechnic. The project came to fruition in a recording entitled *Proud*, subtitled an 'Urban Pacific Streetsoul Compilation' of South Auckland Polynesian rap, reggae, soul, a cappella, swing beat and traditional musicians which topped the New Zealand compilation charts for three weeks in 1994. The project, which involved Samoan, Tongan, Niuean, Fijian and Cook Islander, as well as Maori, musicians, also included a 25-date nationwide tour by most of the artists featured on the album.

Produced by Alan Jansson for Second Nature, the New Zealand branch of Sydney-based Volition Records, the album included Sisters Underground, a Samoan and African-American a cappella duo whose feisty, street-smart rap 'In the Neighbourhood' set the tone for the compilation. This song later received a nomination for best single in the 1995 New Zealand Music Awards, as well for 'Most Promising Group' for Sisters Underground. With the exception of the Semi MCs, a mixed Maori and Samoan swing-beat group whose 'lover's rap' single 'Trust Me' had been released on Volition in 1993; and DJ Payback, who had been involved in one of New Zealand's first rap groups, Double J and Twice the T; the groups featured on the *Proud* album had not previously recorded, and many had been involved in the local Otara Music and Arts Centre. The ironically-named Otara Millionaires Club had done a number of live performances, as had the Pacifican Descendants, who, along with Radio Backstab and DJ Playback, were regarded as one of New Zealand's leading rap acts. The Samoan a cappella group Di-Na-Ve, the Gospel-based Rhythm Harmony, and the seven-man team of log drummers Puka Puka, completed the line-up. Perhaps the most distinctively local, community-oriented track on the album is MC Slam's rap about street violence in Auckland, 'Prove Me Wrong'. This was adopted as a theme song by the Manukau 'Safer Communities' Council, and includes the lyrics:

> Our city streets are tainted with thugs
> Cruising around selling off their drugs
> This wonderful city used to be safe
> You could walk around from dawn til late
> Nut these days nobody's caring
> You want to crack me for something that I'm wearing?

Proud was regarded by music reviewers as a new landmark in New Zealand popular music, despite its release on an Australian label, and 'cringe' reactions to the final track, an a cappella version of the national anthem 'God Defend New Zealand'. This was performed by the Vocal Five, one of a wide range of mainly Polynesian a cappella street performers featured along with Di-Na-Ve, Purest Form and others in a TVNZ programme, *Strictly Acappella* in 1993. Colin Hogg of the *Sunday Star Times* described *Proud* as 'the best compilation of new Kiwi music in a decade' (17 April 1994). Hogg also suggested that the album's 'Otara sound' may have ushered in a 'new era' of New Zealand music, displacing and supplanting 'the challenging new sounds of New Zealand contemporary music ... from the bedsits of Dunedin, the garrets of Grey Lynn and the garages of Christchurch' (*ibid.*). Russell Baillie in the *NZ Herald* found it 'a truly ground-breaking and purposeful local compilation... that captures a time and an attitude, and one to point to as a starting point in years to come' (25 April 1994). But the fact that by 1995 only one of the groups involved in the *Proud* project, the Otara Millionaires Club (who consisted of only one member, Pauly Fuemana), was still in existence, indicates that the album was an expression of potential rather than actuality. Jeremy To'omata, formerly known as DJ Payback, also resurfaced in a hard-core rap group called Overdose, who released a cassette album, *The First Chapter*, in 1996. This was described by Grant Smithies as 'pulling no punches in their portrayal of the violence, poverty, racial tension and urban desolation that is the flip-side to south Auckland's cultural pride and creativity' (1996: 18).

Nonetheless, Hogg's comments suggest that the extent of young Polynesian musical talent which the *Proud* project revealed indicated that the hip-hop, swing-beat, soul and funk music of the loosely-defined 'South Auckland sound' of the 1990s may have replaced the jangling guitars of 'the Dunedin sound' (see Mitchell, 1994: 28–52 and McLeay, 1994 for further discussion) which emerged in the mid-1980s as a major new national direction in New Zealand popular music . But it is arguable that Polynesian hip-hop has been around at least since the Dalvanius Prime and the Patea Maori Club topped the New Zealand charts with their combination of Maori chants and percussions and break-dancing, 'Poi E'. The local and international success in 1995 of the young Auckland-based Pakeha hard-core funk group Supergroove, who sounded a little like a local version of US rappers the Beastie Boys, and sold more albums than Crowded House in New Zealand, indicates that a combination of both the areas of American influence to which these two musical directions can be traced has proved to be a successful formula. As the group's singer Karl Steven has indicated:

> I think people in and around our age group ... are a bit sick of the black hole in music. There's a separation between the white rock thing and the black dance thing. We were influenced for a long time by the white alternative guitar thing coming from the States and at the same time the Public Enemy thing and the rest of that heavier black American rap thing. A lot of people don't want to subscribe to either completely, instead they want a bit of both and we are a bit of both. (Tingwell, 1995: 25)

Steven's reference to Supergroove's music solely in terms of US musical influences runs counter to one of the producers of the *Proud* project's main concerns. This was to create music that was distinctively local and reflected Polynesian musical traditions and influences such as the ukulele, percussion, acoustic guitars and body slaps. Jansson described how a certain amount of weaning away from American influences and coaching and encouragement in Pacific and Polynesian musical culture was necessary to produce the recording:

> a lot of those contributing to the album are Samoans, American Samoans, so they drew off that because they see what's happening in the States with things

like Boo Ya Tribe and they think that's what they should be doing. Pacifican Descendants were pressed by a friend of mine, Andy Vann, a white DJ, to come up with something innovative to the region, not just copying the Americans, because that's all we were getting, a lot of cloning. And I've had to turn them around and tell them to get the Polynesian drum thing happening, and we forced Pacifican Descendants to bring the ukulele into it. We were literally about a third of the way into the album when we started to bring the more Pacific elements out of them and then the other bands saw it. Now they've actually started going back and studying their culture, learning about their roots, and I think you'll see more and more of that coming out as it catches on. When the Proud bands started their tour they were wearing Reeboks and Nikes and back-to-front baseball caps, and when they came back they had lava lavas and tapu cloth headgear and I was absolutely blown away. What they discovered when they went on the road is that New Zealand is not America, and Radio Backstab have written a song called 'This is Not America', so they're really getting into where they're from. (Smith, 1994: 12)

A major contributor to the *Proud* project, and the manager of the *Proud* tour, was 29-year-old Niuean-Maori musician, songwriter and producer, Philip Fuemana, who fronts the soul group Fuemana with his sister Christina, and his brother Pauly, who fronts the Otara Millionaires Club. Fuemana's 1994 debut album, *New Urban Polynesian*, featured covers of the Roberta Flack composition 'Closer' and Stevie Wonder's 'Rocket Love'. Philip Fuemana, a practising Christian, insisted on a clause in his contract allowing him to put Christian songs on the B-sides of the group's singles. Reacting against the 'indigenizing' pressures exerted by Jansson and others, he has pursued a resolutely urban American style of soul and gospel music, resisting suggested incorporations of traditional Maori and Polynesian elements into his music. In retrospect, Fuemana was outspoken about what he regarded as a lack of autonomy in the *Proud* project due to its Pakeha producers' pursuit of a strictly Polynesian musical agenda:

white guys sabotaged the whole thing – hardly any of the bands were happy with the finished product. The Pacifican Descendants hated that version of 'Pass It Over'. But it was a case of people taking over because they thought they knew better than the band. (Farry, 1994: 14)

Fuemana's comments illustrate the dangers of pursuing strictly polarized positions for or against the desirability of distinctively local, indigenous forms of popular music (in preference to American influences). The American influences in the *Proud* compilation (Arrested Development, Cypress Hill, A Tribe Called Quest, Sly Stone, KRS1, Teddy Riley, etc.) are unmistakable. Similarly, the distinctively Polynesian rhythms and harmonies in Fuemana's singing are just as discernible. A desirable solution to the anxieties of influence expressed in the *Proud* project may be a balance between the indigenous and the imported, as Philip Fuemana stated in an interview in the *NZ Herald* in March 1994, after the *Proud* tour:

[t]he performers were all dressed like Americans when we first went out and I don't diss that because we're all affected by American music and culture ... but the trick is to get something of ourselves into the music. It might take a couple of *Proud* albums to do it, but it'll happen. We are aware that at the moment we are Polynesians using Polynesian culture and it's just a token right now. We can sometimes be accused of using our culture as a fashion and we make no apology for how we sound now because that's where we're at. (Reid, G., 1994)

Take away the log drums and ukuleles from *Proud* and what is left is a group of English-language songs and raps which reflect the Pacific Island, migrant status of most the performers. It expresses a strong 'urban Polynesian' perspective, but lacks any equivalent to the use of *te reo Maori* (Maori language) by artists such as Moana Jackson, Hapeta, Survival and Maree Sheehan, who are all featured performing songs in Maori in styles ranging from soul to hard-core rap on the *Once Were Warriors* soundtrack. As James Ritchie (1992) has pointed out, there are fundamental differences between Maori and Polynesian inhabitants of New Zealand:

Polynesian groups are members of one larger Pacific family, with similar languages and cultural elements and patterns ... But, whatever regional connections there may be to create Polynesian goodwill, filial warmth and friendliness, all have other homelands. Their historical and cultural roots bind them to other lands. For the Maori, this is the homeland; there is nowhere else to go. (*ibid.*: 8)

Although many of the Polynesian musicians featured on *Proud* and elsewhere were born in Aotearoa/New Zealand, this separation is reflected in the Auckland music scene, with many Maori artists being linked to the Tangata label, and increasingly making use of Maori language (1995 was designated *Te Tau o te Reo Maori*, the year of the Maori language, but the Maori language content of New Zealand television is still less than 0.1 per cent (Muru, 1994: 28)). Even hybrid Maori-Pacific performers like Fuemana and the Semi MCs tend to be less influenced by Maori culture than by a more generalized 'urban Polynesian' experience.

Multicultural noise: Auckland hip-hop

And what about Mangere? the 'lazy'
volcano, quarried for its scoria,
renowned for significant suburban wildlife: punks, streetkids, rastas,
heavy metal, Ronald McDonald is headmaster of the local primary
(it's true!)
...In Mangere
the PMs's the MP:

everyone and everything's in an inverse universe: you get karanga'd on
the shopping malls, the tangata phenua live in genuine chipboard
        whares
overlooking the beautiful hei-tiki-shaped sewerage system,
the streetkids pop smack, listen to Grandmaster Flash, rap Michael
        Jackson's BAD LP:
I'm Bad, shimon you know it, and of course they sleep in the public
dunnies with the hole in the cubicle to prick your dick through.
    Yeah Columbus
discovered Mangere, but meaty chicken breasts in sesame seed burger
buns are really insensitive: it's just the way, aha aha, you like it?
        No wonder
they spraybombed KILL A WHITE on the local Kentucky Fried.
        (Robert Sullivan, 'Message from Mangere' from *Jazz Waiata*, 1990.)

The young Maori poet Robert Sullivan shows the direct impact of black
American hip-hop culture along with other less welcome forms of US
import culture, on the predominantly Maori, Polynesian and poor white
population of the sprawling, topsy-turvy South Auckland suburb of
Mangere. Situated near the airport, Mangere is largely made up of what
David Eggleton has described, quoting another Sullivan poem, as

state houses for the urban dispossessed where 'the Mongrel mob fights the
power' of the dominant culture ... In a way the deracinated centreless sprawl
of Mangere is repeated all over Auckland, as if the whole city is merely some
Los Angeles spillover. (1991: 380–1)

The affinities with Los Angeles extend to Auckland street gangs, named
Crips and Bloods after their LA prototypes, and featured in February 1995
in *Families at War*, a two-part exposé on NZ TV2's *Sixty Minutes*. This
offered, in the words of the American-accented announcer, 'a rare and
disturbing glimpse into the mind of an active gang member'. Although the
teenaged gang member in question was white, musical accompaniment to
the story was by unidentified Polynesian rappers. Mangere, Otara and a
number of other South Auckland suburbs seem appropriate centres for the
New Zealand hip-hop scene, which is mostly confined to Auckland, but
which involves many Maori, Samoan, Niuean, European and even
Malaysian-Chinese performers. As with a cappella, the essentially oral
and vocal dynamics of rap have been adopted with ease by both Maori
and Pacific Island performers.
    In an examination by the Maori cultural magazine *Mana*, in 1993, of
the adoption by Maori youth of African-American music, films, television
programmes and clothes such as baseball caps, baggies, T-shirts and
jackets, Moana Maniapoto Jackson in part confirms this view in
suggesting that this acculturation of the artefacts of another black
minority by Maori young people was partly due to the absence of Maori
culture from the mass media:

[it] comes down to what you see on TV and what you hear on the radio. We don't hear enough of our own culture, so we co-opt the next closest thing ... Maori kids identify with the stereotypical Afro-American they see on TV, who's funny, sassy, streetwise, who's funky, who plays sports, who's into music, who's got all the quick one-liners and who's got all the gear on. (Ihaka, 1993, 12)

Maori filmmaker Merata Mita blamed the absence of strong Maori leadership and the enforcement of *tapu* (taboos) and preservation restrictions on aspects of Maori culture by Maori elders for alienating Maori youth and forcing them to seek black American role models and cultural icons:

If you put a Maori pattern on your shirt, people accuse you of prostituting the culture or selling out or it's too tapu. We've created such a mystique and negative enforcement that it's much easier for young Maori to take Afro-American symbols and wear them. Nobody's going to attack them for it. (*ibid.*: 13)

But as Jansson has indicated, the adoption of hip-hop by Maori and Pacific Islander youth in New Zealand is part of a universal youth culture involving the hybridization of US influences with local cultural inflections: '[Maori and Polynesians] can listen to a rap track from the States and straight away they can start rapping too ... Rap now is not just an American thing, it's a new universal language' (Walker, 1995: 28). Rap music and hip-hop culture quickly became an inevitable medium for musical expressions of Maori militancy, sometimes expressed in the Maori language. As Kerry Buchanan (1993) has argued, hip-hop's associations with African-American culture quickly became an important reference point and example for musical expressions of a local Maori and Pacific Islander vernacular culture, with which it shared strong roots in church and gospel singing:

with our links to the land broken, our alienation from the mode of production complete, our culture objectified, we have become marginalised and lost ... This is not to say beaten. And this is what we have in common with black America. When Maori hip-hop activists Upper Hutt Posse visited America recently, these political, social and racial links were brought into perspective. Upper Hutt Posse were welcomed as people involved in a common struggle, linked symbolically through hip-hop culture. (*ibid.*: 27)

A 1994 survey of the local rap scene by Otis Frizzell, of the Pakeha group M.C.O.J. and Rhythm Slave, featured a dozen groups and individuals and mentioned five more,[2] many of whom have released recordings. Frizzel emphasizes the multicultural heterogeneity of the scene, but cites Upper Hutt Posse's 1988 rap about Maori rebellion, 'E Tu' (Stand Proud), the first New Zealand rap track to be released on a 12-inch single, as an important influence on the development of a distinctively local style.

(Upper Hutt Posse are also virtually the only hip-hop group to use *te reo Maori*.) Frizzell stated:

> I believe Hip-Hop in Aotearoa is still growing and improving, and has an authentic and original style. We have a lot to thank Maori and Pacific Islanders for, in as much as a South Pacific feel goes, but us honkies have definitely also helped to form the New Zealand rap culture we have today. New Zealand is a multi-cultural society, and this is reflected in most music, but none more so than Hip-Hop. (*ibid.*: 45)

One of the most successful local hip-hop groups has been West Auckland Maori rappers 3 the Hard Way, whose pop-rap single 'Hip Hop Holiday', a hip-hop transposition of 10CC's 'Dreadlock Holiday' (1978) topped the charts for several weeks and went gold in New Zealand in 1994. Describing themselves as 'Old School Prankstas' (the title of their debut album), 3 the Hard Way maintained a commercial, accessible sound which suggested that, despite their name, they may have got to the top of the charts 'the easy way'. Their second single was a soft-edged pastiche of UB40's 1983 version of the Jimmy Cliff song 'Many Rivers to Cross'; and much of the album was produced by Anthony Ioassa, who with his two brothers fronts a smooth 'Samoan soul' group called Grace, who have been described as 'a Polynesian Crowded House' (Pett, 1995: 25). 3 the Hard Way's view of the local hip-hop scene suggests a superficially harmonious homogeneity:

> NZ I think culturally has a really good environment. It really is a multicultural country and when you look at other countries racially and culturally things really are quite smooth over here in comparison to a lot of places. As far as the music goes there's really been a massive resurgence of local bands who are starting to really start raiding the charts over here, which didn't happen before. (Dinnen, 1994: 52)

But they were the exception that proved the rule as far as 'raiding the charts' is concerned, as few other local hip-hop groups had any chart success until 1996, apart from fellow Auckland Deepgrooves label-mates Urban Disturbance, who were voted most promising group at the 1994 NZ Music Awards.

At the other extreme to 3 the Hard Way is Dean Hapeta (D Word), whose uncompromising, *kia kaha* (Be Strong) style of hip-hop is the most distinctive blend of traditional aspects of Maori musical culture, local urban realities and African-American rap music in Aotearoa/New Zealand. Hapeta's 'Whakakotahi' (To Make One) was first released as a single in 1993 by E Tu, an offshoot of Upper Hutt Posse, on Tangata Records to mark the United Nations' International Year for Indigenous People. Like Jane Campion's 1994 film *The Piano*, its video was filmed on a West Coast Auckland beach, but by Hapeta himself at a cost of $1200

(Zepke, 1993: 41). While it includes some snatches of rugged bush and coastline, its uncompromisingly rough, 'in-your-face' indictment of colonialist violence against Maori, presented in the style of 'traditional Maori challenges of stance and gestures' (Shopland, 1993: 38), meant it got little air play. Incorporating quotations from speeches by Louis Farrakhan and Khallid Mohammed of the Nation of Islam along with a *haka* and the sound of the *purerehua* and *ngutu* (nose flute), its message of unity 'to the indigenous people of the world' was also barely noticed in the local music press. The lines 'Fuck New Zealand, ya call me a Kiwi/ Aotearoa's the name of this country' necessitated a specially edited version with expletives deleted for radio play.

A definitively hybridized version of 'Whakakotahi' opens the Upper Hutt Posse's 1995 album *Movement in Demand* (a title derived from Louis Farrakhan), welding together Maori traditional instruments and militant *patere* and *karanga* (raps and shouts) and invocations of the spirits of the forest (*Tane Mohuta*) and the guardian of the sea (*Tangaroa*) combined with Nation of Islam rhetoric. This version also draws on the group's reggae and ragga inclinations (they started off as a reggae group in 1985), funk bass rhythms, blues guitar riffs and hard-core, gangsta-style rapping which switches from English to *te reo Maori*. It ends with a *patere* – for which, like all the other *te reo Maori* lyrics on the album, no English translation is provided – exhorting the Pakeha to leave the land, the sea, the indigenous people and the world, and to get away from Maori space and children at once for ever. One of the album's tracks, the 'tangi (lament) Tangata Whenua', is entirely in Maori.

The cover of *Movement in Demand* assembles images of fourteen Maori chiefs, warriors, prophets and leaders from Hone Heke in the early nineteenth century to Princess Te Puea Herangi in the twentieth century. The album includes historical notes on all of them, under the banner of a slogan appropriated from Rewi Maniapoto and used in Maori demonstrations: *Ka whawhai tonu matou, ake, ake, ake* ('We will continue to fight for evermore'). Knowledge of past Maori battles, struggles and victories over the Pakeha informs the whole album, while reference is made in 'Hardcore' to Bob Marley, Marcus Garvey and English dub poet Linton Kwesi Johnson, along with Malcolm X, Steve Biko, Crazy Horse and a number of Maori militants past and present, all of whom D Word claims as part of his *whakapapa* (lineage). The heterogeneity of the album's musical influences mirrors its political array of black militant role models. The track 'Gun in My Hand' disturbingly adapts the violent rhetoric of African-American gangsta rap and ragga boasting into a biblical-styled diatribe against the evils of Babylon:

> The way you go on and on
> Murdering mis-education fornicating and creating
> Pain and strife for the people of the land
> I'm lettin' ya know there's a gun in my hand

These sentiments are particularly alarming when taken in the light of Hapeta's statement at the end of an Australian radio programme, *Background Briefing*, in November 1995 (which used 'Whakakotahi' as a theme song), that

> guns are going to come into this country sooner or later and they're going to come in in a big way, and people should be really thankful they're not here now ... because I just know a lot of brothers who would be shooting people in a big way if they were as available as they are in the States.

Both the song and the statement suggest a rhetorical confluence between the ritualized Maori challenge and the US gangsta rap threat.

Due to their uncompromising political stance of total support by whatever means necessary for *mana* (authority) and *tino rangatiratanga* (absolute Maori sovereignty), and their musical and political strategy of 'push(ing) it furtherer', the Upper Hutt Posse have never been far from controversy. Hapeta sued the *Auckland Star* (and won) over claims that they had barred two Pakeha youths from one of their shows – while *The Truth* newspaper claimed in 1990 that the group had behaved in a racist fashion in telling Samoans at a concert to 'go home' (Gracewood, 1995: 11). Influenced by his trip to the USA and meeting with Farrakhan and hard-core US rappers, Hapeta's comments about the local hip-hop scene emphasize its smallness, fragility and deracination, but also rap's compatability with Maori formations of oral discourse, illustrated by the way concepts such as *patere* (rap), *whakarongo mai* (listen up) and *wainua* (attitude) are easily assimilated into hip-hop discourse:

> NZ Hip-Hop is a fallacy! Hip-Hop is a culture – rap music, breakdancing, graffiti, clothes, language. This country lacks a connection between, and a socialization of, these components of Hip-Hop. True Hip-Hop will only exist, for the moment at least, in the inner city suburbs of Black America where it was created as an everyday 'living' thing ... We can emulate certain areas of Hip-Hop, as we do with rap music, and did with breakdancing back in the early 80s, and still do with other components of Hip-Hop today, but, just as experiencing Maori culture today is done best on the Marae, Hip-Hop can only truly be experienced fully at its home ... Although I love and respect Hip-Hop, being Maori I only take from it what doesn't compromise my own culture. But in spite of this I have found them both very compatible. (Frizzell, 1994: 48, 50)

Hapeta denies that hip-hop is merely a musical style, emphasizing that the music is an expression of a culture and way of life which originated in inner-city black ghettos in the USA, making it difficult, if not impossible, to transpose to an isolated country at the bottom of the world like Aotearoa/New Zealand. But what Hapeta and other Maori and Pacific Islander rappers and musicians have done is attempt to substitute Maori and Polynesian cultural expressions for the black American context of hip-hop, while borrowing freely from the hybrid US musical styles of the genre. (And it is an indication of the strong position traditionally held by women in Maori and Pacific Islander societies that the misogynist aspects of US hard-core rap are totally absent from its Maori and Pacific Islander appropriations.) The result is a further hybridization of an already hybrid form, but one which is capable of having strong musical, political and cultural resonances in Aotearoa. As the Maori rapper of the group Dam Native (aka Danny Haimona) has stated 'We don't own [hip hop]. All we can do is inject our own culture into it. *Kia kaha.*' (Frizzell, 1994: 50). The importance with which rap music and reggae are regarded by Maori as legitimate forms of expressing 'official' Maori oral *kaupapa* (culture) is illustrated by the inclusion of song lyrics by Hapeta, Herbs and others in *Te Ao Marama* ('The Dawning of the Light') (1993), a five-volume anthology of Maori literature edited by novelist and former New Zealand consul Witi Ihimaera.

By 1995 the 'urban Polynesian' label had become a 'buzz word' in the New Zealand music industry, and was not always to the liking of the musicians it was used to refer to. The young Mangere-based Tokeleaunan singer Sulata, for example, who was voted most promising female vocalist in the 1995 New Zealand Music Awards, indicated her concern at being described in the awards programme as an 'urban Polynesian': 'I went "Uhhh!" I'm trying to get away from the South Auckland scene, away from that music' (McDonald, 1995: 14.) Sulata's debut single 'Never' is an example of 'Samoan soul', with more US than local musical influences, in the style of Phil Fuemana, who co-wrote the B-side, 'Motion'. On the other hand, Wellington-based Samoan recording artist Igelese explores 'Polynesian fusion' on his 1995 debut single 'Groovalation', which incorporates a native language dialogue between Maori and Samoan rappers with US soul, funk, dance and rhythm and blues influences, as well as including Polynesian log drumming and Maori chants. A church choirmaster, pianist and university music graduate, Igelese claimed he 'had some fresh ideas that nobody else had done and was getting sick of watching Polynesians imitating African Americans' (Hunter, 1995: 24). 'Groovalation' advocates racial unity, reworking the slogan 'One nation under a groove', and its albeit self-consciously national, multi-hybridity indicates a possible future musical direction, combining different elements of the multicultural diversity of Polynesian Aotearoa. It represents a landmark in an historical process in which a complex but distinctively Pacific and indigenous local identity has emerged in formations of popular music in Aotearoa/New Zealand.

In July 1996 news of the first major mainstream crossover of 'the cross-cultural sound of urban Polynesia' reached the front page of *Billboard* in an article by Graham Reid recounting the success of Pauly Fuemana's OMC's (Otara Millionaires Club's) dance/rap single 'How Bizarre'.

OMC's single, a catchy, up-beat pop-dance song with similarities to Mink DeVille's 'Spanish Stroll' (1977), co-written and produced by *Proud* producer Alan Jansson, won a 1995 NZ music industry award for Single of the Year (while Pauly Fuemana managed to win both the Most Promising Male Vocalist and Most Promising Group awards). The single sold 142,000 units in Australia and New Zealand, was in the New Zealand Top Ten for three months, and stayed at number one in the Australian charts for five weeks in April and May 1996 – the first New Zealand-produced single to reach number one in Australia since Ray Columbus' 'She's a Mod' in 1965.

By August 1996 'How Bizarre' had also sold 65,000 copies in the UK, risen to number 11 on the UK singles charts, and been released in 21 countries. Fuemana became an overnight celebrity, with local media coverage emphasizing his past involvement in gangs, drugs and petty crime in Sydney and Auckland, and he was flown to London for two appearances on the BBC TV programme *Top of the Pops*. As Atama Raganivatu (1996) commented in a profile of Fuemana in the *Pacific Islands Monthly*, the originally wry and ironic band name Otara Millionaires Club (already abbreviated to OMC for those outside New Zealand who didn't get the joke) was showing signs of becoming 'a self-fulfilling prophecy' (*ibid.*: 57).

OMC's follow-up single, 'Right On', which failed to repeat the success of 'How Bizarre', suggesting it had been something of a novelty hit with its Latino-styled beats and lyrics, was succeeded by 'On the Run' (1996) which appeared to refer to Fuemana's criminal past. (As Raganivatu (1996) has pointed out, Fuemana formed the group in 1992 as a hard-core rap act modelled on Public Enemy, and developed a reputation for brawls at their gigs. After being part of the *Proud* tour, and undertaking a brief tour of Australia, Fuemana began to draw more on his late Niuean father's musical influences, such as Tom Jones, Elvis Presley and Dean Martin, and the group became a solo act.) But in the wake of 'How Bizarre''s success, other hip-hop style releases by Polynesian artists began getting more media and chart attention.

In August 1996, 'Chains', a single by DLT, aka Darryl Thompson, a founder-member of the Upper Hutt Posse, with vocals by former chart-topping group Supergroove member Che Fu, went to number one in the local charts, after debuting at number two. Described by Andy Pickering (1996) in *Rip It Up* as 'possibly the strongest hip-hop single ever released in New Zealand' (1996: 20), 'Chains' featured soul- and Gospel-like vocals from Che augmented by ragga-rap segments by reggae artists the Mighty Asterix and Ras Daan. It combined tuneful melody with slow, loping beats and lyrics about the hardships of life in the city. Thompson is a prominent member of the Trueschool Posse, who present a hip-hop programme on the Auckland music video channel Max TV and student radio station bFM, as well as being a producer for other hip-hop groups such as Joint Force (featuring MC OJ and Rhythm Slave) and Native Bass. 'Chains' is the most commercially-oriented track on his top 20 album *The True School*, which incorporates a wide range of styles from the blues-funk of Maori guitarist Billy TK, through old school hip-hop to jungle, and illustrates Thompson's perception that successful charting songs in New Zealand require US-styled R 'n' B elements rather than Polynesian rhythms to be prominent (Pickering, 1996: 20). DLT's follow-up single, 'One Love' (1996) was in a similar vein, featuring stripped-back jungle-style beats and more ragga toasting from Asterix. Unlike the more hard-core beats of Upper Hutt Posse and Dam Native, with their prominent use of Maori language raps, instrumentation and striking political video imagery, DLT's less threatening and less noticeably Polynesian hip-hop was more inclined to gain acceptance in the mainstream. As Reid pointed out in his *Billboard* profile of Pauly Fuemana:

> while the sound of urban Polynesia has long been part of the substructure of New Zealand's music ... there have been only fleeting glimpses of Polynesian artists cracking the charts ... Maori and Polynesian music is a constant in the cultural landscape, if not on the country's radio stations. (1996: 16)

These fleeting glimpses of Polynesian artists in the charts illustrate that while there is a rich variety of black musical idioms and styles in Maori and Polynesian popular music in Aotearoa, it remains a relatively marginal phenomenon in commercial and industrial terms due to its limited accessibility within Aotearoa/New Zealand, and almost total inaccessibility abroad. The struggle for independence and self-determination contained within the hybridization of Maori and Polynesian popular music has made its presence felt in Aotearoa in the wake of the success of Herbs in the 1970s and 1980s and Moana and the Moahunters, whose cultural profile in New Zealand might be compared, on a minor scale, to that of Yothu Yindi in Australia in the 1990s. But outside Aotearoa, a country still marked by its geographical isolation as a peripheral 'other' in the global economy of popular music, the growing international attention being paid to the independent label Flying Nun and the Pakeha noise-oriented bands and musicians of the 'deep south' of New Zealand has yet to be extended to indigenous Maori and Polynesian groups and performers.

Notes

1. An earlier version of this chapter originally appeared under the title 'New Urban Polynesians' in *Perfect Beat*, vol. 2, no. 3 (July 1995).
2. The rappers featured in the *Pavement* article were Urban Disturbance (European and Niuean), 3 the Hard Way (Maori & Samoan), Upper Hutt Posse (Maori), Dam Native (Maori & Samoan/Maori), Otara Millionaires Club (Niuean/Maori), Ehrman (Samoan), Field Style Orator (Samoan),

Rhythm Slave (European), Teremoana Rapley (Maori), Man Chu (Chinese Malaysian), DLT (European/Maori) and Justice (European). Also mentioned were Sisters Underground (Samoan and African-American), Gifted & Brown (Maori & Samoan), Pacifican Descendants (Samoan), Rough Opinion (Maori) and the Semi MCs (Maori & Samoan). Of these, all are from or based in Auckland with the exception of Dam Native, Gifted and Brown, Upper Hutt Posse, DLT and Rough Opinion, who are from Wellington.

Discography

Ahurangi, *Sanctuary*, Ahurangi Music Collective, 1992.
Crowded House, *Together Alone*, Capitol Records, 1993.
Dam Native, 'Hori'fied One', Tangata Records, 1995.
—'Behold My Cool Style', Tangata, 1996.
DLT, featuring Che Fu, 'Chains', BMG, 1996.
DLT, featuring the Mighty Asterix, 'One Love', BMG, 1996.
DLT, *The True School*, BMG, 1996.
Double J and Twice the T, *All Wrapped Up*, Definitive Records, 1989.
—*Def to be Green*, EMI, 1990.
E Tu, 'Whakakotahi', Tangata Records, 1993.
Fuemana, *New Urban Polynesian*, Deepgrooves, 1994.
—'Closer', Deepgrooves, 1994.
—'Rocket Love', Deepgrooves, 1994.
Gifted and Brown, 'So Much Soul', Tangata Records, 1993.
Grace, *Black Sand Shore*, Deepgrooves, 1995.
Igelese, 'Groovalation', Papa Pacific Records, 1995.
The Mighty Asterix, *The Sweetest Girl*, Deepgrooves, 1993.
Temuera Morrison, *Waiata Poi*, Virgin, 1995.
OMC (Otara Millionaires Club), 'How Bizarre', Huh!, 1996.
—'Right On', Huh!, 1996.
—'On the Run', Huh!, 1996.
Overdose,*The First Chapter*, A&R Entertainment Cassette, 1996.
Emma Paki, 'Greenstone', Virgin, 1994.
—*Oxygen of Love*, Virgin, 1996.
Purest Form, 'Message to My Girl', Madame X, 1994.
Semi MCs, 'Trust Me', Volition, 1993.
Maree Sheehan, 'Dare to be Different', Tangata, 1992.
—'Make U My Own', Tangata, 1992.
—'Past to the Present', Roadshow, 1995.
Sisters Underground, 'In the Neighbourhood', Second Nature, 1994.
Sulata, 'Never', Deepgrooves, 1995.
Supergroove, *Traction*, BMG, 1994.
3 the Hard Way, *Old Skool Prankstas*, Deepgrooves, 1994.
12 Tribes of Israel Band, 'Make It Better', 1991.
Upper Hutt Posse, 'E Tu', Jayrem, 1987.
—*Against the Flow*, Southside, 1989.
—'Whakamutungia Tebei mahi Te Patupatu Tangata', Alcoholic Liquor Advisory Council, 1992.

—'Ragga Girl', Tangata, 1992.
—*Movement in Demand*, Tangata, 1995.
Urban Disturbance, *No Flint, No Flame*, Deepgrooves, 1993.
—*37 (degrees) a-ttitude*, Deepgrooves, 1994.
Various, *Tribal Stomp*, Tangata Records, 1992.
—*Unzipped: Prime Sex*, BMG, 1992.
—*Deep in the Pacific of Bass*, Deepgrooves, 1993.
—*Once Were Warriors*, Soundtrack Album, Tangata Records, 1994.
—*Proud, An Urban-Pacific Streetsoul Compilation*, Second Nature, 1994.
—*Urban Pacific Christmas*, Papa Pacific Records, 1994.

PART III

Access to the Mainstream: The Case of Yothu Yindi

12

Yothu Yindi: Context and Significance

Philip Hayward and Karl Neuenfeldt

Being black is political ... Our music has to be political because it tells our story and our story is one of survival. (Mandawuy Yunupingu, comment made on a visit to South Africa, 1996, cited in Meade 1996a: 4)

Part III of this anthology offers a sequence of chapters which debate and assess the impact and complexities of the most significant Australian, and, arguably, trans-Pacific, pop group of the 1990s, the Australian band Yothu Yindi.

Yothu Yindi were formed in 1986 in the Yolngu community of Yirrkala, in Arnhem Land, in the Northern Territory (see Knopoff, 1997: 49–53 for further discussion). Their first recordings, the single 'Mainstream' and the album *Homeland Movement*, were released in 1989. While these recordings attracted a degree of media attention, Yothu Yindi did not rise to national, and later international prominence until their single 'Treaty' was released in 1991. The first version of the single was released in February, and received limited radio and television exposure (mainly on ABC radio and television and SBS TV) and failed to chart. Disappointed with the single's performance, the band's record company released a dance remix in an attempt to re-promote the single. Tagged the 'Filthy Lucre' remix, the new version was released in June. This fared substantially better than its predecessor, entering the Australian singles charts in July and peaking at number eleven in September.

The single spent 30 weeks in the Top 100. Its success, and the wave of publicity which followed an Aboriginal group's access to the pop mainstream (for the first time[1]), promoted sales of their album *Tribal Voice*, which peaked at number four in the album charts. The 'Treaty' remix and its video also won a series of industry awards in 1991. The single won the APRA (Australasian Performing Rights Association) Song of the Year Award; three awards at the ARIA (Australian Record Industry Association) Awards ceremony: Australian Song of the Year; Best

Australian Single; and (for the Filthy Lucre team) Best Engineer award. The video was voted Best Australian Video at the Australian Music Awards in Melbourne and was also awarded Best Australian Video of the Year (Viewer's Choice) in the MTV International Awards.

Despite this commercial breakthrough, Yothu Yindi's chart success in Australia has declined since the peak of the 'Treaty' remix and the *Tribal Voice* album; with their two subsequent albums, *Freedom* (1993) and *Birrkuta – Wild Honey* (1996) – and various singles extracted from them – failing to match the sales of their 1991 releases. The public profile of the band has, by contrast, remained high. Yothu Yindi, and especially their vocalist/bandleader Mandawuy Yunupingu, have become high-profile cultural performers and icons of Aboriginal achievement, with Yunupingu receiving the Australian of the Year Award in 1992. The band's frequent national and international tours have also kept them in the public eye, as did their involvement in such popular cultural activities as the launch of the (Rugby) Super League sports competition in March 1997. Above all, however, it is the political implications of Yothu Yindi's rise and achievements which have proved most resonant.

In the case of Yothu Yindi, the accidents of history and the nitty-gritty of contemporary politics are crucial to understanding the group and how their music can function as a musical means to extramusical ends. Without an appreciation of the politics of Yothu Yindi, they are too readily reduced either to a commercial product or a haphazard process. In the case of Yolngu, the accidents of history include their culture not having been ravaged by Western colonialism to the extent of many other Aboriginal cultures. Until the 1930s they lived on a reserve with somewhat limited contact with outsiders (first from the Indonesian archipelago and then 'settled' Australia), and have been able to retain some level of independence and a way of life that was not under constant threat. Also, Christian missionaries did not disparage or totally destroy traditional lifestyle and arts as was commonplace elsewhere. Overall, as Berndt observes: 'this concatenation of events made it possible for the north-east Arnhem Landers to keep something of their arts and, what was more, much of their social relevance' (1973: 38). Therefore, Yolngu have retained much of the traditional culture that was decimated elsewhere, despite the growing influence of western culture and economy.

Historical accidents of location and colonization were further complicated by an accident of geology. In the 1960s, a large bauxite deposit was identified in north-eastern Arnhem Land. Watson notes some of the epistemological and political repercussions that followed:

> In 1970 members of the Yolngu Aboriginal communities ... attempted to gain some control over the process by which Aboriginal Australia comes to be known by non-Aboriginal Australia. They began a legal challenge to the invasion of their lands by a mining company [Nabalco] and instituted a public

elaboration [partially through artworks] of the logical and moral basis of Yolngu ownership of land (1990: 125).

However, as the communities discovered:

> their elaboration was not heeded by non-Aboriginal legal authorities [and] the challenge was unsuccessful ... [However,] complex social institutions – Land Rights Acts, Lands Councils, sacred sites legislation and so on – have developed from this initiative. (*ibid*.: 127)

These events in which Yolngu were involved were precursors to later legal and political developments such as the High Court ruling regarding Native Title in Common Law (1992) (commonly known as the 'Mabo decision'); the passage of the Native Title Act (1993); and the High Court ruling that pastoral leases and native title can coexist (1996) (commonly known as the 'Wik decision'). Today the Yolngu are in a unique and sometimes equivocal position: in the past they fought to halt mining but now receive royalties and help service the industry. But they have also been able to retain and sustain core cultural activities, assisted in part by being in a somewhat better economic position than many other Aboriginal peoples. As well, they have considerable input into important local matters such as education and dispute resolution.

When locating Yothu Yindi within contemporary politics, it is important to acknowledge the uniqueness of long-term, proactive, sophisticated and highly politicized Yolngu media campaigns (see Williams, 1986 for a detailed discussion). These have encouraged cultural vitality and movements towards self-determination and Yothu Yindi have played an important part via their music. The success of these campaigns can be appreciated as arising partly out of extensive experience dealing with land rights issues and thus government, indigenous and business stakeholders. However, success also arises out of the political roles of certain extended-family and clan groups and individual Yolngu. The Yunupingu family in particular has been influential. Munggurawuy Yunupingu was involved in the Bark Petition (1963) and the Gove Land Claim (1971). His sons Galarrwuy and Mandawuy have been deeply involved in politics and music: Galarrwuy as head of the powerful Northern Land Council and a contributor to Yothu Yindi's recording projects; and Mandawuy as an educator and the lead singer and spokesman for Yothu Yindi. They have both been voted Australians of the Year and have received adulation and denunciation for their accomplishments. As well, in 1996, a senior Yolngu man, Gatjil Djerrkura, was appointed chairman of the Aboriginal and Torres Strait Islander Commission, the peak national indigenous organization. Yolngu, therefore, are very well represented at the upper levels of indigenous politics both locally and nationally.

In the context of contemporary national politics in Australia, indigenous peoples number only approximately 2 per cent of the population. However, they occupy a unique moral and political position by being the continent's original inhabitants, as well as being ongoing reminders that invasion/settlement was a violent and traumatic process. Vast areas of the continent were literally cleared of Aborigines to make way for sheep and cattle and the pastoralists and farmers who claimed the land Aborigines had occupied for 60,000 years or more. This was expedited by Britain claiming the land was *terra nullius* ('empty land'). In effect, contemporary politics is dealing with the detritus of colonialism: the long-term repercussions of genocide, ethnocide, forced assimilation, the wholesale expropriation of land and the expulsion of Aborigines to government settlements and missions. They remain the most disadvantaged groups in society. There is also an entrepreneurial and vociferous anti-Aboriginal industry (e.g. some media commentators, talk-radio hosts, politicians, mining organizations, pastoralists) which represents vested interests which feel threatened by Aboriginal agendas and aspirations.

In important ways, the experience of Yothu Yindi and the Yolngu are anomalous to the experience of many Aborigines. Therefore, care must be taken when extrapolating from their situation and experiences to those of an often vague and romanticized notion of pan-Aboriginality. The variety of Aboriginal experiences of colonialism is considerable, as are the accidents of history and geology. The Yolngu have avoided some of the worst of the excesses of the 'civilizing process'. Although they experience many of the same challenges found in other Aboriginal groups, and are by no means a monolithic community, they are unique and have used that to their advantage. Publicity and success in indigenous affairs (and popular music), however, is a double-edged sword. Yothu Yindi and individual high-profile Yolngu (such as Galarrwuy and Mandawuy Yunupingu) have reached a point where they are perhaps celebrated and criticized equally. This is especially true in the context of the recent resurgence of race-based hatred that followed the 1996 election of a conservative federal Coalition (Liberal and National) national government which has actively asserted Anglo-Australian hegemony via the denigration of difference and diversity.

A recent 'Letter to the Editor', published in a national newspaper provides a good example of this dynamic at work. It criticized Mandawuy Yunupingu for statements he made while Yothu Yindi were touring in South Africa in support of the Australian-based Fred Hollows Foundation, which has a blindness prevention programme. Yunupingu asked the independent charity AusAid, which usually works only overseas, if it could help Aborigines in Australia by providing health workers and doctors trained in developing world medicine. The letter to the editor stated sarcastically and dismissively:

[Yunupingu] is truly a fine ambassador for our country. If he can possibly fit it into his undeniably tight schedule he might be well advised to make a dash across to Rwanda or Zaire and find out first-hand what genocide is all about. Half a million desperate, destitute people trying to get away from wholesale slaughter, starvation and deadly epidemics might appreciate Yothu Yindi's blend of funk and tribal song cycles. There will never be a better opportunity. (Hill, 1996: 20).

Yunupingu had made the statement because Aboriginal peoples in Australia have the worst health profile of any indigenous population in a First World nation (Meade, 1996b). However, in the current political climate, such truths seem deemed to be divisive.

The cultural production and discourse of Yothu Yindi can be appreciated as an important ingredient in Yolngu and Aboriginal politics. Songs and music have always been sites of political power in Aboriginal society (Von Sturmer, 1987) and Yothu Yindi are continuing in that tradition in a different but not dissimilar way. The secular songs they write and sing and the albums they record are public documents, widely disseminated. They literally record a way of life, a view of the world, and, importantly, establish links between land, the natural environment and Yolngu – the precise issues that were not readily recognized by Australian governments and courts in the past. Yothu Yindi provide a soundtrack to inherently politicized agendas and aspirations that are facilitated by the polished presentation of Yothu Yindi as successful media operators.

From their earliest incarnation, the band attracted considerable critical attention as to their nature, impact and effectiveness as a group whose cultural politics was both overt and an important part of their public image (and, thereby, marketability) (Lawe-Davies, 1993). Amongst the earliest commentators was Muecke (1990), who identified and analysed the complexity of lyrical, musical and visual significance in the video produced by Axolotl for Yothu Yindi's debut single 'Mainstream'. The release of the band's second album, *Tribal Voice*, and, particularly, the release of different versions of the single 'Treaty' – and its videos – prompted further analyses, most notably, for the purposes of this anthology, in Hayward (1992) and Mitchell (1992). The (relatively brief) mention of 'Treaty' in these two pieces prompted Nicol (1993, reproduced in this anthology, in edited form, as Chapter 13) to produce both an in-depth study of the production of the 'Treaty' videos and an ideological critique of the video's critics' political positions and motivations. Nicol's article,[2] and a response by Hayward (1993) (included here as Chapter 14), subsequently became reference points for a number of further discussions (such as Shoemaker, 1994a; Turner, 1995; and Mitchell, 1996). Chapter 15 of this anthology provides both an update of the Nicol–Hayward debate and an expansion of their terms of analysis with regard to a wider sphere of circulation and signification for Yothu Yindi's music and image. (Other significant publications on Yothu Yindi include Magowan, 1996, which provides an analysis of Yothu Yindi's *Tribal Voice* video; and Stubington and Dunbar-Hall, 1994, who provide a detailed musical analysis of 'Treaty'.)

Notes

1. Despite the limited success of predecessors such as No Fixed Address and Coloured Stone, Yothu Yindi were the first Aboriginal band to chart in Australia.
2. Accompanied, in its original version, by a short reply from Mitchell (1993).

Discography

Homeland Movement, Mushroom Records, 1989.
Tribal Voice, Mushroom Records, 1991.
Freedom, Mushroom Records, 1993.
Birrkuta – Wild Honey, Mushroom Records, 1996.

The Filthy Lucre remix of 'Treaty' was released, together with a radio mix and dub version of the track, on *Treaty – The Filthy Lucre Remix*, a three-track Mushroom Records CD and cassette EP, in 1993.

13

Culture, Custom and Collaboration: The Production of Yothu Yindi's 'Treaty' Videos[1]

Lisa Nicol

Today, remixes of songs are a common phenomenon. They are produced for a specific commercial purpose. Remixes extend the commercial life of a music track by re-targeting it at consumer groups who might not have purchased the original version, usually intended for mass exposure radio broadcast. Remixes facilitate the contextual versatility of songs by making them suitable for a variety of contexts, such as the dance floor or lounge room *in addition* to the radio. In recent years there has also been an increasing tendency for remixed music tracks, particularly those produced by prominent and/or 'breaking' acts, to be accompanied by a different, or at least reconstructed, version of the original video. Since there are clear economic reasons behind record companies and artists going for such remixes, little comment is passed on the practice (unless it is by consumers confused as to which version they actually wish to purchase at their local record store). One particular case of remixing however has been singled out for sustained critical address, that of the Aboriginal band Yothu Yindi and the two versions of their single 'Treaty' (see Hayward, 1992 and Mitchell, 1992). As this chapter will argue, the criticisms of this particular example highlight the extent to which Aboriginal acts are subject to a degree of scrutiny not accorded to mainstream Western musicians and, like many other indigenous artists, are plagued by accusations of their 'selling-out' their own cultures and being contaminated by the values of the market and western culture in general.

Analysis of 'world' or indigenous music and its entry into the Western popular music mainstream is fraught with difficulties because it is based on underlying assumptions of similarity and analogy. The agenda is set firmly within a paradigm which sees non-Western musicians struggling to succeed in a white mainstream-dominated market. The assumption is that the cost of such cross-over success is often personal, artistic, musical and – significantly for this analysis – *political* compromise. Such criticisms are of course not restricted to the music industry (and academic critiques of it) alone. In *Out of Africa – Spike Lee* (1991), a documentary about the film producer, director, writer and actor, Lee recounted an anecdote of being approached by a black woman in the street who requested that he make a movie about Afro-Americans that her children could watch. As he pointed out, no-one would ever suggest that David Lynch should make a film for children.

It often seems that non-Western artists are not permitted to be individuals but, more often than not, are seen as representatives of their racial groups. They are then compared to other representatives of (often highly distinct) racial groups, and parallels, conclusions and generalizations are made. Such an approach is questionable, often highly inappropriate and objectionable. Histories of oppression or colour-identity are not sound grounds for comparison, especially in connection with music and art which are often extremely individual and personal expressions (although of course contextualized and nourished in social situations). It is necessary to escape restrictive mind-sets of defining people by colour, whether in a positive or negative light, and to look at the work of cultural producers on its own merits.

It is from this perspective that I will attempt to analyse the two versions of the video for Yothu Yindi's single 'Treaty', both of which were directed by Darwin-based filmmaker Stephen Johnson. The remix of the song and reconstruction of the video have been subject to analysis by Hayward (1992) and Mitchell (1992). The tenor of these analyses has been markedly critical (see pp. 187–9, 'Treaty I to Treaty II', for detailed discussion) and has centred on the shifts in polemic address between the two versions of the single (henceforth 'Treaty I' and 'Treaty II'). The context and underlying assumptions of Hayward and Mitchell's pieces, informed as they are by Marxist-derived traditions of Cultural Studies, engender negative assessments of the changes between the 'Treaty I' and 'II' videos as a matter of course. They also seem to deny Aboriginal performers the same degree of artistic freedom they would presumably accord Western artists. Approaching Aboriginal cultural forms such as the 'Treaty' texts from a different, and less determined position, does not deny the importance of their Aboriginal, and specifically Yolngu, tribal cultural and historical experience to the music and media representations of Yothu Yindi. The history of degradation, abuse and resistance is essential for an understanding of contemporary Aboriginal life and music. These influences, however, should be explored from the perspective of Aboriginal people, not simply used as a basis for comparison. Similarly, Yothu Yindi's music and videos should be analysed on their own terms and not pre-empted or pre-judged by analyses arising out of a pre-defined ideological agenda.

(NB. All quotations attributed to Johnson in the following sections are taken from an interview conducted by the author in Sydney in August 1992.)

'Treaty I'

'Treaty I' was released in February 1991. As the title suggests, the song addresses the unfulfilled promises of a treaty between settlers and indigenous Australian peoples. This was first discussed between (then) Prime Minister Bob Hawke and Northern Lands Council chairman Galarrwuy Yunupingu during meetings between government officials and Aboriginal elders at the Barunga Sports and Cultural Festival in the Northern Territory in June 1988. It was agreed by both sides that the treaty should be concluded in 1990. Yothu Yindi's connection with the treaty proposal, and formal negotiations between Aboriginal and non-Aboriginal Australians, dates back to the 1960s when the fathers of the Yolngu members of the band initiated, from their homelands around Yirrkala in north-east Arnhem Land, the process that led to the first Land Rights legislation. Galarrwuy Yunupingu was, in fact, lead singer Mandawuy Yunupingu's brother. The English language lyrics of 'Treaty I' reflect this history:

> Well I heard it on the radio
> And I saw it on the television
> Back in 1988, all those talking politicians
> Words are easy, words are cheap
> Much cheaper than our priceless land
> But promises can disappear
> Just like writing in the sand...
>
> Treaty Yeh, Treaty Now, Treaty Yeh, Treaty Now ...
>
> This land was never given up
> This land was never bought and sold
> The planting of the Union Jack[2]
> Never changed our law at all ...

'Treaty' was the third of Yothu Yindi's songs to have a video made for it, videos for the previous two being produced by the Sydney-based production group Axolotl. (For discussion of the previous videos see Muecke, 1990 and Hayward, 1992.) Both 'Treaty I' and 'II' were directed by the (Euro-Australian) filmmaker Stephen Johnson. Whereas Axolotl were flown up to the Northern Territory from Sydney to work with Yothu Yindi, Johnson was a director with far closer ties to the band, community and locality. Johnson, who spent time in Darwin and went to school with Stuart Kellaway, one of the Euro-Australian members of the band, developed close ties with Yothu Yindi and the Yolngu tribe during the making of the two 'Treaty' videos. The degree of his involvement with both the band and their cultural context and traditions in making the two music videos is remarkable in both a national and global context. Music video, a form often dismissed by critics as banal, superficial and hastily assembled according to a set of standard (and clichéd) industrial criteria, is given a whole new meaning in this context. Instead of simply being made *for* the band, Johnson's two videos were the result of a sustained creative and communicative process, which even involved Johnson's formal adoption into the Gumatj clan from which the majority of Yothu Yindi are drawn.

In contrast to the standard industrial procedure whereby music videos are pitched and commissioned on the strength of storyboarded treatments, Johnson approached the production process with a set of ideas which he was ready and willing to modify as the project took shape. As he has constantly emphasized, the end product videos were the result of collaboration and collective improvisation. Before any shooting took place, he conducted long and involved negotiations with not only the band themselves but the four families connected to band members and Gumatj tribal elders. Such discussions served both to facilitate the co-operation of the tribe in the production and to establish what was permissible under tribal law. Subsequent to these discussions, further briefing sessions were held in order to explain the filming processes for agreed sections. This process of production is important to keep in mind in order to understand and analyse the nature of individual and collective input into the videos.

The 'Treaty I' video visually supports and reinforces the song's lyrics, often directly visualizing them – as in the sequence when the lyrics 'And I saw it on the television' are accompanied by footage of Yolngu children watching a TV in a school classroom. This image in turn cuts to off-air footage of Bob Hawke throwing a spear and playing the yid̲aki (didjeridu)[3] during a visit to a tribal community. The political charge of such sequences is further reinforced by footage of a self-originated Aboriginal treaty being painted and images of open-cut mining shot in Arnhem Land. These forceful pictures are inserted between positive and spirited images of contemporary Aboriginality with a strong emphasis on youth. Resilience, strength and spirit are conveyed through images of young Aboriginal children dancing and playing on the beach to the sounds of a ghetto-blaster and bouncing and tumbling acrobatically on a beachside trampoline. The vitality and resilience of their culture is glorified by potent and mesmerizing tribal dance sequences set in lush bushland with close-ups of painted faces and body parts in motion. The tenacity of their culture is confirmed by images of young and old dancing in both traditional and contemporary styles at a Yothu Yindi concert. The footage of Yothu Yindi in concert focuses predominantly on Mandawuy

Yunupingu singing, but also features low-angle shots of other band members and dancers. These serve to bring everything back to the ground, signifying the central importance of the land to Aboriginal culture.

With the exception of the footage of Hawke and brief, 'flash' inserts of Aboriginal street protests, the entire video was shot on Aboriginal land in Arnhem Land. According to Johnson it was never his intention to make a consciously 'political' video. He was instead concerned to project Yothu Yindi in a generally affirmative style. As he has emphasized:

> For me it is political enough in the sense that it is showing a positive, healthy and strong side of Aboriginal culture ... The words, who they are and what they are doing, in the context in which they are doing it, is strong enough.

'Treaty II' – The Filthy Lucre Remix

The Filthy Lucre 12-inch dance remix was released in June 1991 and went on to reach number four in the Australian singles charts. The unprecedented success of the second version of 'Treaty' was all the more remarkable since it was achieved with a remix which featured a version of the song sung almost entirely in an indigenous Aboriginal language (Gumatj). The audio remix was not simply an afterthought, prompted by the disappointing chart performance of 'Treaty I', but was decided upon before the 'Treaty I' video was shot. Mushroom Records saw the potential of a dance-orientated remix and hired the services of Melbourne-based sound mixers and producers Gavin Campbell, Robert Goodge and Paul Main in order to produce one. The Filthy Lucre remix was produced without the band's involvement but with the understanding that the 'Yolngu side' of the music was preserved. The final remix was submitted to Mandawuy Yunupingu for approval and subsequently released.

The remix did not just modify the musical track behind the vocals but also substantially edited the vocal track, dispensing with the majority of the English language lyrics. The remix only retains three phrases of the original English lyrics and an extended version of the chorus:

> Well I heard it on the radio
> And I saw it on the television
> Back in 1988, all those talking politicians
> Treaty Yeh, Treaty Yeh, Treaty Now [repeat]

The remix begins with a female voice shouting 'Clap your hands and dance' which then blends into a Sixties-style electric organ riff. The Gumatj lyrics from the original are retained, extended, made more prominent and elevated in the mix; as are the yidaki and bilma (clapsticks). Additional elements include the prominent use of synthesizer, bass and drum machine, and occasional samples.

The visual images of the 'Treaty II' video concentrate on movement and dance. The overtly political shots of Hawke, the treaty painting, the street protests and mining from 'Treaty I' (as well as static sequences such as the children watching TV) are dispensed with. This reflects Johnson's response to the Filthy Lucre audio remix. Discussing his ideas for the video he recalled that 'the first time I heard [the track] I thought and felt: colour, movement, chaos, kids, dancing ... there was nothing political that needed to be portrayed'.

The video's images are framed by horizontal 'cinemascope' cut-off lines at the top and bottom of the frame, giving them a filmic effect which enhances the idea of space. The colour of the mask sections accentuates yellow shades, a symbolically important colour for the Gumatj people. Rapid editing makes the video's visual rhythms appear much faster than the 'Treaty I' video and the camera is moved in swirling, often jerky, motions to mirror the tribal dance styles and music rhythms it represents. The video is a montage of dance, movement and energy; again with a strong emphasis on healthy, strong, beaming youth, dancing and tumbling on the beach. As in 'Treaty I, tribal dancing amidst lush bushland is heavily featured but this time with close-ups of torsos, feet, hands and faces in motion, often backlit by white, red or yellow lighting creating a silhouette which defines outline and movement more distinctly. Aboriginal instruments take on a life of their own as they are prominently featured. The opening sequences of the video, for instance, capture two musicians on the beach, setting their playing of the yidaki and bilma against the striking blue of the water behind them. This image sequence is frequently returned to throughout the video, though subsequent sequences focus more on the instruments, with slow-motion pans along the length of the yidaki.

The new footage in the 'Treaty II' video, also shot in Arnhem Land, is more scenic and colourful than much of the original, with dramatic and spectacular images of land, vegetation and sea. Fire is also used extensively as an image. This provides both dramatic colour and visual effects and is also tribally significant. Children feature more prominently in the second video with new footage of kids dancing on the beach and there are, notably, more young, happy and healthy *girls*. Unlike 'Treaty I', which featured images of children mouthing the words 'Treaty Yeh, Treaty Now' and shaking their fists at the screen, in this version they play, frolic and push each other in the water. The images of the children are powerful nonetheless. Their faces glow and smiles abound, highlighting vitality and optimism for a better future. Children are a central focus for Yothu Yindi – which literally translates as 'Child and Mother' – and the band itself is conceived as a continuing project. It is envisaged that younger members will replace existing musicians in the future, maintaining Yothu Yindi as a musical and educational resource and continuing to provide inspiration and strength for Yolngu people.

'Treaty I' to 'Treaty II' – changes and criticisms

As I have outlined, the musical and visual changes between 'Treaty I' and 'II' have attracted significant critical discussion, much of it based on specific political positions. Criticism, in the main, has focused on the removal of overtly political English language lyrics and imagery from 'Treaty II'. In an article entitled 'World Music, Indigenous Music and Music Television in Australia' (1992), Tony Mitchell discusses the manner in which the erosion of original musical 'force' in the 'Treaty II' remix is paralleled by the visual emphasis of the video which, he argues, foregrounds the exotic in place of political sentiments. He suggests that these changes benefited the band commercially, negatively implying that Yothu Yindi gave in to commercial pressure and suggesting that 'the removal of potentially confronting political material has paid off in terms of popularity' (*ibid.*: 14). The underlying assumption seems to be that Aboriginal musicians should make overtly confronting political music and videos. This seems to deny them the artistic and commercial freedoms that Anglo-Celtic musicians enjoy. Sure enough, the song *is* about a treaty, but the words of Johnson spring to mind: 'who they are, and what they are doing, in the context they are doing it, is strong enough'.

In Philip Hayward's 'Music Video, The Bicentenary (and After)' (1992), criticisms of selling-out and compromise due to the commercial pressures of entering the world music market are again levelled at 'Treaty II'. Similar to Mitchell's critique, Hayward's analysis again represents the application of a pre-set agenda to 'Treaty'. A study of the Bicentenary (and After), centring on the politicization of a popular cultural discourse, was, after all, unlikely to view the removal of overtly political imagery from the video as anything other than a cop-out by an Aboriginal band. However, both accounts do recognize the positive outcomes of Yothu Yindi's success, such as the introduction of indigenous modes of popular music to both listeners and viewers. Hayward also emphasizes the use of optimistic and positive images of Yolngu people for furthering Aboriginal political projects. Despite such acknowledgments, these authors' critiques assess 'Treaty II' in a fundamentally negative manner which principally represents the imposition of their own personal radical politics on material produced by artists from outside their social and cultural milieu.

Assessments of the political 'correctness' of 'Treaty II' are largely the product of personal convictions but undoubtedly mitigate against the freedom of artistic choice of the musicians and video makers involved in its production. Judgements on whether 'Treaty II' is 'political enough' are based on the premise that it *has to be* overtly political in the first place. A contextual reading can produce different emphases. As Johnson explained, the remix dictated the changes he made to the second video:

> We wanted to portray Yolngu people having a good time ... we had the political stuff in the first clip ... it is political enough in the sense that it is

> showing a positive, healthy and strong side of Aboriginal culture – that's the
> best message of all ... I wanted people to dance, pick up on the movements
> and Yolngu style of dancing.

The Filthy Lucre remix of 'Treaty' is a dance song, the (English) lyrics are
more fragmented and less prominent than in 'Treaty I' and the political
force of the video's images is far more subtle. The visuals focus
(unsurprisingly enough) on dance and movement, in both traditional and
contemporary style; and Yolngu people, especially the young, are shown
having a great time, enjoying the land and celebrating the music of Yothu
Yindi.

Criticisms based on the alleged loss of overt political messages are
simplistic because they ignore the nature of the song(s') and videos'
production and the complexity of the individuals and collaborative groups
involved. The philosophy of bandleader Mandawuy Yunupingu is one
which requires the blending of both Yolngu and Balanda (European) ways
and was summarized in the final line of their debut single 'Mainstream'
(1989), with its lyrical call 'Yolngu, Balanda = Australia' ('Yolngu
Aboriginal culture (*together* with) Euro-Australian culture = contemporary Australia). 'Treaty I' reaffirmed this with its lyrics:

> Now two rivers run their course
> Separated for so long
> I'm dreaming of a brighter day
> When the waters will be one

The song itself enshrines this principle, being written in collaboration
with established Euro-Australian singer-songwriters Paul Kelly and Peter
Garrett. This collaboration is the manifestation of 'bothways' in action.
The importance for Mandawuy is the maintenance of 'our values, beliefs
and principles ... and I think we have the strength to do that ... We aim
to make people aware that we have a unique culture that can coexist with
western culture' (unattributed, 1991: 27).

'Treaty I' and 'Treaty II' illustrate the philosophy of Mandawuy
Yunupingu, capture the uniqueness of Yolngu culture and, in the process,
strengthen and preserve it. Importantly too, the production of 'Treaty I'
and 'II' serve to maintain the values, beliefs and principles that are central
concerns for Yunupingu and the Yolngu people. Rather than simply
representing Yolngu-Aboriginal politics in a simplistic and visually
obtrusive way, the *process of production* of the videos is paramount,
and its procedures faithful, and even submissive to, Yolngu ways and
philosophy. As Johnson emphasized in his interview, the production of
the videos respected Yolngu society's distinct time and pace, rather than
the hectic, forced schedules of metropolitan Balanda culture. Consultation
on all aspects of the production process was carried out with elders and
translations were carefully arranged, with Johnson himself learning

Gumatj to facilitate the process. Careful scrutiny was extended to all visual images featured, however fleetingly, so as to ensure that sacred images would not be represented to a general audience. Unlike standard music video fare, there is a careful choice of what is *not* shown as well as what is.

In the production of the 'Treaty' videos, modern technology and modes of production were utilized to work with, and be affected by, tribal customs. In the process, each culture learnt from and enriched the other. 'Bothways' is therefore evident not just in the images on offer but in the production processes which produced them. At a time when artistic freedom is limited by numerous economic, legal, social and cultural restraints, the 'Treaty' singles and videos are remarkable for their accomplishments and collaborative enterprise. To castigate them for a perceived diffusion of overt politics between 'Treaty I' and 'II' is to deny their specific achievements. In the world of MTV and globally exploited world music, the production of the 'Treaty' videos in ways faithful to Yolngu custom and tradition is far more of an achievement – 'political' or otherwise – than the simple lyrical or visual sloganeering which have so preoccupied their critics.

Notes

Academics wishing to use the 'Treaty' videos for teaching purposes should contact Alan James, manager of Yothu Yindi (fax: +61 (0) 89 411088; e-mail: < YothuYindi@YothuYindi.com >).

1. This chapter originally appeared in *Perfect Beat* vol. 1, no. 2, January 1993 (accompanied by a short response by Tony Mitchell).
2. The British national flag.
3. The Yolngu refer to the didjeridu as the yid̲aki – the word 'didjeridu' (in various spellings) was one initially coined and popularized by Euro-Australians.

14

Safe, Exotic and Somewhere Else: Yothu Yindi, 'Treaty' and the Mediation of Aboriginality[1]

Philip Hayward

On 26 October 1992 The *Sydney Morning Herald* featured a wide-angle photo across eight columns under the headline NO TREATY YET, BUT TWO AUSTRALIAN SYMBOLS GETTING ON FINE (unattributed, 1992: 5). The photo showed (then) Prime Minister Paul Keating alongside Yothu Yindi front-man Mandawuy Yunupingu. Shot facing south from the grounds of the official prime ministerial residence in Sydney, Kirribilli House, the two figures were pictured against a classic Sydney skyscape. Spanning (from left to right), this comprised the Royal Botanic Gardens, the Opera House, Circular Quay, The Rocks and the Harbour Bridge – a cityscape erected around the location of the first European settlement/ invasion of (pre-colonial) Aboriginal Australia. The occasion of the meeting was the Federal Government's grant of $30,000 to the band to enable them to play at a concert in New York marking the launch of the United Nations International Year of the World's Indigenous People. Fittingly, in this context, the photo showed Keating in theatrical pose, pointing east, towards the harbour entrance and towards the Americas where Yothu Yindi were bound as officially sanctioned representatives of Aboriginal people and of Australia.

The award and associated publicity underlined Yothu Yindi's achievement as both performers and cultural ambassadors for the Gumatj people, Aboriginal culture and – in an international context – Australia itself. Their achievements are considerable and their ascendancy has been all the more marked given the previous absence of Aboriginal figures in the vanguard of Australian popular music. Such success is undoubtedly a sign of these (post-Bicentennial) times. But we need to ask questions about what this sign signifies in Australia, how its meanings circulate and how these meanings are publicly understood and subsequently represented.

Nicol's analysis of Yothu Yindi's 'Treaty' videos (see Chapter 13) provides a starting point for this. Her study is notable for detailing a degree of careful collaboration surely unmatched in any other previous music video production projects. Her analysis also comments on previous critical readings of Yothu Yindi's 'Treaty' song and videos (specifically Hayward and Mitchell, both 1992). Although her article documents the collaboration between (Euro-Australian) videomaker Stephen Johnson and the band, her critique of previous analyses of the video is based on a model which sees the different (audio and video) versions of 'Treaty' as somehow 'authentic' expressions of Gumatj and Aboriginal culture to which Mitchell's and my critiques are addressed. We are seen thereby to apply (Western) liberal-left cultural analyses to a product originating from a markedly different context to that of our own positions. In this context, Nicol argues that we seem to require Aboriginal cultural forms to carry the burden of being politically 'correct' – i.e. 'oppositional' – and thereby seek to limit their expressive potential. As this chapter will argue, however, political readings of the 'Treaty' texts – far from being *external* to its project – are fundamental to the production, circulation and reception of the audio and visual versions. And further, the reception and, most notably, success of the second 'remixed' versions of the song and video (henceforth referred to as 'Treaty II') are a significant index of the type of representation of Aboriginality deemed acceptable in contemporary Australian society and its media.

The analysis and critique of this process of representation is therefore one which addresses a dominant culture's representation and mediation of its 'other'. The various 'Treaty' texts are, arguably *primarily*, a set of elaborated representations of particular aspects of Aboriginality mediated through a succession of Euro-Australian cultural perceptions. Nicol's chapter openly acknowledges this through its study of Johnson's method of collaborative video production with the band and their tribal elders. It also goes further and accedes to Johnson's assertions that his closeness to Yothu Yindi and their broader community allows him, *de facto, to become one* with his represented group and subsequently relay their experience through his skills and sensibilities. In this manner Johnson is posed as a new figure, as a kind of ethno-music-video-cologist. Such a notion is an intriguing one but the parallel with the discipline of ethnomusicology can only be pushed so far. Perhaps the recording of live music performance on video might be considered a legitimate ethno-music-video-cological enterprise but the sort of complex representations on offer in the 'Treaty' videos clearly transcend documentation and belong to the realm of representation (with all the mediation that this involves).

When considering Yothu Yindi's 'Treaty' texts as mediated objects, we need to start further back than Johnson's mediation of the music texts through the interpretative medium of music video. Taking the first released audio track of 'Treaty' (henceforth 'Treaty I') as the initial version, what is perhaps most significant is that the initial text is already (at least) a triply-mediated expression of Aboriginality. First, as John Castles clearly argues in Chapter 1 in this anthology, *all* contemporary Aboriginal musics, let alone Aboriginal adaptations of imported forms such as Country, rock, rap or reggae, are the product of contact with foreign cultures, forever changed and recontextualized by that contact. 'Treaty', despite its use of traditional Aboriginal instrumentation, vocal intonations, rhythms and percussion sounds, combines aspects of rock, funk and house music. This is specifically foregrounded in Yothu Yindi by the group's (often forgotten) composition, in the early 1990s at least, as a multiracial band, also featuring Euro-Australian musicians (and, in the mid-1990s, Papua New Guinean performers). These musicians underscore the cross-cultural collaboration of the band by their playing of standard western (rhythm) instruments, the guitar, bass and drums, alongside Aboriginal musicians playing the yiḏaki (didjeridu) and bilma (clapsticks).

In the case of 'Treaty', the original English-language lyrics of 'Treaty I' are themselves the result of a collaboration between bandleader Mandawuy Yunupingu and noted Euro-Australian songwriters Peter Garrett and Paul Kelly.[2] In 'Treaty II', this cross-cultural traffic is further elaborated by the substitution of original English-language lyrics for Gumatj ones, where the lyrics function as an expression of the Aboriginality of the band. As is now well known, the lyrics of 'Treaty I' (reproduced by Nicol) address themselves to then prime minister Bob Hawke's 1988 promise to conclude a treaty between Aboriginal and non-Aboriginal Australians. More specifically, the lyrics demand that Hawke's promise be fulfilled *now*. The 'Treaty I' video visualizes these points with footage of Bob Hawke visiting an Aboriginal settlement, Aboriginal artists working on their own treaty document and miners scarring the outback landscape. As Nicol's chapter emphasizes, the political aspect of the 'Treaty I' video is further enhanced by sequences of children chanting and gesticulating to camera in support of the 'Treaty' refrain. Analyses of 'Treaty I' which refer to its political aspects therefore cannot be said to represent any forced 'reading in' but rather address levels of overt textual signification. It is only with the audio and video remixes, the 'Treaty II' texts, that critical dispute arises.

'Treaty II' is significantly different from its predecessor. In the video accompanying the remix, the inserted images referred to above are dispensed with − (literally) rendered invisible in tandem with a substitution of the English-language lyrics that render the song's vocals unintelligible to all but Gumatj speakers. As the narration in Godard and Gorin's film essay on Czechoslovakia, *Pravda* (1969), puts it, 'if you don't understand Czech you better learn quickly'. Of course, anglophone audiences can't and don't, and therefore do not understand what is sung. The same with 'Treaty II'. Shorn of the political groundings of 'Treaty I', 'Treaty II' provides a significantly different set of representations.

'Treaty II', like Yothu Yindi's other videos 'Mainstream' and 'Djapana', locates them as literally 'somewhere else'. The beaches and bush of Arnhem Land in the far Top End are as distant from the eastern metropolitan areas which comprise Australia's principal population centres as Bali – perhaps even more so, since the latter are more easily accessible. The band's cheerful and confident occupation of this territory signifies a healthy base to Aboriginal culture in Australia. In many ways the video is an Australian establishment Public Relations dream after the troubling presence of Aborigines at the Bicentennial celebrations of 1988 (which led Yothu Yindi, together with Peter Garrett and Paul Kelly, to write and record 'Treaty I' in the first place).

While 'Treaty II's' success and the rise in popularity of Yothu Yindi and other Aboriginal acts in the 1990s can be seen to draw on the pioneering work of many 1980s bands (such as Us Mob, No Fixed Address and Scrap Metal), their ascendancy can also be seen to deviate from, and in some aspects, reverse many of the fundamental character-istics Breen observed in the growth of distinct new Aboriginal music forms in the 1980s (Breen, 1992). But while the developments of the 1990s are in accord with the tendency identified by Breen whereby 'young Aborigines, buoyed by the 1979 visit of Bob Marley, began to see music as a form of black celebration and resistance' (160); they are clearly at one remove from that 1980s tendency whereby 'popular music ... took on a new meaning ... music became an overt vehicle for political use' (ibid.). The central shift in the 'Treaty' texts is the suppression of 'overt' politics between versions I and II in favour of representations of untroubled Aboriginal vitality. Breen's characterization of the transformation from the 1970s to the more pointed political address of the 1980s notes precisely those tendencies which are reversed again in 'Treaty II'. Discussing Aboriginal music in the early 1980s, Breen observes:

> Aboriginal use of popular music no longer allowed the cultural and anthropological indulgences of the exotic desert people and their tribal musics to be filed somewhere in the background of the European experience of Australia. There was no strange language or instrumentation to isolate the black person's experience from that of the European. (ibid.: 160–1).

Times have obviously changed. Now with Yothu Yindi, the yiḏaki (didjeridu) is prominent in the mix, the language is Gumatj and the place 'somewhere else'. With world music now fashionable in Australia, the mainstream market context for Aboriginal pop has shifted. As befits that market, there's little in the 'Mainstream' – 'Treaty II' – 'Djapana' singles and videos to suggest a history of the Euro-Australian genocide of Aboriginal people, the brief history of full Aboriginal citizenship or the continuing tragedy of black deaths in custody. They are all essentially 'feel good' videos. And why not, of course? As Nicol emphasizes, there's no mandatory responsibility for contemporary Aboriginal music or music video (or any other examples) to make overtly polemic points. Yothu Yindi's achievements and their role in promoting a positive image of black culture and identity is undeniable and beyond dispute, a major gain of the post-Bicentennial era.

But the tale of two versions won't conveniently disappear. 'Treaty I' represents the other side of Aboriginal politics to 'Treaty II' – political demand as opposed to subtler cultural assertion. And there is no doubt as to which is more broadly in tune with Australian society and the media that represents it. Even without the ghost of 'Treaty I' resonating angrily from the receding shadows of the Bicentenary year, it is clear that the images and associations of 'Treaty II' and 'Djapana' suit, and are employed by, agencies with particular agendas and political projects. The locales and milieu of Yothu Yindi's recent videos are at one remove from white Australian urban culture. This distance ensures safety; the exotic stays put; the politics are below the surface. The highly political lyrics of the original 'Treaty' are buried and/or replaced in the hit Filthy Lucre remix where the prominent vocals are passionately declared in the obscure Gumatj tongue and thereby become sounds as wonderfully exotic as those of Nusrat Fateh Ali Khan or the Mysterious Voices of Bulgaria – generic World Music for jaded cosmopolitan palates.

In the early 1990s there was something reassuringly comforting for Euro-Australians in an Aboriginal band singing in their own tongue amidst dream holiday/exotic surroundings at a time when the USA was convulsed by the Los Angeles riots that followed the Rodney King case; when Ice-T's band, Body Count, were the centre of a national controversy over the (subsequently dropped) album track 'Cop Killer'; and when Public Enemy's Sister Souljah attracted the ire of (then) US presidential candidate Bill Clinton for her statement that blacks should take a week off killing fellow blacks and gives whites a turn. At that historic moment Rage and MTV Australia were screening Yothu Yindi's 'Djapana' – a song of 'Sunset Dreaming'.

To reiterate, the critiques advanced in this chapter are not directed at the band themselves but rather their *representation* and *representing agencies*. To note the nature of their representation is not to foist a Euro-Australian radical project upon them but to recognize the Euro-Australian hegemonic discourses which have created their cultural identity, and thus, context of reception. There is, after all, a consensual convenience to their elevation as Australian cultural ambassadors in the post-Bicentennial period. Their colourful ethnicity has rendered them highly 'media friendly' in an environment whose institutions are, more than ever before, aware of the political correctness of including *occasional* representations of Aboriginality in their material. The public broadcasters, ABC and SBS, have been notable in this, greatly aiding Yothu Yindi through interview features on programmes such as SBS TV's *First In Line* (1989) and 'specials' such as the ABC TV's *First Australians – Yothu Yindi On Tour* (1990).

It is some measure of the progress made since 1988 that the ABC chose to televise *Stompem Ground '92* – the Kimberley Aboriginal Music and Cultural Festival in Broome, as part of its celebration of its Sixtieth Anniversary as a broadcaster. This was a bold and imaginative move on the part of the corporation (and a welcome respite from the station's orgies of opera). It was also good news, a symbolic coming-of-media-age, for the bands and communities involved. Yet the promotional pre-packaging of the event again returned the concert and attendant media event to the safe picturesque 'exoticness' displayed in Yothu Yindi videos. The ABC TV trailer played in the lead-up to the event featured brief visual snippets of the bands (specifically Yothu Yindi and Scrap Metal) in graphic slices montaged with images of 'wild nature' and Northern Territory natural landscapes. Here, bracketed by desert lightning, waterfalls and mountains – all highly reminiscent (if not directly sourced from) the ABC's sell-through video 'Kimberley: Land of Wandjina' – the different bands were effectively rendered part of the landscape, as organic cultural outcrops. Rock music's manufactured qualities, so often cited by the cultural establishment, are miraculously dissolved by the cultural authenticity of Aboriginality and Aboriginal rock rendered unproblematically indigenous.

Viewed positively, the telecast of the event and the airplay of videos such as 'Treaty II' and 'Djapana' can be seen to affirm and foster Aboriginal solidarity. They can be understood to communicate affectively, that is to reinforce the traditional *feeling* identified by Archie Roach who argues, of his own music, that

> the spiritual values are still there. That's what I'd rather get across to people. If the spirit dies nothing else is going to be much use. (Breen, 1992: 170)

It could also be argued that the affirmative representation of the *Stompem Ground* coverage also served to forge affective alliances by showing positive role models and images to the broader viewing public, or rather, and more accurately, the type of audience who would watch a seven-hour midnight-to-dawn show on a Friday night. Significantly, despite the cultural value placed on the bands and music in the programme, ABC TV steered clear of anything truly daring such as taking over Peter Ross's Sunday afternoon culture slot to show highlights of the event to a different, and arguably less informed, audience. Aboriginal rock may function as 'culture' in the Rage slot, but it clearly is not perceived to do so elsewhere. In this way, the *Stompem Ground* coverage was as safely remote in its overnight slot as the Yirrkala lands of 'Treaty' and Broome itself are from the metropolitan East Coast. *Stompem Ground*, like Yothu Yindi and 'Treaty II' thereby was resolutely safe, exotic and somewhere else.

Ultimately Nicol is right in asserting that the 'Treaty' videos have been singled out for unusually sustained analysis by critics intent on probing and characterizing the politics of the videos' representations. But such a concentration is not surprising. 'Treaty' is not just any old song or video, it's a new high water mark for Aboriginal culture's access to the popular cultural mainstream. The political shift which marks the transition from 'Treaty I' to 'Treaty II' is also the shift which moved the band from musical fringe dwellers to dance party darlings. The symmetry of this shift is, at the very least, unsettling.

What we have with 'Treaty' is not just a tale of two versions but rather a clash of two socio-cultural–economic paradigms. The *signifying text* – 'Treaty I' – missed its mark in the broad pop arena and proved awkward and dissonant. 'Treaty II', by contrast, with its politics rendered opaque by its linguistic and stylistic substitutions, hit home and hit the charts. As Yothu Yindi's manager Alan James, video director Stephen Johnson and Mushroom Records boss Michael Gudinski have variously and repeatedly argued, this broad commercial success is also a positive affirmation of the band's Aboriginality. They are obviously right. This lends support to the view that the overtly signified politics of 'Treaty I' were naïve, unnecessary, heavy-handed and counter-productive. Overt political commentary in popular music is seen as a commercial 'turn-off' here, a hindrance to Yothu Yindi's push for broader acceptance. But here we hit the problems. This 'common sense' assessment betrays a more specific market calculation. It is not signified politics *per se* that are the problem, it is radical – or almost *any* other kind of – Aboriginal politics that are perceived to grate on mass market sensibilities.

A brief catalogue of examples of Western popular music proves illuminating in this regard. Midnight Oil, champions and lyrical polemicists for a raft of socio-political causes, achieved considerable commercial success in the late 1980s and early 1990s. And internationally, to name but two celebrated examples, the Special AKA's UK hit single 'Free Nelson Mandela' (1984) and Artists United Against Apartheid's US hit single 'Sun City' (1985), lit and stoked the anti-apartheid cause in Western pop (and eventually resulted in the high-profile Mandela festivals held at London's Wembley Stadium in 1988 and 1990, which were televised worldwide). The bottom line is that it is *Aboriginal* politics, in all but the most subtly rendered shapes, that is still too confrontational for Australian sensibilities. In this regard, it is increasingly apparent that it is only the celebratory cultural vision of 'Treaty II' and Yothu Yindi's general public image that have a hope in hell of mobilizing broad-based affective alliances around Aboriginal culture and rights in contemporary Australia. But the danger with Yothu Yindi's public acceptance – and the softening of their call for treaty promises to be honoured – is that it allows mainstream Australian culture to congratulate itself on its new-found tolerance and receptiveness to (one) Aboriginal band.

Reinscribed into the international media space, the political signification of Yothu Yindi and their success with mainstream Australian pop audiences inevitably becomes dissipated. It evaporates like morning mist under a hot Northern Territory sun. The band's fleeting inclusion in the global broadcast of the 1991 MTV International Awards show exemplified this. Included in a rapid montage of sequences from Best International Videos, voted by viewers from the regions concerned, an extract from 'Treaty II' was sandwiched between Sepultera's 'Orgasmatron' (Best Brazilian video) and Cui Jin's 'Wild in the Snow' (Best Asian video). Returning to the kinds of visual symbolism referred to in the introduction to this chapter, the video was introduced by MTV Australia VJ Richard Wilkins in a brief sequence. This was shot – with sublime irony – on Sydney Harbour Bridge, with its scenic background of the Opera House and Sydney Cove, the geographical and symbolic epicentre of the 1988 Bicentenary celebrations. To all but a few, such ironies were lost in a kaleidoscope of the exotic – the 'other' that gave the MTV Awards their global colour and verified their international appeal. In this context, the fleeting rehabilitation of Pee Wee Herman, fresh from arrest on a public indecency charge in the USA, was a hotter issue than 200 years of Aboriginal oppression and 'Treaty' just another chant echoing across the global dance floor.

As Tony Mitchell (1992) has pointed out, in the international context the danger is not simply marginalization, the fragmentation of (loaded) signifiers in a global media bricolage of superficial affect – it is of reassignation, the re-reading of signifiers within re-figured discourses of racism and primitivism. As Mitchell has identified, the most notable culprit here is the 1993 Hollywood film *Encino Man*. The film relates the story of a prehistoric cave dweller who materializes in present day Los Angeles and encounters a deeply confusing world. Adrift from his primitive roots he searches for points of identification. Standing in a lounge room peering puzzled at a TV set he suddenly finds one. Yothu Yindi's 'Treaty II' video comes on screen. Instinctively his body picks up the beat and begins to imitate the stiff-limbed movements of the band's dancers. Albeit momentarily, he reconnects to his past and – simultaneously – reveals the filmmaker's ideological casting of Yothu Yindi as (latterday) primitives; 'holdovers' from pre-history.[3]

If Yothu Yindi, the Gumatj and Aboriginal peoples of Australia cannot be expected to carry radical cultural struggle in all their artefacts – and they undoubtedly cannot – critics can, through our 'left-liberal' discourses, examine the nature of mediations accomplished by Euro-Australian cultural representatives, agencies and media. If Cultural Studies is to be anything other than an exercise in passive consumption and banal commentary, we must retain a focus on the relation of cultural production to social change. It is clearly important to applaud Yothu Yindi's success but it is just as important to retain a critical focus and to recognize that the singling out of Yothu Yindi as (in manager Alan James's words) 'the flagship for Aboriginal Australia' (unattributed, 1992: 5), conveniently serves to elide all that is troubling to Euro-Australian culture.

Notes

Academics wishing to use the 'Treaty' videos for teaching purposes should contact Alan James, manager of Yothu Yindi (fax: +61 (0) 89 411088; on e-mail: < YothuYindi@YothuYindi.com >).

1. An extended version of this chapter originally appeared in *Perfect Beat* vol. 1, no. 2, January 1993.
2. NB. Garrett, however, is omitted from the list of credited composers for the song, who are listed on the CD sleeve as: Yunupingu, M.; Kelly; Mununggur; Kellaway; Williams; and Yunupingu, G.
3. The (supposedly well-respected) American music writer John Schaefer (1990) describes the didjeridu as a 'holdover from the Pleistocene Era – like the duckbill platypus and the dingo' (134). See Hayward and Neuenfeldt (1997: 1–3) for further discussion.

15

Yothu Yindi: Agendas and Aspirations

Karl Neuenfeldt

There is a fear of losing one's culture because of the white man's influence. So what we've tried to do with Yothu Yindi is creating something about [Aborigines] taking pride in their identity, taking pride in their music, taking pride in their dance, taking pride in their rituals, taking pride in their secret sacred ceremonies. All those aspects of reality one should take seriously, [which] shouldn't be considered as if trivial. (Mandawuy Yunupingu, interview with the author, 1996)

Introduction

In June 1995 the Australian Aboriginal music group Yothu Yindi went on-line globally over the Internet with the following message:

Welcome to Yothu Yindi on the web. Download a message from Mandawuy Yunupingu – 1992 Australian of the Year – on the significance of the worldwide web in preserving the 40,000-year-old Yolngu wisdom and culture for future generations. We invite you to explore the Yolngu music, art and stories in our site. (http://www.yothuyindi.com)[1]

Distinctive features of the World Wide Website are the chance to learn about the Yolngu Aborigines of north-eastern Arnhem Land in the Northern Territory and to hear Yothu Yindi's music. However, the Web site offers more than entertainment. It also provides education about the culture and land that is vital to Yolngu identity, and how Yothu Yindi's music can provide a point of contact, a 'bothways' perspective, to empower Aboriginal and non-Aboriginal Australians.

By providing an Aboriginal voice on the Internet, Yothu Yindi are weaving World Wide Webs of significance, not only about their particular brand of syncretic music, but also more generally about Yolngu and other Aboriginal societies and cultures.[2] Their use of the Internet is noteworthy for several reasons. First, with over 500 visitors a week it affords access to a potentially large commercial audience for its music, as well as a potentially influential constituency for its extra-musical objectives. Second, it shows how contemporary artistic expression has helped move Aboriginal agendas and aspirations out of traditional cultural practice and into cyberspace, the global cultural economy and the universal pop aesthetic.

At the time Yothu Yindi went on-line, manager Alan James noted: 'We believe it is fitting that Yothu Yindi, a band dedicated to improving communication among peoples and cultures, is using the latest technological advancements to share its message with the world' (promotional fax, July 1995). The Internet is only part of their multimedia use of modern technology to promote Yolngu connections to land, its ownership and spiritual and physical resources, and to promote inter-cultural co-operation. They also use recordings, print and video in a concerted and co-ordinated campaign to disseminate their message as widely and to as many stakeholders as possible.

This chapter examines Yothu Yindi on several interwoven levels of cultural production and discourse: as a socio-cultural and musical phenomenon; as an example of how indigenous popular music informs the social construction of the soundscape and humanscape of Australia; and as a case study of how their career and strategies might provide insights into similar situations elsewhere. I argue that in the all-important 'business of culture' Yothu Yindi remain successful, although in commercial and critical terms they may have peaked in popularity. I also argue that Yolngu and Aboriginal cultural vitality is a much more valid gauge of success than either the whims of international media, audiences and industries, or the caprices of academic infatuation.

This chapter complements the observations of Hayward and Nicol in Chapters 12 and 13. They deal more directly with debates that accompanied the group's rise to prominence at a particular confluence of (local, national and international) socio-cultural and political events, which provided a favourable climate for their agendas and aspirations, and the emergence of the transnational popular music genre of world music, which provided a commercial and aesthetic outlet for their music. Hayward's and Nicol's chapters – and this study, for that matter – are examples of the provisional and contested nature of Yothu Yindi, who mean different things to different people at different times. They will continue to do so because they have become a metonym, located at the interstices of popular music, technology and contemporary indigeneity. Yothu Yindi is a cogent example of the multiple, interwoven and vital roles of popular music in shaping individual, group and national identity.

In addition to providing an update on academic debates that were prominent in 1992–94,[3] this chapter focuses more specifically on some of the small, but cumulatively crucial details of cultural production and discourse. Consequently, I describe and discuss how Yothu Yindi operates simultaneously as a product and a process through the multiple use of media. Yothu Yindi is a product in the international music market and on the Internet and a process in the evolution of Yolngu, pan-Aboriginal and 'mainstream' Australian societies and cultures. The quotations at the beginning of each section demonstrate this simultaneity.

Yothu Yindi as a product

The struggle [previously] was to find ways of explaining our laws and beliefs to white Australia in an attempt to retain all that is important and sacred in Yolngu life – our land. That struggle ... is what you hear in Yothu Yindi's songs ... In our songs we have found a way to help people hear us today. (Yunupingu, 1994: 4)

Through a combination of hard work and good luck Yothu Yindi have reached a level of success unequalled by any other Aboriginal music group to date. They have won numerous industry, songwriting and humanitarian awards and have toured internationally in North and South America, Oceania, Asia, Europe and Africa. However, as indigenous music groups and their sounds (and sentiments) move away from their origins they can be reshaped and reinterpreted until their self-representations (Langton, 1993) may end up bearing little resemblance to their original intentions (Feld, 1994).[4] This is a not uncommon outcome when the local engages with the national and the transnational. There is ultimately no control over reception, but there is some control at the levels of product and production, some agency, albeit mediated.

Yothu Yindi have released four albums: *Homeland Movement* (1989), *Tribal Voice* (1991, *Freedom* (1993) and *Birrkuta – Wild Honey* (1996). From the beginning of their recording career, their albums have tried to integrate Yolngu and Western musics and to develop a syncretic form of their own. A Yolngu music form which appears on some Yothu Yindi recordings is *djatpangarri*. Knopoff describes it as 'a song form that developed at Yirrkala during the Mission era (late 1930s through early 1970s)' (1997: 66), and adds that 'in contrast to the religious, ceremonial nature of clan songs, *djatpangarri* songs are purely recreational in nature' (*ibid.*). *Djatpangarri* songs deal with commonplace or current phenomena, and can imply 'personal relations between individuals through reference to the names of particular secondary kinship groups (*malk*) that the individuals belong to' (*ibid.*). The Western music forms used by Yothu Yindi on their albums range across the spectrum of contemporary styles: folk, rock, country rock, heavy metal, dance and ambient. This reflects the eclecticism found in many indigenous peoples' popular music tastes and exhibited on many indigenous recordings.

It is valuable to examine closely the cultural production and discourse of the albums themselves. They are central to the public face of Yothu Yindi and reflect the evolution of their music, sound, visual style and marketing strategies. They also reinforce extra-musical objectives. The first album, *Homeland Movement* (in cassette format), features one full side each of (predominantly) Western- and Yolngu-influenced music. The songs on side one are recorded in standard pop-rock style with minimal production. They are predominantly sung in English, although the themes are Yolngu, such as in the song 'Homeland Movement' which deals with Yolngu people returning to ancestral areas from settlements to which they had been forcibly moved. Most of these songs have been subsequently re-recorded with fuller production. The songs on side two are mostly traditional, feature clapsticks and didjeridu accompaniment, and are sung in Yolngu. Thematically, they deal with the natural environment and Yolngu relationships to it. On *Homeland Movement* the integration of the two main music influences is limited, and somewhat stilted at times, but indicates future directions.

The second album, *Tribal Voice*, shows increasing musical sophistication and integration. This reflects the use of high-quality recording technology, an experienced producer in Mark Moffitt, and the addition of musicians such as Ricki Fataar (Beach Boys, Bonny Raitt) and Tim Finn (Crowded House). The songs are once again sung in English and Yolngu *Matha* but the musical integration is smoother. The Yolngu and Western songs are no longer separated from each other but are sequenced or integrated together in a coherent whole. Sonically, the clapsticks and didjeridu are consolidated within the pop-rhythm section to establish the pulse of many of the songs (see Neuenfeldt, 1993). *Tribal Voice* also features two versions of the song 'Treaty' (see Chapters 12 and 13 and Lawe-Davies, 1993). There are several anthemic songs, such as 'Tribal Voice' and 'My Kind of Life' which explicitly celebrate indigeneity and promote cultural vitality.

The third album, *Freedom*, continues in the same fashion as *Tribal Voice* but is more diverse given the input of four producers (Ian Faith, Bill Laswell, Lamar Lowder, Robert Musso); the use of different studios and guest musicians; and song co-writers such as David Bridie (Not Drowning, Waving), Ian Faith, Andrew Farriss (INXS) and Neil Finn (Crowded House). Anthemic songs such as 'Timeless Land', 'World of Innocence', 'Freedom', 'World Turning' and 'Our Generation' once again celebrate indigeneity but in a more global sense than just Arnhem Land or Australia. A noteworthy stylistic refinement is displayed in 'Gapu' ('Tidal Mix') which augments a traditional-style vocal with sound effects and an elaborate and rhythmic arrangement to create the hypnotic ambience of 'the ocean water coming in and creating the full tide then going out again' (*Freedom* liner notes).[5]

The latest album, *Birrkuta – Wild Honey*, further extends Yothu Yindi's musical syncretism. It features a core of long-term musicians and singers (Jodie Cockatoo Creed, Stuart Kellaway, Milkayngu Mununggurr and Galarrwuy, Gurrumul, Makuma and Mandawuy Yunupingu) augmented by the musical and songwriting input of keyboardist/guitarist Andrew Farriss (INXS) and the production of Lamar Lowder. Of special note is the contribution of the Papua New Guinean members of the group, Baruka Tau-Matagu and Ben Hakalits, who are accomplished arrangers, writers and multi-instrumentalists. Aside from playing Western instru- ments they also contribute kundu drum and woodwinds. This new influence is most apparent on the chant-like 'Spirit of Peace' which begins with a traditional-style Papua New Guinean flute passage. On *Birrkuta – Wild Honey* the Yolngu and Western songs are mixed together, with a variety of lead singers and songwriters. Overall, there are fewer anthemic songs, more rhythmic variety, and a sense of allowing core members of the group to take on a variety of musical and songwriting roles.

Just as Yothu Yindi's musical style has become progressively more integrated and sophisticated, so too has their visual style and iconography.[6] These are integral to the group's overall presentation as a product. Their album packaging has won awards for design excellence and features original paintings and high-quality photography. Liner notes go beyond the usual acknowledgment of song copyright and performance/ songwriting credits. The cultural politics of arts funding is acknowledged by noting organizations that have assisted the recording projects (e.g. the Aboriginal and Torres Strait Islander Commission; the Department of Employment, Education and Training; and the Aboriginal Arts Board).

Importantly, liner notes also include specific and essential Yolngu cultural information. For example, indicating the clan affiliation of Yolngu songs, providing a brief précis in English for songs in Yolngu *Matha*, and crediting Galarrwuy Yunupingu's contribution on the *Freedom* album as vocals, bilma (clapsticks) and clan leader. The intricacy of protocols of use and acknowledgment is shown in the information provided for the cover painting of *Birrkuta – Wild Honey*. It cites Gawirrin Gumana (a senior elder from Gangan) and Wuyal Wirrpanda (the *Djungaya* songman for the design) for permission to use Trevor Warralka Wunungmurra's cover art. Also cited are the assistant painter (Mitjayna Wunungmurra) and the conceptual and background painting (Yalmay Yunupingu).

The packaging of the Yothu Yindi Website is similarly informative and of high quality. Along with introductory data, there is additional cultural information, and sound samples and visuals are available under the categories of The Band, Discography, Tour Dates, Sound and Video, Art Gallery, Our Home, Our Vision and Web Links. As well as being able to order albums and video tapes direct, other products are on offer such as T-shirts, didjeridus and videos. Throughout the album and Website packaging there is consistent emphasis on the interconnections between land, music, art and Yolngu, and the possibility of 'bothways' co-operation between Yolngu and Balanda (Europeans). In order to meet the demands of the market-place and thus facilitate the dissemination of Yolngu (and pan-Aboriginal) political agendas and aspirations, Yothu Yindi may be packaged as a product. However, successfully exploiting available technologies also contributes to Yothu Yindi's polysemy as a process.

Yothu Yindi as a process

> Your parents and grandparents saw us [Aborigines] as utterly mysterious and incomprehensible. For you lot [of people] we had to be different and inferior, otherwise your lot could not have treated us the way they did. They refused to see us as civilised people who owned land. Your lot wanted us to be just a blur on the land, like a smudge on paper that could be rubbed out. That was an important part of your colonising us. I am saying that it is time for those attitudes to be left behind. It is time you understood us as we are. (Yunupingu, 1994: 11)

There are different layers operating concurrently in the cultural production and discourse of Yothu Yindi as a process. There are several that are useful to note here. The first is the notion of what Hamilton (1993) refers to as 'anti-colonialist cultural criticism', defined as 'a practical commitment to the political consequences of representation [that] requires a rupture and a positive awareness of the way colonial representation has shaped, and mis-shaped, reality for colonizer and colonized alike' (ibid.: 5). The quotation at the beginning of this section is a persuasive example of Yothu Yindi as anti-colonialist cultural criticism. It points out the underlying premise of Western colonialism and the necessity of trying to move beyond a singular Eurocentric version of Australian history to re-represent its multiple histories. Yothu Yindi's songs, both in English and Yolngu *Matha* offer one of those histories. As identity narratives they chronicle the past and present experience of colonialism and offer templates for changing Australian society.

Similarly, the informational content of Yothu Yindi's packaging sometimes overtly critiques colonialism. For example, the story behind the use of the cover art work for *Birrkuta – Wild Honey* (noted above) is that the design belongs to the Manatja people, most of whom

> never recovered from a massacre in the early 1900s when most of its members were shot by intruders with guns and horses. Later, the skulls of some of those murdered were collected and sold to museums and universities for scientific study. (*Birrkuta – Wild Honey* liner notes)

One of the only two survivors is the mother of Mandawuy Yunupingu's wife Yalmay, who (as noted above) provided the conceptual and background painting for the cover artwork. Anti-colonialist cultural criticism is a consistent thread running through the discourse of Yothu Yindi (such as the song 'Luku – Wangawuy Manikay' [1788] on *Homeland Movement*), although its rhetoric is sometimes either circumspect or subsumed by the music and rhythm of the songs.

A second layer of Yothu Yindi as a process concerns notions of self-representation. In an Aboriginal context applicable directly to Yothu Yindi, Langton asserts that 'it is clearly unrealistic for Aboriginal people to expect that others will stop portraying us in photographs, films, on television, in newspapers, literature and so on' (1993: 10). So rather than demanding the impossibility of total control over representations, Langton suggests that 'it would be more useful to identify those points where it is possible to control the means of production and to make our own self-representations' (*ibid.*). In this sense, Yothu Yindi have had access to the means of production, either in the sense of technologies of musical production and reproduction or the promotional skills to disseminate their product and link it effectively to political objectives.

Other Aboriginal groups and soloists also have had access to the means of production (e.g. Archie Roach, Coloured Stone, Kev Carmody, Blek Bela Mujik), but Yothu Yindi have moulded a musical, visual and political image that contributes to a sense of a cohesive whole. They have survived and prospered while arguably more talented musicians and groups have not, perhaps because of being perceived, accurately or inaccurately, as rooted in something that transcends the moment. To draw momentarily on one of the false but persistent stereotypes of Aborigines, they have been perceived and often represented in the media as 'real blackfellas' with 'authentic' connections to 'tradition', unlike their urban counterparts.

Yothu Yindi are predicated on a notion of *self*-representation, even though, if necessary, this may take the form of technologically and industrially mediated syncretic music and Westernized rhetorical, lyrical and/or audio-visual styles. However, Yothu Yindi's self-representation is problematic in some respects in that the band are not *all* Aborigines, nor do they speak *for* all Aborigines. Similarly, accommodation and resistance within self-representation are fluid and relative concepts, especially when the relations of power (coercive and moral) are asymmetrical yet (somewhat) open to negotiation. If there is recognition of a level of agency in indigenous music groups such as Yothu Yindi, then accommodation is not necessarily antithetical to resistance. It may be an essential adjunct that neither demeans nor impedes the achievement of desirable end results.

A notable aspect of Yothu Yindi is the consistent emphasis that real, positive change in Australian society can only come about through dialogue, and that the two major cultural logics and world views (i.e. indigenous and Euro-Australian) do have some points of contact – places where boundaries can be crossed and bridges built. Yothu Yindi have consistently offered themselves as one of those points of contact. However, there is a sense that they also are well aware that their appeal as exotica can be useful in challenging what the Western world lacks (or thinks it lacks). Taken in a broader context, their efforts are part of indigenous peoples' efforts to 'seize the means of cultural expression to redefine a positive image of themselves' (Young, 1990:11). Yothu Yindi are consistently positive about the future even when recounting the negatives of the past. It is not a Pollyanna-ish or haphazard approach. It has been consistent throughout their career regardless of the ebb and flow of 'street-cred(ibility)', popularity, airplay or academic interest.

Conclusion

In this chapter I have described and discussed the cultural production and discourse of Yothu Yindi across various media, showing how the group operates simultaneously as a product and a process. These interwoven facets of Yothu Yindi help to fashion them into a cohesive whole in pursuit of specific agendas and aspirations. These revolve around land, Yolngu relationships with it and the roles of Aboriginal and non-Aboriginal Australians in creating a socio-cultural, musical and political climate where difference is accepted as valuable and diverse knowledges are recognized as valid.

For this (or any other) analysis to avoid uncritical lionization or over-critical dismissal, it is important to place Yothu Yindi in perspective. They are like any other popular music group, with a 'shelf-life' and a 'use-by' date, similar to other musical commodities on offer in the marketplace. It is rare for a group or soloist to sustain a career over any length of time and failures are more common than successes. That is the reality of the music business. In this context Yothu Yindi are no different when understood solely as a product. Their career has had a predictable, if somewhat meteoric, entertainment industry trajectory. They have gone from being a *cause célèbre* in the early 1990s to a present in which they are subject to equivocal and sometimes disparaging reviews.[7]

When popular music groups – especially indigenous ones – are also understood as a process, however, notions of what constitutes success have to be considered differently. Attention needs to be given to how consistent they have remained either to themselves (e.g. musically and aesthetically) or to the often politicized agendas and aspirations that may have inspired them. For indigenous artists, it is often in this latter sense, the all-important 'business of culture', that success is gauged, although commercial and critical success is certainly not irrelevant. Yothu Yindi have remained focused on what constitutes success to them and what roles their music can play in the pursuit of extra-musical objectives. The interconnection of the business of culture and the business of music is crucial to understanding indigenous groups such as Yothu Yindi. They may end up as culture brokers serving several masters simultaneously because they operate at the interstice of popular music, technology and contemporary indigeneity. However, they also can pursue their own agendas and aspirations within the parameters of Western cultural production and discourse. They are often fluently bi- or tri-cultural.

What has been left out of this analysis thus far is the effect and affect of Yothu Yindi on individuals. Although not all Aborigines would have the same views on Yothu Yindi.[8] Western Australian Aboriginal (Nyungar) educator and musician Clinton Quartermaine provided a compelling personal perspective on the role of Yothu Yindi, in particular, and indigenous popular music and musicians in general, when interviewed by the author at Edith Cowan University (Bunbury, Western Australia) in October 1992. His comments provide a fitting conclusion to this chapter because when all the trappings of cultural production and discourse are stripped away and analysis is set aside, it is still individuals who use popular music to fashion identity and help make sense of the private and public worlds in which they live.

> If you listen to [Aboriginal artists such as singer-songwriter] Archie Roach it reminds you of what happened in the past and the struggle still going on. But if you listen to Yothu Yindi, it gives you hope that somewhere along the line things have got to change. And if both [Aboriginal and non-Aboriginal] cultures can get together, like the Yothu Yindi band, then that relationship should come closer. Yothu Yindi do remind you [of the past] on one hand, but on the other hand they give you hope for what the future holds.

Acknowledgments

Special thanks to Steve Knopoff and Fiona Magowan for their suggestions, Cal Williams for Internet information and Ian Faith for insights on music production.

Notes

1. Yothu Yindi (pronounced 'yo-thoo-yin-dee') is a kinship-related term meaning 'child/mother'. 'Yolngu' is the term for 'human being' in related, regional Arnhem Land dialects. As a music group Yothu Yindi is a paradox in that it is considered (and celebrated as) an 'Aboriginal' band although it has always had both Aboriginal and non-Aboriginal members and management. As Beach (1995) argues, it has been commercially and critically successful and also has had a demonstrable positive effect in promoting the Northern Territory as a tourist destination.
2. There are several useful World Wide Websites that contain information on Australian indigenous peoples:

Australian National University < http//coombs.anu.edu.au/wwwvl-Aboriginal > ; Council for Aboriginal Reconciliation < http://www.austlii.edu.au/car/ > ; National Library of Australia < http://www.nla.gov.au/dnc/^aboriginal/ ^aborigrt.html > ;

indigenous peoples in general < http://www.halcyon.com/FWDP/ fwdp.html >

3. See, particularly, Castles (1992), Hayward (1992), Lipsitz (1994), Muecke (1992), Nicol (1993), Shoemaker (1994a and 1994b), Stubington and Dunbar-Hall (1994) and Turner (1995).

4. Langton offers an influential discussion of this process at work in Australia. The title of her book, *Well I Heard it on the Radio and Saw it on the Television* is taken from the Yothu Yindi song 'Treaty'. Feld (1994) provides a useful frame for understanding the splitting of sounds from their sources, while Feld (1996) uses 'pygmy pop' as an instructive case study of the process he labels 'schizophonia to schismogenesis'.

5. See Neuenfeldt (1993) for a discussion of the importance of water metaphors in Yothu Yindi's songs.

6. Dunbar-Hall (forthcoming, 1998) addresses this specifically in the context of Yothu Yindi album designs.

7. Examples of recent equivocal or negative reviews (supplied to the author by Mushroom Records) are: 'Yothu Yindi are to be credited for remaining optimistic ... But then, [their] strength has always been in couching their "messages" in upbeat and easily digestible formats ... The only question remaining is whether or not Yothu Yindi are still saying what their fans – loyal and fickle alike – want to hear' (Stafford, 1996 npd); and 'the hopes "Treaty" once so conjured for a truly original Australian music have dissipated ... something obviously went wrong while we were congratulating ourselves over [Yothu Yindi]' (unattributed, 1996).

8. See Aboriginal singer-songwriter Kev Carmody's comments on some of the paradoxical side effects of Yothu Yindi's success for other Aboriginal artists (cited in Johnson, 1993).

Bibliography

Avei, P. (1989) 'Copyright Law Issue Gets Mixed Reaction', *Post-Courier* (PNG) (13 January).

Averill, G. (1994) ' "Se Krèyol Nou Ye"/"We're Creole": Musical Discourse on Haitian Identities', in G. Behague (ed.) *Music and Black Ethnicity: The Caribbean and South America* (Boulder (USA): Lynne Rienner).

Babadzan, A. (1988) '*Kastom* and Nation Building in the South Pacific', in R. Guideri, F. Pellizi and S. Tambiah (eds) *Ethnicities and Nations: Processes of Interethnic Relations in Latin America, Southeast Asia, and the Pacific* (Houston: University of Texas Press).

Babiracki, C. (1985) 'Indigenizers', in B. Nettl (ed.) *The Western Impact on World Music: Change, Adaptation, and Survival* (New York: Schirmer).

Baillie, R. (1994) 'Our Streets are Grooving', *NZ Herald* (25 March).

—(1996) 'Getting DeaLT To ...', *Real Groove* (NZ) no. 43 (6-7 September).

Baltersby, M. and Valtwier, M. (1992) 'Music Video, Marketing and Misadventure', *Perfect Beat*, vol. 1, no. 1 (July).

'Barbie' (1993) 'Moana and the Moahunters', *Rip It Up* (NZ) no. 192 (16–17 July).

'BB Kings Fan' (1984) ' "Stolen" Song', *Post-Courier* (PNG) (28 December).

Beach, C. (1995) 'Yothu Yindi Tunes into Internet', *The Australian* (30 June).

Berndt, R. (1973) 'The Arts of Life: An Introduction', in R. Berndt, and E. Phillips, (eds) *The Australian Aboriginal Heritage: An Introduction through the Arts* (Sydney: Ure Smith).

Bollinger, N. (1992) 'South of the Border', *Rip It Up* (NZ) no. 181 (August).

—(1994) 'Emma Paki's *Greenstone*' (review), *Real Groove* (NZ) no. 25 (25 December).

Bourke, C. (1992) 'Brothers and Sisters', *Rip It Up* (NZ) no. 179 (June).

Breen, M. (ed.) (1989) *Our Place, Our Music – Aboriginal Music: Australian Popular Music in Perspective* (Canberra: Australian Institute of Aboriginal Studies).

—(1992) 'Desert Dreams, Media, and Interventions in Reality: Australian Aboriginal Music', in R. Garofalo, (ed.) (1992) *Rockin' the Boat – Mass Music and Mass Movements* (Boston: Southend Press).

Broughton, S., Ellingham, M., Muddyman, D. and Trillo, R., with Burton, K. (eds) (1994) *World Music: The Rough Guide* (London: Rough Guides Inc.).

Brown, S. (1989) 'The Rock of Ages Past', *The Weekend Australian* (27–28 May).

Buchanan, K. (1988) 'The Upper Hutt Posse: Music with a Message', *Music in New Zealand* (Summer).

—(1993) 'Ain't Nothing But a G Thing', *Midwest* (NZ) no. 3.

Buck, E. (1984) 'The Hawaii Music Industry', *Social Process in Hawaii* no. 31.

Burlingame, B. (1991) 'Helemano Jams to Beat of Own Drum', *Honolulu Star Bulletin* (1 May).

Campbell, D. (1991) 'Rasta Reggae', *Rip It Up* (NZ) (September).

— (1993) ' "Jah Life" and "Dread Beat" ', *Planet* (NZ) no. 10 (Autumn).

Castles, J. (1992) 'Tjungaringanyi: Aboriginal Rock', in P. Hayward (ed.) (1992) (reproduced, in revised form, as Chapter 1 of this anthology).

Chun, G. (1991) 'A Closer Look at "Jawaiian" ', *Honolulu Advertiser* (31 October).

Creighton, K. (1988) *Koori Relationship to the Land in Traditional Song and Modern Poetry* (unpublished Monash University research paper).

Crotty, J. (1992) *Aspects of Detribalized Koori Music History in Victoria Prior to 1988* (unpublished Monash University research paper).

Cubey, M. (1994) 'Pure Independents', *Real Groove* (NZ) no. 23 (October).

Dart, W. (1994) '*Te Ku Te Whe*: Rediscovering a Tradition', *Music in New Zealand* no. 24 (Autumn).

Dinnen, N. (1994) 'Hip Hop Hooray', *Drum Media* (Sydney) (19 July).

Dix, J. (1988) *Stranded in Paradise: New Zealand Rock and Roll, 1955–1988* (Paradise Publications).

— (1992) 'E Hoa Kaa Hongi Aahau I Te Rangi' , *Rap* (NZ) (November).

Dunbar-Hall, P. (1995) *Discography of Aboriginal and Torres Strait Islander Performers* (Sydney: Sounds Australian).

Dunbar-Hall, P. (1997) 'Music and Meaning: the Aboriginal Rock Album', *Australian Aboriginal Studies*, no. 1.

Eggleton, D. (1991) '*Jazz Waiata*' (review), *Landfall* (NZ) vol. 45, no. 3 (September).

Ellis, C. (1985) *Aboriginal Music: Education for Living* (Brisbane: University of Queensland Press).

— Brunton, M. and Barwick, L. (1988) 'From the Dreaming Rock to Reggae Rock', in McCredie, A. (ed.) *From Colonel Light into the Footlights: The Performing Arts in S.A. from 1836 to the Present* (Adelaide: Pagel Books).

Ewings, S. (1989) '*Koori Beat*' (Review) *Ots* (*On the street*) (Sydney) (18 October).

Farry, E. (1994) 'The Producers: 5 go Mad in a Studio', *Rip It Up* (NZ) no. 204 (14–15 August).

Feld, S. (1981) ' "Flow Like a Waterfall": the Metaphors of Kaluli Musical Theory', *Yearbook for Traditional Music,* vol. 13.

— (1988) 'Notes On World Beat', *Public Culture Bulletin* vol. 1, no. 1 (Fall).

— (1994) 'Schizophonia to Schismogenesis: On the Discourses and Commodification Practices of "World Music" and "World Beat" ', in C. Keil, and S. Feld (1994) *Music Grooves* (Chicago: University of Chicago Press).

— (1996) 'Pygmy Pop: A Genealogy of Schizophonic Mimesis', *Yearbook for Traditional Music*, vol. 28.

Fleras, A. (1991) ' "Tuku Rangatatatiratanga": Devolution in Iwi–Government Relations', in P. Spoonley, et al. (eds).

Fraser, H. (1988) *New Caledonia – Anti-Colonialism in a Pacific Territory* (Canberra: Peace Research Centre).

Frith, S. (1991) 'Critical Response', in D. Robinson et al. (eds).

Frizzell, O. (1994) 'Hip Hop Hype', *Pavement* (NZ) no. 8 (December).

Fujikane, C. (1994) 'Between Nationalisms: Hawai'i's Local Nation and Its Troubled Racial Paradise', *Critical Mass*, no. 1/2 (Spring).

Fyfe, A. (1994) 'The House that Roared', *New Musical Express* (UK) (11 June).

Garofalo, R. (1992) *Rockin' the Boat: Mass Music and Mass Movements* (Boston: South End Press).

Gee, A. (1991) 'Contact, Change and the Church', unpublished MA dissertation, University of New England, Australia.

Gee, K. (1990) 'DAT's the Way I Like It: Upper Hutt Posse', *Rip It Up* (NZ) no. 142 (January).

Gracewood, G. (1995) 'What's New Posse Cat?', *Real Groove* (NZ) (August).

Hamilton, A. (1993) 'Foreword' to Langton, M.

Handler, R. and Linnekin, J. (1984) 'Tradition, Genuine or Spurious', *Journal of American Folklore*, vol. 97.

Hansen, G. (1990) 'Interview with Archie Roach, Musician', *Koorier 3* (Melbourne) (21 June).

Hanson, A. (1989) 'The Making of the Maori: Culture Invention and Its Logic', *American Anthropologist*, no. 91.

Hayward, P. (1990) 'Industrial Light and Magic: Style, Technology and Special Effects in Music Video and Music Television', in P. Hayward (ed.) (1991).

— (ed.) (1991) *Culture, Technology and Creativity in the Late Twentieth Century* (London: Arts Council of Great Britain/John Libbey Publications).

— (1992) 'Music Video, The Bicentennial (and After)', in P. Hayward, (ed.) *From Pop to Punk to Postmodernism: Popular Music and Australian Culture from the 1960s to the 1990s* (Sydney: Allen and Unwin).

— (1993a) 'After the Record: *Tabaran*, Television and the Politics of Collaboration', *Perfect Beat*, vol. 1, no. 3 (July).

— (1993b) 'Safe, Exotic and Somewhere Else', *Pefect Beat*, vol. 1, no. 2 (January: Reproduced as Chapter 14 of this anthology).

— (ed.) (1994) *From pop to Punk to Postmodernism – Popular Music and Australian Culture from the 1960s to the 1990s* (Sydney: Allen and Unwin).

— (1998) *Music at the Borders: Not Drowning, Waving and Their Engagement with Papua New Guinean Culture (1986–96)* (Sydney: John Libbey and Co.).

Hayward, P., Mitchell, T. and Shuker, R. (eds) (1994) *North Meets South: Popular Music in Aotearoa/New Zealand* (Umina NSW: Perfect Beat Publications).

Hayward, P. and Neuenfeldt, K. (1997) 'Introduction: One Instrument, Many Voices', in K. Neuenfeldt (ed.).

Henry (1983) 'A Sour Note', *Post-Courier* (PNG) (23 September).

Hill, A. (1996) 'There's a Thing or Two that Rwanda Can Show Yunupingu', *The Australian* (1 November).

Hitchings, S. (1990) 'Dream Time's Over', *The Edge* (NZ) (November).

Hogg, C. (1995) 'Greenstone Girl', *The NZ Listener* (21 January).

— (1994) '"Otara sound" Creates Proud New Kiwi Era', *Sunday Star Times* (NZ) (17 April).

Horsfield, J. and Horsfield, B. (1988) 'Australia Penetrates the South Pacific: A Comparative Analysis of the Introduction of Commercial Television into Fiji and Papua New Guinea' (unpublished paper presented to the 1988

International Television Studies Conference, University of London Institute of Education, July 1988).

Hulme, K. (1985) *The Penguin Book of New Zealand Verse* (review), *Landfall* (NZ) vol. 34, no. 3 (September).

Hunter, S. (1995) 'Grooving to Sounds Rooted in the Pacific', *Evening Post* (NZ) (9 March).

Ihaka, J. (1993) 'Why the Kids Wanna be Black', *Mana* (NZ) (August/September).

Ihimaera, W. (ed.) (1993) *Te Ao Marama: Contemporary Maori Writing, Volume 3: Te Puawaitanga o Te Korero, The Flowering* (Auckland: Reed Books).

Jackomos, A. and Fowell, D. (1991) *Living Aboriginal History of Victoria, Stories in the Oral Tradition* (Melbourne: Cambridge University Press).

Johnson, R. (1993) 'Looking Out: An Interview with Kev Carmody', *Perfect Beat*, vol. 1, no. 2 (July).

Joku, H. (1983) 'Black Brothers Stole Our Yalikoe – Sanguma', *Niugini Nius* (PNG) (11 March).

Jolly, M. (1992) 'Specters of Inauthenticity', *Contemporary Pacific*, vol. 4, no. 1.

Jolly, M. and Thomas, N. (1992) 'The Politics of Tradition in the Pacific', *Oceania*, vol. 62, no. 4.

Kalo, K. (ed.) (1987) 'The Report of the Board of Inquiry into Broadcasting (including Television) in Papua New Guinea' (Port Moresby: Government Printer).

Kanahele, G. (ed.) (1979) *Hawaiian Music and Musicians* (Honolulu: University of Hawaii Press).

Kange, A. (1985) 'Stevie Unique', *Post-Courier* (PNG) (8 March).

Kapferer, B. (1988) *Legends of People, Myths of State* (Washington: Smithsonian Institute Press).

Karecki, M. (1993) 'Inculturation: An Imperative of Mission,' *Missionalia*, vol. 21, no. 2.

Kartomi, M. (1981) 'The Processes and Results of Musical Culture Contact: a Discussion of Terminology and Concepts', *Ethnomusicology*, vol. 25, no. 2.

Kelsey, J. (1991) 'Treaty Justice in the 1980s', in P. Spoonley *et al.* (eds) *Between the Lines* (Auckland: Heinemann Reed).

King, A. (1980) 'Innovation, Creativity, and Performance', in N. McLeod and M. Herndon (eds) *The Ethnography of Musical Performance* (Norwood (USA): Norwood Editions).

King, M. (1993) 'Books: Ethnic Cleansing', *Metro* (NZ) no. 139 (January).

Kirkpatrick, J. (1989) 'Trials of Identity in America', *Cultural Anthropology*, vol. 4, no. 3.

Knopoff, S. (1997) 'Accompanying the Dreaming: Determinants of Didjeridu Style in Traditional and Popular Yolngu Song', in Neuenfeldt, K. (ed.).

Kombi, J. (1984) 'Painim nek bilong Wes Sepik', *Wantok Niuspepa* (PNG), (4 February).

Kopytko, T. (1986) 'Breakdance as an Identity Marker in New Zealand', *Yearbook for Traditional Music*, vxviii.

Kornhauser, B. (1978) 'In Defence of *kroncong*', in M. Kartomi (ed.) *Studies in Indonesian Music* (Carlton (Australia): Monash Papers on Southeast Asia), no. 7.

Krempl-Pereira, S. (1984) 'The Urban Music Situation in Papua New Guinea, 1977–1984' (Port Moresby: Music Department, National Arts School).

Lamb, J. (1990) 'The New Zealand Sublime', *Meanjin* (Australia), vol. 49, no. 4.

Langton, M. (1993) *Well I Heard It on the Radio and I Saw It on the Television* (Sydney: Australian Film Commission).

Lawe-Davies, C. (1993) 'Aboriginal Rock Music: Space and Place', in T. Bennett, S. Frith, L. Grossberg, J. Shepherd and G. Turner (eds) *Rock and Popular Music* (London: Routledge).

Lealand, G. (1988) *A Foreign Egg in Our Nest? American Popular Culture in New Zealand* (Victoria (NZ): Victoria University Press).

Lester, L. (1989) 'Black Marks on the White Man's Blues', *The Sunday Age (Agenda)* (Australia) (31 December).

Linnekin, J. (1992) 'On the Theory and Politics of Cultural Construction in the Pacific', *Oceania*, vol. 62, no. 4.

Lipsitz, G. (1994) *Dangerous Crossroads: Popular Music: Postmodernism and the Poetics of Place* (London: Verso).

Lull, J. (1987) 'Communicative Uses of Popular Music', in J. Lull (ed.) *Popular Music and Communication* (California: Sage).

Lulungan, T. (1983) 'Tolai Music', *Bikmaus* (PNG), vol. 4, no. 3.

McDonald, B. (1995) 'Now or Never', *Pavement* (NZ) no. 11 (June/July).

McGuinness, B. (1989) 'Rock Against Racism', in *Koorier 3* (Melbourne) (12 September).

McGuinness, K. and Brown, B. (1985) 'Rock Against Racism', in *Koorier 2* (Melbourne), vol. 1, no. 6.

McLeay, C. (1994) 'The "Dunedin Sound" New Zealand Rock and Cultural Geography, *Perfect Beat*, vol. 2, no. 1 (July).

McManus, K. (1992) 'Teeth Gritted Harmonies: Music Policy on Australian Public Radio', *Perfect Beat*, vol. 1, no. 1 (July).

McMillan, A. (1988) *Strict Rules* (Sydney: Hodder and Stoughton).

McQueen, H. (1993) 'Dreaming and Reality', *24 Hours* (NZ) (May).

Magowan, F. (1996) 'Traditions of the Mind or the Music Video: Imaging the Imagination in Yothu Yindi's *Tribal Voice*', *Arena*, no. 7.

Malm, K. (1992) *Media Policy and Music Activity* (London: Routledge).

—(1993) 'Music on the Move: Traditions and Mass Media', *Ethnomusicology*, vol. 37, no. 3.

Malone, A. (1991) *Contemporary Urban Popular Aboriginal Music: A Survey of Melbourne and Broome* (unpublished Monash University Music Department thesis).

Manuel, S. (1991) 'Bright, Israel Top Vocalists: The 14th Annual Hoku Awards Honor Tradition', *Honolulu Star Bulletin*, B1; B3 (8 May).

Martin, D. (1995) 'The Choices of Identity', *Local Identities*, vol. 1, no. 1.

Martin, G. (1989) 'Aboriginal Soundtrack', *New Musical Express* (18 March).

Meade, A. (1996a) 'Outback Rhythms Strike Chord with Soweto Youth', *The Australian* (30 October).

— (1996b) 'Charity May Begin at Home for Blacks', *The Australian* (2–3 November).

Meyer, L. (1989) *Style and Music Theory, History, and Ideology* (Philadelphia: University of Pennsylvania Press).

Miller, D. (1994) *Modernity: An Ethnographic Approach* (Oxford: Berg).

Miller, R. (1992) 'Is this the birth of Koori Cool?', *Songlines*, no. 3 (Australia) (May).

Mitchell, T. (1992) 'World Music, Indigenous Music and Music Television in Australia', *Perfect Beat*, vol. 1, no. 1 (July).

— (1993) 'Reply' (to Nicol), *Pefect Beat*, vol. 1, no. 2 (January).

—(1994) 'He Waiata Na Aotearoa: Maori and Polynesian Music in New Zealand', in P. Hayward, T. Mitchell and R. Shuker (eds) *North Meets South: Popular Music in Aotearoa/New Zealand* (Umina, NSW: Perfect Beat Publications.

— (1995) 'New Urban Polynesians: *Once Were Warriors*, the *Proud* Project and the South Auckland Music Scene', *Perfect Beat*, vol. 2, no. 3 (July).

— (1996) *Popular Music and Local Identity* (London: Leicester University Press).

— (1997) 'New Zealand Music on the Internet: A Study of the NZPOP Mailing List', *Perfect Beat*, vol. 3, no. 2 (January).

Molnar, Helen (1994) 'Indigenous Broadcasting in Australia and the Pacific' (unpublished PhD thesis, Monash University, Melbourne).

Moore, L. (1994) 'Crowded House Makes Room for More Talent', *NZ Herald* (28 February).

Morley, B. (1993) 'The Launching of Nga Matua: A Personal View', *Music in New Zealand*, no. 21 (Spring).

Morris, B. (1989) *Domesticating Resistance: The Dhan Gadi Aborigines and the Australian State* (Oxford: Berg).

Muecke, S. (1990) 'Yolngu Culture in the Age of MTV', *Independent Media* (UK) no. 92 (October).

— (1992) *Textual Spaces: Aboriginality and Cultural Studies* (Kensington Australia: New South Wales University Press).

Mulgan, G. (1991) *Communication and Control* (London: Polity).

Murphie, A. (1996) 'Music at the End of the World', *Perfect Beat*, vol. 2, no. 4 (January).

Muru, S. (1994) 'Maori and the Media', *Planet* (NZ), no. 15 (Summer).

Narogin, M. (1990) *Writing from the Fringe* (Melbourne: Hyland).

National Information and Communication Policy Committee (1993) 'National Information and Communication Policy of Papua New Guinea' (Port Moresby: Division of Policy Research, Department of Information and Communication).

Nettl, B. (1978) *Eight Urban Musical Cultures: Tradition and Change* (Chicago: University of Illinois Press).

Neuenfeldt, K. (1991) 'To Sing a Song of Otherness: Anthros, Ethno-Pop and the Mediation of Public Problems', *Canadian Ethnic Studies*, vol. xxiii, no. 3.

— (1993) 'Yothu Yindi and Ganma: The Cultural Transposition of Aboriginal Agenda Through Metaphor and Music', *Journal of Australian Studies*, no. 38.

Neuenfeldt, K. (ed.) (1997) *The Didjeridu: From Arnhem Land to Internet*, (Sydney: John Libbey/Perfect Beat Publications).

Nicol, L. (1993) 'Culture, Custom and Collaboration', *Pefect Beat*. vol. 1, no. 2 (January) (Reproduced as Chapter 13 of this anthology).

Niles, D. (1992) 'Traditional and Contemporary Concerns Relating to Copyright in Papua New Guinea', *Phonographic Bulletin*, no. 61 (November).

Noble, J. (1929) *Royal Collection of Hawaiian Songs* (Honolulu: Johnny Noble).

Nonggorr, J. (1990) 'The Introduction of Copyright Law in Papua New Guinea', *Melanesian Law Journal*, no. 18.

'Novorab Kid' (1984) 'Compose Your Own', *Post-Courier* (PNG) (8 June).

NZ On Air Annual Report (1991), no. 2 (Auckland: NZ on Air).

Oedin, J. (1991) 'Mission d'expertise, d'assistance technique et artistique' (unpublished paper).

Okamura, J. (1980) 'Aloha Kanaka Me Ke Aloha 'Aina: Local Culture and Society in Hawaii', *Amerasia*, vol. 7, no. 2.

— (1994) 'Why there are no Asian Americans in Hawai'i: The Continuing Significance of Local Identity', *Social Process in Hawaii*, no. 35.

Pett, R. (1995) 'They're by the Grace', *NZ Musician*, vol. 5, no. 4 (March).

Philpott, M. (1992) 'Revival and Restructuring : The NBC of Papua New Guinea', *Media Information Australia*, no. 66 (November).

— (1993) 'Papua New Guinea: Developing a National Communication Policy', *Media Information Australia*, no. 68 (May).

Pickering, A. (1996) 'Walking the Razor Blade', *Rip It Up* (NZ) no. 228 (20 August).

Potiki, R. (1991) 'A Maori Point of View: The Journey from Anxiety to Confidence', *Australasian Drama Studies*, no. 18 (April).

Rae, F. (1992) 'Annie Crummer', *Rip It Up* (NZ) no. 185 (December).

Raganivatu, A. (1996) 'Fuemana's *Bizarre* rise to fame and glory', *Pacific Islands Monthly* (September).

Reedy, E. (1993) 'A Passion for Maori Music', *Mana* (NZ) vol. 1, no. 1 (January).

Reid, G. (1992a) 'New Zealand's Maori Music a Genre Melange', *Billboard*, vol. 104, no. 22 (30 May).

— (1992b) 'New Zealand Awards Display Diversity', *Billboard*, vol. 104, no. 1 (25 April).

— (1994) 'Tour Teaches Pride', *NZ Herald* (25 March).

— (1996) 'Polygram's OMC Unearths Polynesia', *Billboard*, vol. 108, no. 27 (6 July).

Reid, V. (1994) 'Phil Fuemana Interview', *Giveway* (NZ) no. 4 (November/December).

Ritchie, J. (1992) *Becoming Bicultural* (Wellington: Huia Publishers).

Robinson, D., Buck, E. and Cuthbert, M. (eds) (1991) *Music at the Margins: Popular Music and Global Cultural Diversity* (Newbury Park, California: Sage).

Ruina, B. (1986) 'Kopiket na bagarapim musik', *Wantok Niuspepa* (PNG) (1 February).

Schaefer, J. (1990) *New Sounds: The Virgin Guide to New Music* (London: Virgin).

Schmidt, A. (1994) 'Rad Attitude', *Metro* (NZ), no. 152 (February).

Sheridan, B. and Hayward, P. (1994) '*Let's Go to Frenzy:* A Brief History of New Zealand Music TV and Music Video', in P. Hayward, T. Mitchell and R. Shuker (eds).

Shoemaker, A. (1994a) 'The Politics of Yothu Yindi', in K. Darian-Smith (ed.) (1992) *Working Papers in Australian Studies*, nos. 88–96 (London: Institute of Commonwealth Studies).

— (1994b) 'Selling Yothu Yindi', in G. Papaellinas (ed.) *Republica* (Sydney: Angus and Robertson).

Shopland, A. (1993) 'E Tu', *NZ Musician*, vol. 4, no. 4 (August).

Shuker, R. (1994) *Understanding Popular Music* (London: Routledge).

Siwi, P. (1990) 'Give PNG Music a Chance!', *Niugini Nius* (PNG) (22 February).

Slobin, M. (1992) 'Micromusics of the West: A Comparative Approach', *Ethnomusicology,* vol. 36, no. 1.

Smith, D. (1989) 'Some Thoughts', in 'Koori Music Club', *Koorier 3* (Melbourne) (8 December).

Smith, M. (1994) 'High on Second Nature', *Drum Media* (Sydney) (21 June).

Smithies, G. (1996) 'Overdose: The First Chapter', *Real Groove* no. 42 (August).

Spearritt, G. (1982) 'The Pairing of Musicians and Instruments in Iatmul Society in Polynesia', *Yearbook for Traditional Music*, vol. 25.

Spoonley, P. and Hirsch, W. (eds) (1991) *Between the Lines: Racism and the New Zealand Media* (Auckland: Heinemann Reed).

Spoonley, P., Hirsch, W. et al. (eds) (1991) *Nga Take: Ethnic Relations and Racism in Aotearoa/New Zealand* (Palmerston North (NZ): Dunmore Press).

Stahl, G. (1997) 'Citing the Sound: New Zealand Indie Rock in North America', *Perfect Beat*, vol. 3, no. 2 (January).

Stead, C. (1985) '*The Penguin Book of New Zealand Verse*' (review), *Landfall* (NZ), vol. 34, no. 3 (September).

Steggels, S. (1992) 'Nothing Ventured, Nothing Gained: Midnight Oil and the Politics of Rock', in P. Hayward (ed.) (1992).

Stewart, J. (1993) 'EM-TV: The First Six Years of Broadcast Television in Papua New Guinea', *Pacific Islands Communication Journal*, vol. 16, no. 1.

Stillman, A. (1993) 'Prelude to a Comparative Investigation of Protestant hymnody in Polynesia', *Yearbook for Traditional Music,* vol. 25.

— (1996) 'Hawaiian Hula Competitions: Event, Repertoire, Performance, Tradition', *Journal of American Folklore*, no. 109.

Stokes, M. (1994) *Ethnicity, Identity and Music* (Oxford: Berg).

Street, J. (1986) *Rebel Rock: The Politics of Popular Music* (Oxford: Basil Blackwell).

Stubington, J. and Dunbar-Hall, P. (1994) 'Yothu Yindi's "Treaty": Ganma in Music', *Popular Music*, vol. 13, no. 3.

Sullivan, C. (1988) 'Non-tribal Dance Music and Song: From First Contact to Citizen Rights', in *Australian Aboriginal Studies*, no. 1.

Sullivan, N. (1993) 'Film and Television Production in Papua New Guinea: How the Medium Became the Message', *Public Culture,* no. 11.

Sullivan, R. (1990) *Jazz Waiata* (Auckland University Press).

Sumida, S. (1991) *And the View from the Shore: Literary Traditions of Hawai'i* (Seattle: University of Washington Press).

Sword, A. (1992) 'Kanaki Strikes Pacific Chords', *Cook Island News – Entertainment This Week* (7 November).

Tauwala, B. (1984) 'Copyright', in S. Krempl-Pereira (ed.) *The Urban Music Situation in Papua New Guinea from 1977 to 1984* (Waigani: National Arts School).

Tein, K. (1993) 'Kanak, Knk, Kaneka', *Mwà Vée* (New Caledonia), no. 2.

Tein, K., Wainebeng, J., Menango, T., Beardet, J.M., Wiyat, T. and Bharat, A. (1993) 'Naissance du Kaneka: la rencontre de 1986', *Mwà Vée* (New Caledonia), no. 2.

Thomson, M. (1991) 'A New Song: Women's Music in Aotearoa', *Music in New Zealand* (Winter).

Thorpe, W. (1985) 'Hard Times in Video Clip', *Koorier 2* (Melbourne), vol. 1, no. 6.

— (1990) 'Koori Kollij', *Koorier 3* (Melbourne) (June).

Tingwell, J. (1995) 'Groove Mania', *Drum Media* (Sydney) (17 January).

Tjibaou, J.-M. (1978) *Kanaké the Melanesian Way* (Tahiti: Les Editions du Pacifique).

Toturi, K. (1985) 'Copycat Musos', *Post-Courier* (PNG) (8 June).

Turner, G. (1995) *Making It National: Nationalism and Australian Popular Culture* (Sydney: Allen and Unwin).

Unattributed (1989) '*Homeland Movement*' (Review), *RAM* (Australia) (28 June).

Unattributed (1991) 'Yothu Yindi', *Ots* (*Out on the Street*) (23 December).

Unattributed (1992) 'No Treaty Yet, But Two Australian Symbols Getting On Fine' *Sydney Morning Herald* (26 October).

Unattributed (1994) 'Urban Disturbance & 3 The Hard Way', *NZ Musician*, vol. 4, no. 8 (April).

Unattributed (1996) Review of Yothu Yindi's *Superhighway* (Mushroom Records press kit).

Von Sturmer, J. (1987) 'Aboriginal Singing and Notions of Power', in M. Clunies-Ross, T. Donaldson and S. Wild (eds) *Songs of Aboriginal Australia* (Sydney: University of Sydney Press).

Vui-Talitu, S. (1996) 'Communication of Polynesian Cultures: An Analysis of Moana and the Moahunters' "AEIOU"', *Perfect Beat*, vol. 2, no. 4 (January).

Waitangi Tribunal (1986) *Te Reo Maori Report*.

— (1990) *Report on Claims Concerning the Allocation of Radio Frequencies* (Spectrum Report).

Walker, C. (1995) 'Pacific Pride', *Rolling Stone* (Australia) no. 510 (June).

Wallis, R. and Malm, K. (1984) *Big Sounds from Small Peoples* (London: Constable).

— (1986) *The Workings of the Phonogram Industry: Three Analytical Perspectives* (Stockholm: Musikmuseet, Report 86).

Ward, A. (1993) 'Blind Justice or Blinkered Vision?', *Meanjin* (Australia), vol. 52, no. 4.

Wark, McKenzie (1992) 'Ornament and Crime: The Hip Hop Avant Garde of the Late 1980s', *Perfect Beat*, vol 1, no. 1 (July).

Watson, H. (1990) 'The Politics of Knowing and Being Known', *Arena* (Australia), no. 92.

Webb, M. (1993) *Lokal Musik: Lingua Franca Song and Identity in Papua New Guinea*, Boroko (PNG): National Research Institute.

Webb, M. and Niles, D. (1987) 'Periods in Papua New Guinea Music History', *Bikmaus* vol. 7, no. 1.

Weintraub, A. (1993) 'Jawaiian and Local Cultural Identity in Hawai'i', *Perfect Beat*, vol. 1, no. 2 (January) (Reproduced as Chapter 5 of this anthology).

Wetherell, M. and Potter, J. (1992) *Mapping the Language of Racism: Discourse and the Legitimation of Exploitation* (Brighton: Harvester/Wheatsheaf).

Whaanga, P. (1990) 'Radio: Capable of Carrying a Bicultural Message?', in P. Spoonley and W. Hirsch (eds) *Between the Lines* (Auckland: Heinemann Reed).

Whiteoak, J. (1993) 'From Jim Crow to Jazz', *Perfect Beat*, vol. 1, no. 3 (July).

— (1998) *Playing Ad Lib: Improvisatory Music in Australia 1836–1970 – A Melbourne Perspective* (Sydney: Currency Press/National Library).

Wild, M. (1993) 'The Growth and Direction of the PNG Music Video Industry' (paper given at the PNG Ethnomusicology Conference, July).

Williams, N. (1986) *The Yolngu and Their Land: A System of Land Tenure and the Fight for Its Recognition* (Canberra: Institute of Aboriginal Studies).

Wilson, C. (1983) 'The Impact of Rock 'n' Roll on the Music Perceptions of Young Papua New Guineans (with particular reference to National High School Students)', *Bikmaus* (PNG), vol. 4, no. 3.

Wilson, H. (ed.) (1994) *The Radio Book* (Christchurch (NZ): Christchurch Polytechnic).

— (1993) 'Broadcasting and the Treaty of Waitangi', *Media Information Australia*, no. 67 (February).

Yamamoto, E. (1979) 'The Significance of Local', *Social Process in Hawaii*, no. 27.

Young, I. (1990) *Justice and the Politics of Difference* (Princeton: Princeton University Press).

Yunupingu, M. (1994) 'Yothu Yindi – Finding Balance', in *Voices from the Land: 1993 Boyer Lectures* (Sydney: ABC Books).

Yuzwalk, D. (1991) 'Black Pearl: Moana and the Moahunters', *Rip It Up* (NZ) no. 162.

— (1992a) 'Margaret Urlich', *Rip It Up* (NZ) no. 183 (October).

— (1992b) 'Maree Sheehan', *Rip It Up* (NZ) no. 185 (December).

Zemp, H. (1978) ''Are 'Are Classification of Musical Types and Instruments', *Ethnomusicology*, vol. 22, no. 1.

Zepke, S. (1993) 'Dean Hapeta: The Medium Is the Message', *Music in New Zealand*, no. 23 (Summer).

Index